Final Cut Express HD 3.5
Editing Workshop

Final Cut Express HD 3.5 Editing Workshop

Tom Wolsky

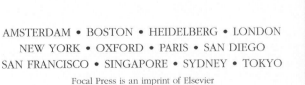

AMSTERDAM • BOSTON • HEIDELBERG • LONDON
NEW YORK • OXFORD • PARIS • SAN DIEGO
SAN FRANCISCO • SINGAPORE • SYDNEY • TOKYO

Focal Press is an imprint of Elsevier

ELSEVIER

Acquisitions Editor:	Paul Temme
Publishing Services Manager:	George Morrison
Project Manager:	Mónica González de Mendoza
Assistant Editor:	Georgia Kennedy
Marketing Manager:	Christine Degon Veroulis
Cover Design:	Alan Studholme
Composition:	Multiscience Press, Inc.

Focal Press is an imprint of Elsevier
30 Corporate Drive, Suite 400, Burlington, MA 01803, USA
Linacre House, Jordan Hill, Oxford OX2 8DP, UK

∞ Recognizing the importance of preserving what has been written, Elsevier prints its books on acid-free paper whenever possible.

Library of Congress Cataloging-in-Publication Data
Application submitted.

British Library Cataloguing-in-Publication Data
A catalogue record for this book is available from the British Library.

ISBN 13: 978-0-240-80945-8
ISBN 10: 0-240-80945-9

For information on all Focal Press publications
visit our website at www.books.elsevier.com

07 08 09 10 11   5 4 3 2

Printed in the United States of America

Working together to grow libraries in developing countries

www.elsevier.com | www.bookaid.org | www.sabre.org

ELSEVIER   BOOK AID International   Sabre Foundation

Table of Contents

Introduction

What Is Editing?

Video or film production is based on the notion of time, usually linear time of a fixed length. Whether it is 10 minutes, 30 minutes, one hour, two hours, or more, the film is seen as a single event of fixed duration. On the other hand, time within the film is infinitely malleable. Events can happen quickly: we fly from one side of the world to another, from one era to a different century, in the blink of an eye. Or every detail and every angle can be slowed down to add up to a far greater amount than the true expanse of time—or seen again and again.

Because film and video production are based on the notion of time, the process of editing—controlling time and space within the story—is of paramount importance. This process of editing, however, does not begin after the film is shot. It begins when the idea is conceived. As soon as you are thinking of your production as a series of shots or scenes, you are mentally editing the movie, arranging the order of the material, juxtaposing one element against another.

The first movies were single, static shots of everyday events. The Lumière brothers' screening in Paris of a train pulling into the La Ciotat train station caused a sensation. Silent and black and white, it still conveyed a gripping reality for the audience. The brothers followed this with a staged comic scene. Georges Méliès expanded this into staging complex tableaux.

It wasn't until Edwin H. Porter and D. W. Griffith in the United States discovered the power of editing one shot next to another that the movies were really born. Griffith also introduced such innovations as the flashback, the first real use of film to manipulate time. Close-ups were used to emphasize the moment of impact and wide shots to establish context. Parallel action was introduced, and other story devices were born, but the real discovery was that the shot is the fundamental building block of film and that the film is built one shot at a time, one after the other.

> **Nonlinear Movies?** The notion of nonlinear presentation of films and videos that DVD offers is antithetical to the idea of film as a progression in time. Over the years there have been many attempts to make films nonlinear or with variable structures and outcomes, much like a game. None have really been successful. I think the reason is that the movies are about storytelling, and that requires a linear presentation. If variability is introduced to the movie, or if the scenes can be seen in any order, then its ethos as a story disappears. We will all see a different story. We'll no longer be able to say, "Did you like *Casablanca*?" The question would then be, "How was your version of *Casablanca*?" It's not quite the same thing and probably doesn't provide the same sense of satisfaction and fulfillment, which is why I think the attempts at nonlinearity or variability have largely failed except in games.

Editing is about three things: selection, arrangement, and timing—selecting which shot to use, determining where that shot should be placed, and deciding how long the shot should be on the screen. The first of these elements, selection, begins in the process of capturing your material. For many editors, the process of logging and capturing material is part of the selection process. In days when hard drives were small and very expensive, this was a critical step in the digital editing process. Now, because drives have become relatively cheap and much larger and faster, the pressure to capture selectively has been greatly reduced.

The moment of the edit is dictated by rhythm: sometimes by an internal rhythm the visuals present, sometimes by a musical track, and often by the rhythm of language. All language, whether it's dialog or narration, has a rhythm, a cadence or pattern, dictated by the words and based on grammar. Grammar marks language with punctuation: commas are short pauses; semicolons are slightly longer pauses; periods are the end of an idea. The new sentence begins a new idea, a new thought, and it is natural that as the new thought begins, a new image is introduced to illustrate that idea. The shot comes, not at the end of the sentence, not in the pause, but at the beginning of the new thought. This is the natural place to cut, and this rhythm of language drives the rhythm of film and video.

Films and videos are made in the moments when one shot changes into another, when one image is replaced by the next, when one point of view becomes someone else's point of view. Without the image changing, you just have moving pictures. The idea of changing from one angle to another or from one scene to another quickly leads to the concept of juxtaposing one idea against another. It soon becomes apparent that the impact of storytelling lies in the way in which the shots are ordered. Editing is about selection, arrangement, and timing. Editing creates the visual and aural juxtaposition between shots. That's what this book is about: how to put together those pieces of picture and sound.

Who Am I To Write This Book?

I have been working in film and video production for longer than I like to admit, about 40 years. A few years ago I left ABC News, for which I'd worked as an operations manager and producer for many years, first in London and then in New York, to take up teaching—video production, of course—at a small high school in rural northern California. I also have written curriculum for Apple's Video Journalism program and taught training sessions for them, and in the summers I have had the pleasure of teaching Final Cut at the Digital Media Academy on the beautiful Stanford University campus.

The structure of this book follows that of my *Final Cut Pro Editing Workshop* books. It is organized as a series of tutorials and lessons that I hope have been written logically to lead the reader from one topic to a more advanced topic. The nature of your work with Final Cut Express, however, may require the information in Lesson 10, for example, right away. You can read that lesson by itself. There may, however, be elements in Lesson 10 that presuppose that you know something about using the Viewer in conjunction with the Canvas.

Who Is This Book For?

This editing workshop is intended for all FCE users. So the broader question should really be: Who is FCE intended for? It appeals, I think, to serious hobbyists, the so-called prosumer market, event producers, and even small companies with video production requirements. I also think it's a great product for education—fully featured, able to go far beyond the limitations that frustrate many students who use iMovie, but without the professional features found in its older sibling Final Cut Pro. Institutional education pricing makes it affordable for schools even in penny-pinching times. Final Cut Express is not a simple application to use; it's not plug-and-play. It requires learning your way around the interface, its tools, and its enormous capabilities.

What's on the DVD?

The DVD included with this book is a hybrid DVD. It contains an introduction to Final Cut aimed at the iMovie user. If you have been using iMovie, I urge you to watch the introduction. It will explain, compare, and contrast the two applications. I hope it will make the transition easier for you. The DVD also has a DVD-ROM portion that contains some of the lessons, projects, and clips used in the book. Not all of the lessons require materials from the DVD. For some, such as Lessons 1, 6, and 7, you don't need any clips at all. For others, you may want to substitute your own material, clips you want to work with or are more familiar with. I hope you find this book useful, informative, and fun. I think it's a good way to learn this kind of application.

Acknowledgments

First, as always, my gratitude to all of the people at CMP Books and now at Focal Press who make this book-writing process relatively painless, particularly Paul Temme, Acquisitions Editor for Focal Press in Kansas, for his thoughtful advice, guidance, and repeated assistance with the vagaries of Microsoft Word; and Dorothy Cox and Gail Saari at CMP Books, for organizing the files I needed. My thanks also to Georgia Kennedy, Associate Editor for Focal Press in Oxford, for her help. Many thanks are due to Tim Donar for his work on the layout, and to Ginjer Clarke for her meticulous copyediting. My thanks to Alan Studholme for his wonderful work on the covers.

So many people helped make this book possible and deserve thanks: Sidney Kramer for his expert advice; Mary Massey, FCE product manager, for her kind assistance; Anne Renehan, formerly at Boris FX, now in charge of Apple pro training, for her excellent suggestions for Calligraphy; Rich Corwin and Anita Lupattelli Corwin for their gracious cooperation; and Toby Malina for her kind help. Thanks also to the creative software engineers who allowed me to put samples of their work on the DVD, especially Graeme Nattress, Christoph Vonrhein, John Wainwright, and Klaus Eiperle; and to Eric Fry, for his Timecode Calculator.

A great many thanks are due to my partner, B. T. Corwin, for her insights, her endless encouragement, her engineering technical support, and her patience with me. Without her, none of this would have been possible. Finally, again my thanks to the wonderful people of Damine, Japan, who welcomed us into their homes and whose lives provided the source material for many of these lessons.

Lesson 1

Installing Final Cut Express HD

Welcome to Final Cut Express HD version 3.5, the newest version of Apple's video editing software for DV and HDV users. This version of the application is based on its older cousin Final Cut Pro 5.1 and has been fully rewritten to be Universal Binary. That means it will run on either older PowerPC Macs or Apple's new Intel-based computers. So if you are using one of Apple's Intel computers, a new iMac, MacBook, or Mac-Book Pro, this is the version of the application you need to be running. This new version brings quite a few changes and even more complexity to the application, together with more real-time capabilities.

Final Cut Express (FCE) has a unique niche in video editing applications; there is nothing else of its caliber at its price point. FCE occupies the space between Apple's free iMovie editing application and its high-end, resolution independent suite of applications called Final Cut Studio. Many Mac users working in video quickly become frustrated by the limitations of iMovie, despite its many improvements since it was first introduced in 2000. There are a few similarities between iMovie and FCE, but there are many, many distinct differences, not only on the surface, but also in the very format in which the applications work.

For more information about making the step from iMovie to Final Cut Express, see the DVD that comes with this book. It is a hybrid DVD, including a section that will play with your Mac's DVD Player. There I'll explain a little about the differences between the two applications and moving from one to the other.

🖎 Note

New Operating System: If you
need to upgrade your operating system to run your new software, most
professionals will always recommend
that you do a clean erase and install
of the new operating system, rather
than simply archiving and installing
it. Professional applications, especially video applications, call on
many system functions to operate,
and a small change, or a failure to
correctly place or update a minor
Library file, will cause the application to function incorrectly. If you
have to upgrade, the best way is to
make a clone of your existing system
using Carbon Copy Cloner or Super-
Duper! Erase your main drive, which
you can do from the system installation disks, and then install a clean,
new operating system. Install your
software, and then from the cloned
drive, move over your users and
other files you need to keep. If you're
really careful you can even move
over and install many simple applications this way, but NOT video or
other professional applications.

I'm sure you want to dive right into it, but FCE 3.5 first must be installed properly on a properly functioning system. Video editing software is not simple shareware, but a complex, system-integrated piece of software that requires your system to be running in optimal condition. This means that you have to have all of the correct system software installed, and have it installed on hardware, computer and hard drives, that can support digital video. Your hard drives must be fast, clean, and running properly, ready for moving large amounts of data at high speed.

What You Really Need

Final Cut Express 3.5 will work only with Apple's OS X 10.4.6 (Tiger) or higher and will run only on a G4 Mac 500MHz or higher or an Intel dual-core (Core Duo) computer with an AGP or PCI Express graphics card or the Intel GMA integrated processor in the MacBook. It will run on a G4 iBook, PowerBook, MacBook, MacBook Pro, or iMac, and of course it will run beautifully on a top-of-the-line MacPro tower with Intel's dual-core Xeon processors. It is not supported for use with the MacMini, but many users are working with it successfully. To achieve good real-time preview capabilities, and if you're working in HDV, you'll need a 1GHz or faster processor. Final Cut Express allows processor-based real-time transitions, graphics, and motion.

Memory: How Much and What Kind?

Applications have to deal with two distinct types of memory: RAM and storage. They perform quite distinct functions. RAM (random access memory) is the chips that hold the system and applications while they are running. FCE is stored in RAM while it's open, as is the operating system. To do this, you will need at least 512MB of RAM, with 1G required for editing HDV and 2G recommended. The more you can put in, the better, allowing you to have multiple applications open with ease.

You'll also need 500MB of storage space available for installation of applications, Final Cut Express, LiveType 2, the motion graphics application, and Soundtrack 1.5, the music creation and mixing application, which come with FCE. These applications, together with their ancillary application support media, which take up an additional 16G of space, will eat up a good deal of your system drive.

Your finances almost invariably dictate which computer you purchase for editing video. My recommendation is always to get the biggest, fastest, most powerful computer you can afford. If you have budget constraints, get started on an iMac. If you need to be on the road a lot, get a MacBook or a MacBook Pro. If you have a larger budget, go for it: a Quad Core Mac Pro loaded with lots of RAM.

Multiple Drives

Storage is an essential part of any video system. DV consumes about 3.6MB per second of storage space. That translates to 216MB per minute, approximately 1GB for five minutes, and almost 13GB for an hour. Fortunately, cheap hard drives are available in ever-increasing sizes, with platter speeds, seek times, and caches ample for working with DV-quality material. HDV material has the same amount of storage space on tape, but gets converted to a high-resolution format when it's captured into FCE. The material is transcoded into the Apple Intermediate Codec, which is approximately 12MB per second, about 40G per hour of footage.

Because a digital video editing system needs to move large amounts of data at high speeds, you should use separate drives purely for storing video data. You should have one internal hard drive dedicated to your operating system and applications, such as Final Cut Express, LiveType, Soundtrack, Photoshop or Photoshop Elements, your iLife applications, iTunes, iDVD, and so on, and everything else from Internet access software to word processing and spreadsheets. All of these should be on one drive.

You should also have at least one other hard drive, one that's large and fast. This drive—better still, drives—should carry only your media. A separate drive is much more efficient at moving large amounts of data at high speed. The media drive needs to get that data off the drive very quickly and play it back. In addition, it needs to play back multiple tracks of audio from various places on the drive simultaneously. That's quite enough work for any one drive to be doing at any one time. To then have it be accessing the application and the operating system as well is often the straw that breaks the camel's back. You are much less likely to have video playback or capture failure through dropped frames and other issues if you have the media on a separate, dedicated hard drive. This drive should run at 7,200rpm and have at least an 8MB cache. For Mac-Book, MacBook Pro, or iMac users, external FireWire drives are a good

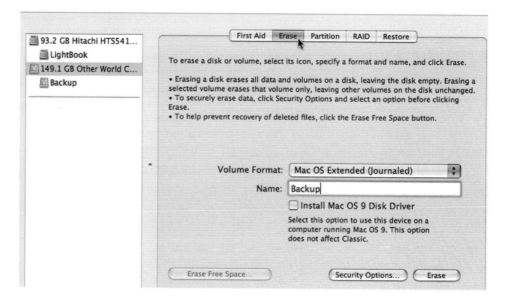

1.1   Disk Utility Erase Panel

solution, such as those from WiebeTech, or boxes from Granite Digital in which you can put a number of different fast, bare drives.

1.2   Zero Out Data

Optimizing Your Computer for FCE

You can optimize your computer for video editing with Final Cut Express in **System Preferences**, mostly by switching off things that might interfere with its operations while it's running. You should set **Software Update** to not check for updates automatically. That way there is no chance it will take off and try to run while you're working in FCE.

For the **Desktop** most professionals recommend switching off screen savers and working in a neutral, usually midtone gray desktop, as this is more restful for the eyes and does not affect the color rendition of your eyes. You'll see this tonal display in the application, mostly midtone grays with little color.

The **Displays** should be set so that your computer monitor is running in **Millions of colors** and at the resolution settings the system recommends for your display, which should be a minimum of 1,024×768. The application will not run properly at lower resolutions.

The **Energy Saver** should be set so that the system never goes to sleep. It's less critical that the monitor doesn't go to sleep. I usually set it around 10 minutes, but the system and the hard drive should never shut down. This can cause havoc with slow renders.

I also recommend that you switch off **AppleTalk** and networking. This is simplest to do by going to **Network Preferences** and creating a new location called **None**. Set up your **None** location without any active connections—no internal modem, no Airport, no Ethernet—everything unavailable and shut off. To reconnect to the network, simply change back to a location from the **Apple** menu that allows access to whatever connection you want to use.

One last step is in **Dashboard and Exposé**. This feature calls up your widgets and allows you to separate your windows to see them all, as well as the desktop. Unfortunately for FCE users, the default shortcuts for Exposé's functions are **F9**, **F10**, and **F11**. These three keys are critical to working efficiently in FCE. I recommend that you change the default Exposé keyboard shortcuts to **Option-F9**, **Option-F10**, and **Option-F11**. You can do this in your **System Preferences** in the Dashboard and Exposé panel as in Figure 1.3. Hold down the **Option** key before selecting the item in the pop-up. You should change the default Dashboard shortcut as well. I like to use **F1**, because it doesn't do anything in FCE.

Monitors

In addition to your computer display, you should also have a video monitor. These monitors, like television sets, reproduce images very differently from computer monitors, which have much greater color depth, resolution, and contrast range. In addition, video monitors have an interlaced scan line display, which computer monitors do not. These attributes are all critical to how your video will finally look. One reason this is so important is because your material is being made into a video format. Whether you shot it with a DV or HDV camera or not, because FCE is resolution specific, it always generates video in one of these formats, which are interlaced video formats designed for display on a television. If your project is intended to be seen on a television set, you must edit with

⟍Note

Reformatting a New Drive:

Most hard drives come formatted for Windows. Before you start to use them, you should reformat them to Mac OS Extended (Journaled). You should use Disk Utility to do this:

1. Open Disk Utility, which should be in the *Utilities* folder of your *Applications* folder.

2. Select the drive you want to format and click on the Erase tab (see Figure 1.1).

3. Set the Volume Format pop-up to Mac OS Extended (Journaled).

4. Name the drive.

5. Switch off OS 9 drivers if you don't need them.

6. Click on Security and check Zero Out Data as in Figure 1.2.

You only have to zero out on a new drive that has not been properly formatted. If you need to reformat it or erase the drive later, you can do a simple erase that deletes the directory file without having to zero out.

1.3 Dashboard and Exposé System Preferences

a video monitor that shows true color and interlacing output. Even if you don't intend the final product to be seen anywhere but on the Internet on a computer, the application is still making it into one of these video formats, so you have to monitor on an interlaced display to properly assess your material's output.

You may also want a second computer display for the large number of windows that video editing applications need. This is helpful for long-form video production, but by no means as essential as a video monitor, or at the very least a television display.

1.4 Typical Connection Layout

To get the video out of your computer and onto the video monitor or TV set, you're going to need to use some kind of digital-to-analog conversion device. The simplest one for most people is a camcorder. The video and audio comes out of the computer's FireWire port, which gets connected to the camcorder, or DV deck, or DV converter box, such as the Data-Video DAC-200. The output of the camcorder in turn is connected to the video monitor. That's the best place to watch your movie while you work. The audio from the camera or the video monitor is fed into speakers. Figure 1.4 shows a typical connection layout. The camera is the hub that passes the digital signal back and forth to and from the computer and sends the analog signal to the video monitor and speakers.

If you are using an external FireWire hard drive, in most cases the system works best by daisy-chaining the FireWire connection. A six-pin to six-pin FireWire cable connects the computer to the hard drive. Then a six-pin to four-pin cable connects the hard drive to the camcorder or converter box, and then standard video cables connect the camcorder to your television set or video monitor. Avoid using USB drives for video work. Although these are fast, they transfer data in bursts, which doesn't work well for video, and is not supported by Apple for use with video applications.

Speakers

Good-quality speakers are very important. They should be connected to the same source as the video you're monitoring. The rule of thumb here is that audio follows video, so if you are looking at your video on a television monitor, you should listen to your audio from the same source. So if you have a deck or a DV camera that is feeding the signal from your computer to your TV monitor, that device should also be feeding your audio speakers. Switchable speakers would be ideal, with two inputs to monitor either the video source or the computer output.

Firing Up the Application

Now it's time to launch that program. Double-click on the icon in the *Applications* folder, or better yet make an alias in the **Dock** and click on that (see Figure 1.5). After you start up the application, the first window asks you to register your application. Once you've done this, the screen will not appear again.

After a new installation or after you have trashed your *Final Cut Preferences* file (see page 102), you will next see the setup preferences screen. The default setting is **DV-NTSC** with audio at 48kHz, as shown in

✎ Note_____
Canon Cameras: Generally, Canon cameras do not support daisy-chaining and require a separate FireWire bus to work correctly with an external FireWire drive. Unfortunately, all Apple computers, although they may have multiple FireWire ports, only have one FireWire bus controlling them. For tower computers, and laptops with cardbus slots, third-party hardware can be added that will add a second bus and allow you to use external drives with these cameras. This is a real problem for iMac users, who don't have these options. Generally, with these setups, it's best to capture your material in the internal drive and then move it to the external drive for editing.

✎ Note_____
Updates: After installing the software, it's probably a good idea to check the Apple Final Cut Express web page http://www.apple.com /finalcutexpress to see if there have been any updates to the application. Applications are constantly being refined and updated to fix problems or to accommodate developments in hardware or the operating system. You can also do this by choosing **Software Update** in the **System Preferences** or directly from under the Apple menu. Also, don't forget to register your new software.

1.5 Final Cut Express Icon

1.6 Choose Setup Dialog Box

Figure 1.6, and you have several settings available to you for NTSC as well as PAL. If you're using HDV, select the appropriate HDV Apple Intermediate Codec preset. If you are working with 12-bit, also called 32kHz audio, more choices are available. If you click on the little Show All checkbox in the upper right of the window, you can select from a longer list of options (see Figure 1.7). For now, choose **DV-NTSC**. That's the format in which we'll be working.

The second pop-up makes you choose your primary scratch disk. The pop-up defaults to your system partition, setting the scratch disk inside the user's *Documents* folder. It also offers you the choice of any hard drives attached to your system. You should set this to your dedicated media drive whenever possible, as in Figure 1.6.

If you do not have a camcorder or DV deck connected to your computer, you will get the warning dialog in Figure 1.8. If you will be working consistently without a deck or camera connected, notice the little checkbox in the lower left that allows you to switch off this warning. You can turn it back on in **User Preferences** under the **Final Cut Express HD** menu.

1.7 FCE Presets

Understanding the Interface

Launching a new application for the first time is always an adventure, especially when it's as complex as Final Cut Express HD. Some software can be intimidating, and some can be downright confusing. When FCE launches, it fills your screen with lots of windows, buttons, and tools to explore. Figure 1.9 shows you the default arrangement called **Standard**.

1.8 External A/V Warning

1.9 The Final
Cut
Express
HD
Interface

The Primary Windows

The screen is divided into four primary windows, with two large empty
screens as your principal monitors:

1. The **Browser** is the first window at the top left of the screen, empty
   except for one sequence. The Browser is the equivalent of the **Clips**
   pane in iMovie.

2. The **Viewer**, the empty black window in the middle of the screen,
   allows you to look at individual video clips, either from the Browser
   or from the Timeline.

3. The **Canvas**, the empty monitor on the right, displays the output of your material as you edit it. The Canvas is linked directly to the Timeline.

4. The **Timeline** for your video is the window with the horizontal sections in the bottom half of the screen. This is where you lay out your video and audio material in the order you want it. The Timeline that's open in the interface is the item called *Sequence 1* in the Browser.

The materials that you're working with in the project, such as video clips, audio files, and imported graphics, are all listed in the Browser. Think of the Browser as a giant folder. You can nest folders within folders, just as you can on the Desktop. You can make folders in FCE and keep them in your Browser to organize your material. The Browser is not where your clips are stored; it is only a list. Your clips are physically stored on your media hard drives.

You'll also notice small vertical bars to the right of the Timeline that contain the **Tools** and **Audio Meters**. Some of the tools are hidden, nested inside the Tools palette. Figure 1.10 shows all the tools displayed. There is a Selection tool, the arrow at the top. There are Edit and Range Selection tools; Track Selection tools; editing tools such as Roll, Ripple, Slip, and Slide; Blade tools; Zoom and Hand tools; Crop and Distort tools; and various Pen tools for creating and editing keyframes.

1.10 Tools Palette

Window Arrangements. Many people like to work with multiple monitors or large Cinema displays, or attach a second monitor when working on a PowerBook. With multiple monitors you can move the Browser onto a separate screen and leave just the Viewer, Canvas, Timeline, and Tools on the main monitor. In FCE you can create new window arrangements by moving the screens into new positions such as in Figure 1.11 with a long tall Browser on the left. You can save this, or any other window arrangement, by holding down the **Option** key and selecting from the **Window** menu, **Arrange>Set Custom Layout** (see Figure 1.12). Here a few other presets are available to you.

Once the arrangement has been set, it can be called up at any time from the **Window>Arrange** menu or by using the listed keyboard shortcut. You can always return to the Standard window arrangement from the **Window** menu or using the keyboard shortcut **Control-U**.

In FCE you can resize windows dynamically by grabbing the edges where the cursor changes to a Resizing tool (see Figure 1.13). When you pull with the **Resizing** tool, the windows will move proportionately, expanding and contracting as needed to fill the available space.

1.11 Long Browser Arrangement

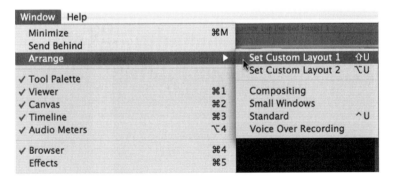

1.12 Window>Arrange>Set Custom Arrangement

> **Tip**
>
> **Open Sequence:** Should your project ever open and you don't see a Canvas or Timeline, it means that no sequence is open. There needs to be at least one sequence in a project. Double-click the sequence icon in the Browser, and it will open the Timeline with its Canvas.

1.13 Resizing Tool for Window Arrangements

Tabbed Palettes

You have probably also noticed that most of these windows have tabs with other windows behind them. Let's take a quick look at what's back there. Tabbed in the Browser is the **Effects** window. Video and audio effects, transitions, and generators are stored here, including any favorites you want to access frequently.

The **Viewer** has tabs behind it as well:

- **Stereo (a1a2)** or **Mono (a1) and Mono (a2)**, which hold the two channels of audio associated with a video clip. This is where you can see a video clip's audio waveform and manipulate the sound by raising and lowering the levels or panning the tracks from left to right.
- **Filters** is where you control effects applied to clips.
- **Motion** lets you view and change settings for properties such as Scale, Rotation, Center, Crop, and others.

Most of the Motion properties can be animated. You can also change the image's Opacity, making it more transparent. At zero opacity it will be invisible. You can add a Drop Shadow that will appear on any underlying layers, and you can add Motion Blur, which simulates the amount of smearing, created by a fast movement across the screen. We will look at these Motion tools in later lessons (see Lessons 13 and 14, which start on pages 215 and 233, respectively).

The Canvas and the Timeline window also have tabs. If you have more than one sequence open at a time, they will appear as tabs in the Timeline window and in the Canvas.

Summary

So ends Lesson 1. The purpose of this lesson has been to get you started correctly, to make sure your system is set up to edit digital video with a professional application. We have looked briefly at the application and its interface. In the next lesson, we'll look at the interface in greater detail with an existing project.

Lesson 2

Exploring the Final Cut Express HD Interface

Now that you've set up your system, we'll take a detailed look at each of the components in its interface. Let's look at each of its windows in turn.

Default Windows

If you have the default window with a new sequence open, there isn't much to look at in the application. The Browser is empty except for the single sequence called *Sequence 1*. You can rename sequences just as you would any file in the Finder. Click on the name to highlight it, and type in a new name. You can also select it and press the **Enter** key on the keyboard to select the name for editing. (See the note on **Clip Name Changes**.) You can have as many sequences as you want in a project, and you can place sequences within sequences, which is called nesting sequences. We'll look at nesting later (page 202 in Lesson 12).

Because there's not much to see here, we'll open an existing project so we can look at each window in greater detail and see what a project in progress looks like. FCE allows you to have more than one project open at a time, which is very useful because it allows you to easily move elements from one project to another. However, you may get confused about which window belongs to which project, so I normally don't have more than one project open at a time unless I really need to.

13

Note
Clip Name Changes: Selecting a clip and pressing the Enter key is the only instance in the application in which the Enter key and the Return key have a different function. While the Enter key will let you rename an item, the Return key will open the item, a clip into the Viewer, and a sequence into the Timeline window.

Note
Right-Clicking: If you do not have a three-button mouse, either an Apple Might Mouse or a third-party mouse, you really should get one. Any inexpensive USB three-button mouse with a scroll wheel will do. The application uses right-clicking to bring up shortcut menus, and the scroll wheel will move sliders as well as window displays. Until you get the three-button mouse, whenever I say right-click you should hold the Control key while clicking to bring up the shortcut menu.

To close the currently open project, click the little round button in the upper left corner of the Browser. This is the **Close** button that in most windows in the Mac operating system is colored red. You can also close the project by right-clicking on the tab and selecting **Close**, or by simply pressing **Command-W** when the Browser is the active window. You can tell which is the active window because the window title bar at the top is highlighted and brighter than the other window title bars in the application.

Loading the Lesson

Let's begin by loading the book's DVD into your DVD drive. When you begin any lesson that needs material from the DVD, you should first drag the needed folders onto the media drive of your computer. The sound and video clips included in those folders will play much better and more smoothly from your computer's high-speed media drive than from any DVD drive. This is a hybrid DVD, and it will probably start up your DVD player application when you mount the disk. The DVD portion contains a short introduction to FCE aimed at iMovie users, but if you double-click on the DVD icon in the Finder, you will find a folder called *Hybrid DVD-ROM Contents*. Inside that folder are several other folders. Open the *FCE3.5EW_Projects_and_Media* folder.

1. From this folder, drag the folder called *Media* onto your media drive. If you don't have a separate media drive, drag the folder onto your computer's system hard drive.

2. Next, drag the *Projects* folder onto your internal system drive. It's not very large. Probably the best place to put it is inside your home *Documents* folder.

3. Before doing anything else, eject the DVD.

4. Open the *Projects* folder on your hard drive, and double-click the project file *Lesson 2* to open the project. There is no project for Lesson 1, so for convenience there's no project named *Lesson 1*.

Reconnect Media

Before the project finishes loading, you will see the dialog box in Figure 2.1. Because the media is in a new location from where it was previously, you will have to reconnect the files:

1. Click on the **Reconnect** button in the Offline Files dialog. Do not click **Continue**.

2. In the next window that comes up, check the box to specify the drive where your media is located (Figure 2.2).

3. Click the **Search** button.

4. FCE will find one of the items. If it's the correct item, make sure it's selected and click the **Choose** button in the dialog box (Figure 2.3). If it doesn't find it, use the **Locate** button to find it manually. It should find the rest of the files as well.

5. All of the files should then have moved to the bottom of the Reconnect Files dialog box. Click the **Connect** button to reconnect the files (Figure 2.4).

You'll have to do this for each of the projects from this book that you open.

2.1   Offline Files Dialog

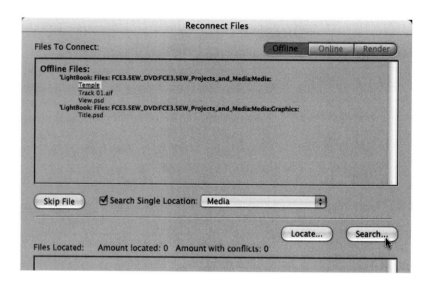

2.2 Reconnect Files Dialog Box

2.3 Reconnect Dialog Box

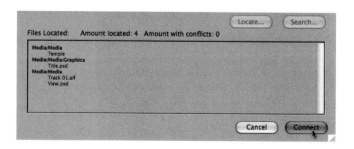

2.4 Items Ready to Be Reconnected

The Browser

When the project called *Lesson 2* has finished loading, the Browser should look like Figure 2.5.

2.5   Lesson 2 Browser Window in Medium Icon View

Browser Views and Buttons

This default view for the Browser in Final Cut Express is called a Medium Icon view. You will see icons for video clips—notice the small speaker to indicate that the clip has audio. You will also see an audio track with its speaker icon, and you will see a couple of folders. Although it uses a folder icon, in FCE-speak this folder is called a *bin*, an old film term. Think of long bits of processed film hanging from pins into a large, cloth-lined bin. Whatever you call it, it behaves like a folder.

You can change the Browser view by clicking one of the tiny buttons in the upper right corner of the window (see Figure 2.6). These buttons let you choose List view or three different icon views, Small, Medium, and Large, as well as buttons for arranging by Name or by Duration. Small icon view is pretty useless, and the large icons take up a lot of screen space.

2.6   Browser Buttons

You can also change views by selecting **View>Browser** Items. Finally, as in much else in FCE, you can use a keyboard shortcut. **Shift-H** will cycle through the four Browser view options.

FCE has the ability to create buttons that you can place in the various windows of the interface. To create a new button, open the **Button List** from the **Tools** menu (or use the keyboard shortcut **Option-J**). This calls up the Button List in Figure 2.7. To find a function for which you want to create a button, start typing in the search field at the top of the list, and all the functions that have that word will appear in the list below.

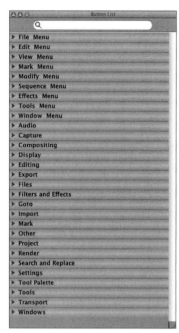

2.7   Button List

✦ *Tip*
Tabbed Bins: You can open a bin tabbed into the project window by holding down the Option key as you double-click to open it. To close a tab, right-click on the tab and select Close Tab.

2.8   Button Holder
        Shortcut Menu

To make a button for Export to QuickTime Movie, for instance, type *export*, and five items will appear. Drag the item you want to any one of the little coffee bean–like holders in the upper right corner of any of FCE's windows. The buttons can be further customized by adding colors to the buttons and spacers to group them into sections. You can even color the spacers by using the shortcut menu, with which you can also save your button configurations for all of your windows (see Figure 2.8). To remove a button, drag it out of the bean. It will disappear, like an item from the Dock, in a puff of smoke.

In the Extras folder on the DVD that came with this book is a Button List called *Editing Workshop Button Bars*. Using the **Load Button Main Button Bars** function and navigating to that file on the DVD, you can load a group of buttons that I find useful to have. There aren't many of them, because I'm not a great advocate of mousing around the desktop and clicking buttons, but you can add your own favorites to any of the button holders.

Let's change the Browser to List view. Right-click in the empty Browser space and select **View as List**. To see the contents of the bins:

- Click the twirly disclosure triangle to expand the folder view *or*
- Double-click on the folder icon

If you double-click the icon, the bin will open in a new window. To close the window, click on the little button in the upper left corner of the window or use the keyboard shortcut **Command-W**.

There are two sequences in the Browser: one called *Sequence 1* and another called *Title.psd*. When opened, a sequence appears in the Timeline window. Here you lay out your video, audio, and graphics clips. A sequence can have multiple tracks of video and audio. You can also place sequences within sequences, as we shall see later. Whenever you create a new project, FCE always creates a default empty sequence called *Sequence 1*. The *Title.psd* also has a sequence icon because FCE imports Photoshop files as layered sequences, with each of the layers in the PSD file appearing as a separate video layer in the Final Cut sequence, one stacked on top of the other. The other PSD file, *View.psd*, is a single-layer file and imports as single-layer graphic and has a different icon. We'll look at working with graphics in Lesson 12 on page 208.

Browser Details

With the Browser in List view and the window arrangements set to Standard, stretch out the Browser window to the right (or use the maximize button, the one on the right of three in the upper left corner), and you will see just some of the many things the Browser displays in List view (see Figure 2.9).

The Browser shows the duration of clips and the In and Out points, which are probably marked Not Set at this stage. You also see track types (whether video and/or audio) and how many audio tracks. Note that the Photoshop sequences tell you how many layers there are in the sequence. Also notice that *Sequence 1* by default has two video tracks and four audio tracks.

2.9   Browser List View

Notice the column Master Clip and items that are checked. We'll look at this more closely in the next lesson on page 38.

Notice in Figure 2.10 that the clips in the bin called *Courtyard* have torn edges on the left and right. These are subclips. We'll look at subclips and how to use and create them in Lesson 3 starting on page 40.

The Browser also shows the type of audio, frame size, and frame rate (in the case of these clips, 29.97 frames per second, the standard frame rate for all NTSC video).

2.10   Subclips in the Browser

Other information displayed in the Browser includes:

- Type of video compression used
- Data rate
- Audio sampling rate
- And much, much more information than you will probably ever need to look at.

⭑ *Tip*

Ordering: You can arrange the order in which clips are shown in List view by selecting the column header. By clicking the little triangle that appears in the header, you can change the order from descending to ascending. Also, if you Shift-click on the header of other columns, another triangle will appear and will be added as secondary ordering lists. Secondary sorting allows you to organize and arrange your material to suit your workflow. To clear secondary sort orders, choose a new primary sort, and click on an unsorted column header without the Shift key.

Only the **Name** column cannot be moved. It stays displayed on the left side of the window. You can move any of the other columns by grabbing the header at the top of the column and pulling it to wherever you want the column to appear.

If your cursor is over the column headers in the Browser and you right-click your mouse, you get a shortcut menu. Figure 2.11 shows the list of available categories, except for Name and Duration, which are active columns in the Browser.

| Hide Column |
| Edit Heading |
| |
| Show Offline |
| Show Length |
| Show Reverse Alpha |
| Show Composite |
| Show Type |
| Show Source |
| Show Size |
| Show Last Modified |
| Show Capture |
| Show Scene |
| Show Shot/Take |
| Show Reel |
| Show Comment 1 |
| Show Comment 2 |
| Show Comment 3 |
| Show Comment 4 |
| Show Pixel Aspect |
| Show Anamorphic |
| Show Thumbnail |
| Show Aux 1 Reel |
| Show Aux 2 Reel |
| Show Creator |
| Show Comment 1 |
| Show Comment 2 |
| Show Master Clip |
| Show In |
| Show Out |
| Show Tracks |
| Show Good |
| Show Log Note |
| Show Audio |
| Show Frame Size |
| Show Vid Rate |
| Show Compressor |
| Show Data Rate |
| Show Aud Rate |
| Show Aud Format |
| Show Alpha |

2.11 List of Available Browser Items

One of the important items you can call up here is Source. This tells you the file path to a clip's location on your hard drive.

The Browser Facade. The FCE Browser is a facade. What you're bringing into the FCE project, the media you are importing into your Browser, is the equivalent of aliases of your media (see Figure 2.12). While you are working with these aliases, you are using them to pass instructions to the computer about which pieces of video and audio to play when and what to do with them. The conveniences created for you in the application are an elaborate way of telling the computer what to do with the media on your hard drives and how to play it back. All of the clips in the project, whether in the Browser, the Viewer, or the Timeline, are simply pointers to the media on the hard drive. This is a non-destructive, completely non-linear, random-access artifice. This means that your media is not modified by anything you do in the application; it means you can arrange the media and work on any portion of your project at any time; and it means that you can access any piece of media from anywhere on your hard drive at any time. The clips are not brought into the Browser or placed in the Timeline. They never leave their place on the hard drives. They are never in the project at all except as a list. You can change the names in the list to anything more convenient, and it has no effect at all on the data stored on your hard drive. All you are doing is changing how you give instructions to the data; you are not changing the data at all. On the other hand, if you change the names of the clips on your hard drive, that will confuse FCE, and you will have to reconnect each clip to establish the links between the two.

2.12 Media and FCE Workflow

Tip
Shortcut Menus: There are shortcut menus available throughout FCE that can be accessed by right-clicking in the application. These are context-sensitive menus that change, depending on where the cursor is. These shortcut menus provide powerful tools for working with the application.

Another item hidden in the shortcut menu is **Show Thumbnail**. This cool feature brings up a thumbnail that shows the first frame of the video. Grab the thumbnail and drag the mouse. This is called *scrubbing*, and you're dragging through the video clip itself so you can see what's in it. Viewing media in the Browser can save time. You can quickly scan through a shot to see if it's the one you're looking for. You can also change the Poster frame, the frame that appears in the thumbnail. The default is the first frame of the video (or the In point), but if you scrub through the video and find a new frame you would like to set as the thumbnail, press the **Control** key and release the mouse. A new Poster frame has been set. If you change the Poster frame for a clip here or in any other Browser window, the poster will change for each instance of that clip anywhere in the Browser and will also display as the poster when the Browser is set to Icon view.

2.13 Scrub Tool

When the Browser is in Icon view, the clips are shown with their Poster frame. Like the thumbnails we saw earlier in List view, these icons have the same scrubbable property. To do this, you have to select the **Scrub** tool from the **Tools** palette (see Figure 2.13). Or, if you hold down **Control-Shift**, the cursor will change to the **Scrub** tool, which is the **Hand** tool with forward and reverse arrows that will let you scrub the icons.

As everywhere in the application, right-clicking in the Browser will call up several useful items, allowing you to make new bins and sequences, as well as importing and arranging material. The clips themselves hold a shortcut menu that can do a variety of useful things, including a new function in v3.5, the ability to **Reveal in Finder** (see Figure 2.14). This is a neat feature that gives you the ability to go directly to the media file in its location on your hard drive.

2.14 Clip Shortcut Menu

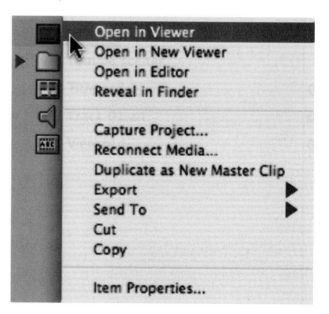

Another very useful option in the clip's shortcut menu is Item Properties. Item Properties, which can also be called up by using the keyboard shortcut **Command-9**, calls up an information window that tells you everything about a clip (see Figure 2.15). You can rename a clip here, as well as see technical information about the clip and its specifications.

In an earlier version of the application, there were two more very important panels behind the Format panel: one for Timing and, even more

Item Properties: Temple

Format	Clip	V1	A1	A2
Name	Temple	Temple	Temple	Temple
Type	Clip			
Source	Media: FCE2 Editing Wor	Media: FCE2 Editing Wor	Media: FCE2 Editing Wor	Media: FCE2 Editing Wor
Offline				
Size	360.8 MB	360.8 MB	360.8 MB	360.8 MB
Last Modified	Tue, Aug 12, 2003, 6:46	Tue, Aug 12, 2003, 6:46	Tue, Aug 12, 2003, 6:46	Tue, Aug 12, 2003, 6:46
Tracks	1V, 2A			
Vid Rate	29.97 fps	29.97 fps		
Frame Size	720 x 480	720 x 480		
Compressor	DV/DVCPRO – NTSC	DV/DVCPRO – NTSC		
Data Rate	3.6 MB/sec	3.6 MB/sec	3.6 MB/sec	3.6 MB/sec
Pixel Aspect	NTSC – CCIR 601	NTSC – CCIR 601		
Anamorphic				
Field Dominance	Not Set	Not Set		
Alpha	None/Ignore	None/Ignore		
Reverse Alpha				
Composite	Normal	Normal		
Audio	A1 + A2		Mono Mix	Mono Mix
Aud Rate	48.0 KHz		48.0 KHz	48.0 KHz
Aud Format	16–bit Integer		16–bit Integer	16–bit Integer

2.15 Item Properties Format Panel

importantly, one for Logging Info. Logging Info was particularly useful because you could enter searchable descriptions and comments and other information about the clip in different windows. Unfortunately, Apple chose to remove this functionality. Fortunately, the descriptive capabilities are still available in FCE; they are just a little more awkward to access. The descriptive information and comments can still be entered in the Browser columns (see Figure 2.16). To get from one comment field to the next, press the **Tab** key, and the cursor will move to the next editable window.

Temple scenes							
Name ▼	Camera	Sound	Comment 1	Comment 2	Comment 3	Comment 4	Log Note
LS incense at the altar	wide angle	quiet	nice shot	LS at altar	from behind	incense smoke	
LS incense up steps	blue		walks up steps	LS to altar	from behind		
man praying							NG
woman praying	exposure change	OK	LS push	good for MS	from the side		
woman with incense			bowing at incense				

2.16 Browser Comments

Notice that two of the column headers have been renamed Camera and Sound to add information about the technical quality of the material. Except for Comments and Comments 2, you can change the names of the other comments columns by right-clicking in the column header and choosing Edit Heading from the shortcut menu (see Figure 2.17). (There seems to be a bug that changes the column names from **Master Com-**

2.17 Editing a Column
        Heading

ment **1** to **4** to **Comment 1** to **4**, giving you duplicate column header names, only one of which can be edited.)

2.18 Log
        Note
        Shortcut
        Menu

✦*Tip*
Shortcut Menus: Using shortcut menus in List view lets you change items for multiple clips with a few clicks of the mouse. For instance, to add a comment to the Log Note, I select a number of clips. Then I use the shortcut menu in the same column, the Log Note column. This will bring up a list with all of my recent notes in that column. I select the one I want, and all of the selected clips will have their log notes changed (see Figure 2.18).

Viewer

The Viewer is one of the primary editing places in Final Cut Express. This is where you manipulate your clips, mark where you want them to start and end, and prepare them for your timeline. To load a clip into the Viewer, double-click on it or select it and press the **Return** key. Start by double-clicking on the clip *Temple* to open it into the Viewer (see Figure 2.19).

Viewer Buttons

Let's look at that array of buttons clustered around the bottom of the Viewer so that you are familiar with them and what they do (see Figure 2.20).

2.19 The
        Viewer

The **Shuttle** tab, on the left just below the video display in the Viewer, lets you shuttle the clip forward and backward. Grab it with the mouse and move right and left. The farther from the default center position you go, the faster the video will play.

The **Jog** wheel on the right, opposite the Shuttle tab, will let you roll back and forth through the frames slowly.

2.20 Viewer Buttons

The central button in the middle is the **Play** button. Starting from the left in the group around the Play button, the first button is **Go to Previous Edit** (**Up** arrow). The next button is quite useful—it lets you play from your In point to your Out point. The keyboard shortcut is **Shift-**.

The next button to the right of the central Play button is **Play Around Current Point** (****). The default is for playback to start five seconds before where the playhead is and play for two seconds past where the playhead is. We'll look at how to use these functions in later lessons.

The last button is **Go to Next Edit** (**Down** arrow).

Another cluster of smaller buttons sits at the bottom left of the Viewer. From the left, the first button is **Match Frame** (**F**). This is a very useful tool, although it won't work for you at the moment. If you open a clip that's in a timeline, it allows you to match back to the same frame in the Canvas.

The next button is **Mark Clip** (**X**), which selects as the In and Out points the entire length of the clip.

The next button, the diamond shape, adds a keyframe, which you need when creating animation, although the Viewer is not the best place to do this.

🐎 *Note*
Match Frame Variations:

Another useful tool to remember is Command-Option-F. This is a variation of Match Frame. This matches back to the same frame from a new clip of the original piece of media called up directly from your hard drive. Another useful shortcut is Shift-F, which doesn't open the clip into the Viewer, but finds it and selects it in the Browser. This can be very handy if you have lots of bins and even bins within bins.

The next button adds a marker to the clip (**M**). Markers are useful. They let you set visible marks on clips that appear in the Timeline window. You can mark the beat of a piece of music, where a phrase appears in dialog, where a pan or zoom starts or ends. Practically anything you can imagine noting about a clip can be made to appear on the screen. Think of them as onscreen Post-It® notes for a video editor.

Next to the **Marker** button is a group of two buttons: **Mark In** (**I**) and **Mark Out** (**O**).

There are two more buttons at the bottom right of the Viewer. The one with the **Clip** icon lets you load recently opened clips. Next to that is a button with a large **A**. This opens a menu that accesses the **Generators**, such as Bars and Tone, Render Gradients, Color Mattes, Slug, Text, Title 3D, and the Title Crawl tool. We'll delve into this button in later lessons.

Put your cursor in the white bar directly below the video image. As you mouse down, the playhead will jump to where you are. The playhead is the little yellow triangle with a line hanging from it. There are other playheads in Final Cut Express. In addition to the Viewer, they're in the Canvas and the Timeline, every place where you can play video.

2.21 Top of the Viewer

Duration — Zoom — View — Current Time

Top of the Viewer

Let's look at the top portion of the Viewer for a moment (see Figure 2.21). In the center are two buttons, actually pop-up menus. The one on the left, the **Zoom** pop-up menu (see Figure 2.22), adjusts the size of the image displayed in the Viewer. You can set it to **Fit to Window** (**Shift-Z**), or to a percentage from very small to so large that you can see all of the pixels at their blocky best.

The other button, the **View** pop-up menu, changes the view from **Image** mode to **Image+Wireframe** (see Figure 2.23). You need this mode especially for compositing in the Canvas when you're combining and animating multiple layers of video. The pop-up also lets you turn on overlays, including the **Title Safe** overlay.

2.22 Zoom Pop-Up Menu

Viewer Time Displays

At the top of the Viewer are two sets of numbers. The time display on the left is the duration of the clip from its marked In point to its marked Out point. If the In and Out are not set, it will show the duration of the media from start to finish.

The time display on the right shows the current time for the frame where its playhead is sitting. This is not the timecode for the clip, which FCE does not display, but timecode is crucial to accurate editing, and FCE does keep track of the timecode internally, although it is not viewable. Like all time displays in FCE, it's addressable. Click in it to type a new number, or add and subtract a value. When you change the time in the current time display, the playhead immediately jumps to that time.

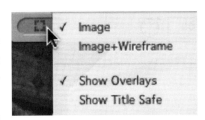

2.23   View Pop-Up Menu

Playing Clips

There are several different ways of playing a clip to look at your video. The most apparent is the big Play button in the middle of the Viewer controls. If you like working with the mouse, this will be for you, but it is not the most efficient way to work by any means.

There are other ways to view your video besides at real speed. The buttons on the Viewer do this, but learn the keyboard. It's your friend, and it's really a much simpler, easier way to control your editing than the mouse.

Spacebar

Press the **Spacebar** to play the clip. To pause, press the spacebar again. **Spacebar** to start, **Spacebar** to stop. To play the clip backward, press **Shift-Spacebar**. This method is much quicker and keeps your hands on the keyboard and off the mouse. You can play and manipulate clips in the **Viewer** with great efficiency using only the keyboard.

What Is Timecode? Timecode is a frame-counting system that is almost universal to video cameras. A number is assigned to every frame of video and is physically recorded on the tape. The numbers represent time and on most consumer cameras begin at 00:00:00:00, zero hours, zero minutes, zero seconds, and zero frames. On professional and some prosumer cameras, the start number can be set to anything you like. A timecode number is assigned to every frame of video—25 frames per second in the European PAL system and 30 frames per second in the North American and Japanese NTSC system.

For NTSC this is a problem, because the true frame rate of all NSTC video isn't 30fps but 29.97fps. Because of this, NTSC has created two ways of counting timecode called Drop Frame and Non-Drop Frame.

Non-Drop Frame (NDF) displays the numbers based on a simple 30fps frame rate. The problem with this is that when your timecode gets to the one-hour mark, one hour of real-world time has already come and gone. The one hour of clock time finished almost four seconds earlier, so your program is running too long.

Drop Frame (DF) uses a complex method of counting that compensates for the difference between 29.97fps and 30fps. No actual frames of video are dropped. DF drops two frames per minute in its count, except every 10th minute. This means that at the one-minute mark, your DF video will go from 59;29 to 1:00;02. There is no 1:00;00 or 1:00;01. Notice the semicolons. The convention is to write DF timecode with semicolons, or at least one semicolon, but NDF is written only with colons. The DV standard uses Drop Frame timecode as its counting method, although some prosumer and all professional cameras can be switched between the two.

Some consumer cameras, particularly inexpensive Canon cameras, are dependent on having their date/time clock set so they can generate timecode. It is crucial that the clock on your camera be set to some date or time; otherwise, every time you press Record, the camera will restart the timecode at 0:00:00;00, which will create a break in what should be continuous timecode.

If you are working in HDV, you should also be aware that in FCE the timecode in that format is unfortunately lost during capture.

Keyboard Shortcuts

Another common way to play the clip is with the **L** key:

- **L** is play forward.
- **K** is pause.
- **J** is play backward.

On your keyboard, the keys are clustered together, but you're probably thinking, "Why not comma, period, and slash?" There is a method to the madness. **J**, **K**, and **L** were chosen because they're directly below **I** and **O**. **I** and **O** are used to mark the In and Out points on clips and in sequences. They are probably the most commonly used keys on the editing keyboard. Hence **J**, **K**, and **L** are positioned conveniently for the fingers of your right hand with the **I** and **O** keys directly above them.

You can view your video at other speeds. You can fast forward by repeatedly pressing the **L** key. The more times you press **L**, the faster the clip will play. Similarly, hitting the **J** key a few times will make the clip play backwards at high speed.

To play a clip one frame at a time, press the **Right** arrow key. To play it slowly, hold down the key. To play slowly backward, hold down the **Left** arrow key. To jump forward or backward one second, use **Shift** with the **Left** or **Right** arrow keys. Pressing **K** and **L** together will give you slow forward, and **K** and **J** together, slow backward. To go back to the previous edit—the cut prior to the point where you are currently—use the **Up** arrow key. To go to the next edit event, use the **Down** arrow key. To go to the beginning of the clip, press the **Home** key; to go to the end, press the **End** key.

Table 2.1   Some Principal Keyboard Shortcuts

Play	L
Pause	K
Play backward	J
Fast forward	Repeat L
Slow forward	L + K or hold Right arrow
Fast backward	Repeat J
Slow backward	J + K or hold Left arrow
Forward one frame	Right arrow
Backward one frame	Left arrow
Forward one second	Shift-Right arrow
Back one second	Shift-Left arrow
Go to previous edit	Up arrow
Go to next edit	Down arrow
Go to beginning	Home
Go to end	End
Mark the In point	I
Mark the Out point	O
Go to In point	Shift-I
Go to Out point	Shift-O
Play Around Current Point	\
Play from In point to Out point	Shift-\

★ *Tip*
Shortcut Help: If trying to remember all of the keyboard shortcuts is shorting out your brain, you can get color-coded special keyboards with keys that display the shortcuts. A great tool is Loren Miller's KeyGuide. No FCE editor should be without one. He makes them for several applications including Final Cut Express. You can find out more about them and order them from http://www.neotrondesign.com.

Table 2.1   Some Principal Keyboard Shortcuts

Match Frame	F
Mark Clip	X
Add Marker	M

This is just the surface of the Viewer. We'll be visiting it repeatedly in the lessons to come, especially the tabbed windows behind the video window.

Exploring the Canvas and Timeline

You'll probably first notice that the Canvas window (see Figure 2.24) is similar to the Viewer. Most controls are duplicated. Some have been placed in mirrored positions, such as the cluster in the lower right corner, which mirrors the cluster in the lower left of the Viewer. The Shuttle and the Jog are also in mirrored positions in Canvas, but they function the same. The time displays at the top function the same as in the Viewer. The two pop-up menus in the top center are also the same. The Canvas is missing the Recent and Generators pop-ups, which are only in the Viewer window.

2.24 The Canvas Window

Timeline Window

Let's look at the Timeline window, which, being empty at this stage, isn't much to look at (see Figure 2.25). The Timeline window is made up of tracks. Above the horizontal central double bar are the video tracks. FCE defaults to two video tracks visible, marked V1 and V2. You can change this in Preferences, which we'll look at in Lesson 6 on page 93. An FCE

2.25   The Timeline Window

sequence can have up to 99 tracks of video and 99 tracks of audio.

At the top of the window is the **Timeline Ruler**, which is marked off like a ruler and displays the current time position for an item in the Timeline window. Just to the left of the ruler is the current time display, where the playhead is at the moment. In an empty sequence that has just been opened, the playhead will be at the beginning at 0:00:00;00.

The Patch Panel

One of the video tracks has a small v1 attached to it. This is the source button and indicates what selected destination track the source video will be sent to. This area, which sets the source video and audio to the destination video and audio tracks, is called the **patch panel**. We'll talk about the patch panel more in later lessons.

There are simple keyboard shortcuts to select each of FCE's windows. The principal windows are shown in Table 2.2.

2.26 Setting Destination Tracks in the Patch Panel

Table 2.2 Principal FCE Windows Shortcuts

Window	Shortcut
Viewer	Command-1
Canvas	Command-2
Timeline	Command-3
Browser	Command-4
Toggle between Viewer and Canvas	Q

Below the horizontal bar are the audio tracks. There are four showing. A1 and A2 are set as destination tracks, awaiting a stereo pair of audio clips. A3 and A4 are ready for additional sound tracks. You can separate the source button from the destination track by clicking the small source button, separating it from the track icon as in Figure 2.26. You can reset the destination track by clicking the link together. You can also reassign source buttons to destination tracks by pulling the patch to the desired track.

More Timeline Functions

To the right of the patch panel are track locks, which let you lock and unlock specific tracks as you need to (see Figure 2.27).

Just to the right of that, next to the tracks themselves, is FCE's Auto Select feature. **Auto Select** is used to perform copy, lift, add edit, and some paste functions to specific tracks. It also controls FCE's match frame function.

2.27 Track Locks and Auto Select Features

To the left of the patch panel are the **Visibility** and **Audibility** buttons, which can be toggled on and off as needed. We'll look at those in later lessons (see Figure 2.28).

There are more controls for the Timeline windows along the bottom and the left edge of the window (see Figure 2.29).

The slider on the far right lets you change the horizontal scale at which your clips are displayed in the Timeline window. Drag the clip *Temple* from the Browser into the Timeline. You don't have to be very precise; just drop it anywhere. It's a pretty long clip, so use the slider to adjust the scale of the Timeline to see how it functions.

2.28 Visibility and Audibility Buttons

The triangle to the left of the slider is a pop-up menu that lets you set different displays in the Timeline window (see Figure 2.30), audio waveforms or filmstrip display.

0.29   Timeline Buttons

Mute/Solo Reveal   **Clip Overlays**   **Track Height**   **Display Popup**   **Horizontal Scale**

2.26   Timeline Pop-Up Menu

2.31   Resizing ndividu al Track Heights

2.32   Mute/Solo Buttons

2.33   Track Mover and Static Display Line Closed

2.34   Track Mover and Static Display Line Split

2.35   Snapping and Linked Selection On

The buttons to the left of that set the track height. There are four settings of track height, which can be toggled with the keyboard shortcut **Shift-T**. Choose whichever height is comfortable for you and your monitor's resolution. You can also set individual track heights by putting the cursor between the tracks and dragging up or down to resize the track height (see Figure 2.31).

The second button from the left displays **Clip Overlays**, which allow you to adjust the clip's audio levels and video opacity.

On the far left edge of the Timeline window is a little button that opens up the Mute/Solo buttons on the left edge of the window (see Figure 2.32). These buttons allow you to selectively mute tracks or solo a track so that you hear only the selected tracks. The difference between muting and switching off audibility is that a muted track will still export or record to tape, while a track with audibility switched off will not export or be heard during recording to tape.

The **Track Mover** tool lets you change the proportions of the video and audio panels in the Timeline window by moving the **Static Display Line** (see Figure 2.33). This can also be split to show different sections of the video and audio panels simultaneously, which can be very useful when you're working with multiple tracks of video or audio. By pulling the tabs on the right edge, you can pull the Static Display Line apart (see Figure 2.34). Much like word processing software, this function lets you keep several tracks displayed while scrolling through the rest of the tracks independently.

In the upper right corner of the Timeline window are two tiny icons that tell you whether **Snapping** and **Linked Selection** are turned on (see Figure 2.35). When these are turned on, the buttons are green; when they're switched off, the buttons are black.

If **Snapping** is on, the playhead, clips, and anything you move in the Timeline will automatically want to butt up against each other as though they had magnetic attraction.

Turn on **Linked Selection** if you want the sound and the picture together when you grab a sync clip. With **Linked Selection** on, they'll move in unison. With it off, the two elements can be moved separately. I recommend leaving **Linked Selection** on at all times, bypassing it only when necessary with a simple keyboard modifier instead of using the button.

The last button in the Timeline window is a little pop-up in the upper left corner, the **RT** pop-up that lets you set your real-time playback capability (Figure 2.36). The default is **Safe RT**, while **Unlimited RT** allows more real-time playback on fast computers, but at the expense of dropped frames during playback. You should leave it on Safe RT for now.

Summary

You should now be familiar with the interface and with the terminology used in Final Cut Express. I know you must have many questions, and I hope to be able to answer most of them over the course of these lessons so that you can work smoothly and efficiently with the application. Spend some time clicking around in the Final Cut Express windows. You can't hurt anything. And remember to try right-clicking to bring up shortcut menus. In the next lesson, you'll learn how to edit your material into a sequence and start to build up your movie.

2.36 RT Pop-Up

Tip
Help: If you have problems with your computer or with Final Cut Express specifically, there are two useful places you can go to for help. One is the Apple Final Cut Express discussion forum, which you can link to from http://discussions.info.apple.com, or through my website at http://www.fcpbook.com.

Lesson 3

Cutting Up Those Shots

In this lesson we're going to look at some video and cut it up. We've looked at the interface in detail, so it's time to learn how to use FCE tools. FCE has several different ways you can work with your video, different ways to do the same function, so that users can find a workflow with which they're comfortable.

Loading the Lesson

If you haven't already done this, if you skipped directly to this lesson, you'll need to load the material from the DVD that accompanies this book.

1. Start by loading the DVD that came with this book into your DVD drive. Open the DVD. This is a hybrid DVD and will probably start up your DVD player application when you mount the disk. If your system is set to start up the DVD player, you should quit that application. Double-click on the DVD icon on your desktop, and you will find a folder called *Hybrid DVD-ROM Contents*. Inside that folder are several other folders.

2. Open the *FCE3.5EW_Projects_and_Media* folder. From this folder drag the folder called *Media* onto your media drive. If you don't have a separate media drive, drag the folder onto your computer's system hard drive.

3. Next, drag the *Projects* folder onto your internal system drive. It's not very large. Probably the best place to put it is inside your home *Documents* folder.

4. Open the *Projects* folder on your system hard drive and double-click the *Lesson 3* project to launch Final Cut Express.

The project is empty except for one sequence that is also blank.

Importing the Movie

Use **File>Import** (**Command-I**) to import the *Temple* file from the folder inside the *Media* folder on your hard drive. Or you can drag the clip directly from the *Media* folder into your Browser. It should appear as in Figure 3.1.

This is a *master clip*. Every time you import a clip or capture a clip or bring a new clip into the Browser, the first instance of that clip is always a master clip. A master clip can be cut up into smaller clips called *affiliate clips*. Any copy or portion of a master clip has an affiliate relationship to the master. All of the pieces made from the master clip, all the affiliates and the master clip, must have the same name. If you change one, they all change.

3.1   Clip in Browser

DV Start/Stop Detect

DV Start/Stop Detect is probably the best way to work with DV material in FCE. HDV material already comes into the Browser broken down into separate clips, but DV material does not. The DV Start/Stop function uses the start/stop information from your camera to create markers on your video. This method works only if your camera has had its clock set. It doesn't have to be the right date or time, but it has to be set. No clock, no DV Start/Stop Detect. Once markers are set with DV Start/Stop Detect, they can be used to segment the master clip. Here's how it works.

1. Bring your long clip of DV material into FCE, either by importing it, capturing it with the Clip method, or with Now.

2. Select the clip or clips. In this case, select the *Temple* clip you imported into your Browser.

3. From the Mark menu, select DV Start/Stop Detect.

You will immediately see the Scanning DV Movie(s) progress bar (see Figure 3.2). It can scan multiple clips at once. It can handle even whole bins. It produces clips with markers at each camera start/stop.

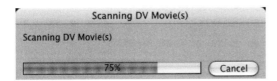

3.2 Scanning DV Movie(s) Progress Bar

After it's finished, nothing seems to have changed, but it has. DV Start/Stop Detect will add markers at every shot change based on that date/time stamp. To see what's happened, double-click the clip *Temple* to open it into the Viewer. In Figure 3.3, notice that the playhead in the Viewer is sitting on the first marker, *Segment 1*; each of the other markers appears in the scrubber bar at the bottom of the Viewer.

3.3 Master Clip with Segments in the Viewer

Once the material has had segment markers added, it's easy enough to change the separate segments in shots:

1. Change the Browser into List view, either from the **View>Browser Items>as List**, or by using **Shift-H** to toggle through the Browser views, or by clicking the List view button in the upper right corner of the Browser as in Figure 3.5.

2. Twirl open the disclosure triangle in the Browser and marquee-drag through all of the markers, as shown in Figure 3.6.

3.4 Markers in Current Time Indicator Box

➤ Note

Marker Shortcuts: You can easily move between segments with keyboard shortcuts:

Shift-M (or Shift-Down arrow) takes you to the next marker.

Option-M (or Shift-Up arrow) takes you to the previous marker.

Command-` (grave key) will delete a marker under the playhead, as will the Delete button in the Marker dialog box. You can call this dialog box by pressing the M key while you're positioned on a marker.

A list of markers can be accessed by right-clicking in the current time indicator window in the upper right of either the Viewer or Canvas (see Figure 3.4). This will allow you to leap from one marker to another.

➤ Tip

Moving Shots Out of Bins: To move a shot out of the bin back to the top level of the Browser, drag the shot out of the bin and pull it onto the Name column header. That puts it at the top level of the project window.

3. Then select from the menu **Modify>Make Subclip** or use the keyboard shortcut **Command-U**.

Before I do that, I often move the master clip into a bin appropriate for its content. To create a new bin, either use **File>New>Bin** or right-click in the Browser and from the shortcut menu choose **New Bin**, or use the keyboard shortcut **Command-B**. I do this so that when I make the subclips from *Temple*, they're already placed in the right bin.

3.5 List View Button

3.6 Marquee-Dragging before Making Subclips

The subclips appear in the Browser with the subclips' torn edges icon as in Figure 3.7. All subclips are master clips, and though you can rename your subclips anything you want, be aware that the underlying media that remains on your hard drive is unchanged in any way. Most important, its name is not changed. So if you ever need to reconnect the media or recapture it, FCE will want to do it under its original naming convention.

At this stage you're breaking down your material, organizing it, arranging it into bins, renaming clips, adding notes, and so on. This is critical if you're working on a project that's longer than 10 minutes or so, or a project with a lot of material, regardless of its finished length. This process of viewing, logging, and organizing should not be skimped on, rushed, or dismissed as drudge work. It is crucial to the editing process.

Using Markers

If you're working with DV material without camera breaks, material captured from an analog-to-digital converter, or material that was dubbed to DV, you can still cut up your material using subclips. There are a few different ways to do this.

You can do this by adding markers to the clip similar to the way DV Start/Stop Detect worked. Open your long capture into the Viewer, and add markers as you play the clip—on the fly if you like—by tapping the **M** key or the ` (grave) key. You can create markers with more precision, as well as set up extended markers to segment your material. Try this with *Temple*.

3.7   Subclips in Browser

1. First, marquee-drag through any segment markers that may already be in the clip.

2. With the segment markers selected, hit the **Delete** key to wipe them out.

3. Double-click *Temple* to open it into the Viewer.

4. Set a marker at the beginning of the clip. Do this by moving the playhead to the beginning of the clip with the **Home** key and pressing either the **M** key or the ` (grave) key.

If you wish, you can label the marker. Press the **M** (or `) key again while sitting over the marker. This brings up the dialog window in Figure 3.8. Change the name of the marker, and add comments if you wish.

This name will carry over into the name of the subclip. In this case, the subclip would be called *WS with memorials from "Temple" subclip*. The marker information and comments will displays in the Viewer. This stays with *Temple* and will appear whenever the playhead is over the marker.

3.8   Edit Marker Dialog Box

5. Play through the clip either with the spacebar or by scrubbing in the scrubber bar until you find the shot change.

6. Use the **Left** and **Right** arrow keys to find the first frame of the next shot at 10;16.

7. Add another marker.

You can work your way through the clip, adding markers at each shot change. As with DV Start/Stop Detect, the markers can be turned quickly into subclips.

8. Marquee-drag to select the markers from *Temple* in List view and press **Command-U**.

⤳*Tip*
Scroll Wheel: FCE allows you to use the scroll wheel of a multibutton mouse like the Apple Mighty Mouse to do a variety of tasks. It's quite a powerful tool. You can scroll the Browser window, but you can also use the scroll wheel to scrub the playhead in the Viewer window, in the Timeline Ruler of the Timeline window, as well as scrubbing the playhead when the cursor is over the Canvas. If the cursor is above one of FCE's sliders, it will move the slider, changing the values.

⤳*Tip*
Edit Marker: If you Shift-click the Marker button in either the Canvas or the Viewer, it not only sets a marker but also opens the Edit Marker dialog box, where you can enter information. You can also use Command-Option-M to open the Edit Marker window for the nearest marker before the current position of the playhead.

If you're working on narrative film or tightly scripted material, or material with lots of excess that you can discard, *extended markers* might be useful. When you capture large sections of material, there are often unnecessary pieces: clapperboards, director's instructions, setting the camera, bad takes. You can avoid adding these into your subclips by extending a marker:

1. Start by finding where you would like the subclip to begin.

2. Add the marker with the **M** or ` key.

3. Play through the shot until the director shouts, "Cut!" or you find the end of the piece you want to make into a subclip.

4. Now extend the marker from the menus by going to **Mark> Markers>Extend**, or extend it even more simply by using the keyboard shortcut **Option-`** (the grave key).

The nice thing about this technique is that when you create your subclips by selecting them and pressing **Command-U** or using the **Modify** menu to **Make Subclip**, the subclips are only for the duration of the extended marker. By extending the markers, you have defined the limits of the media available for each shot, basically defined rough In and Out points.

In the *Temple* clip, for instance, there are some camera bobbles, such as right at the end of the second shot, the glass-fronted hut. The start of the third shot also has a reframing zoom. By using extended markers, you can cut these areas out so they don't appear unexpectedly during a transition. You might also not want to subclip a shot (e.g., the fourth shot in *Temple*). Extend the previous marker to the end of the third shot, and don't add a marker for the fourth shot. This is why there are only seven markers or extended markers as in Figure 3.9.

3.9   Extended Markers

Do not extend markers or define subclips too tightly. This should only be a rough cut covering the entire portion of usable media. FCE will treat the limits of the subclip as the limits of its media and will not allow you to extend the shot farther, so always make the ends of the subclips, the limits of the media, as far as you can without going into another shot or into some rough material, such as a swish pan or a quick zoom, that you don't want to see on the screen.

Markers are an excellent tool for entering information about clips, even if you're not using the markers to edit your material. Here you can add comments, as well as create *chapter markers* to use with iDVD and *scoring markers* to carry over to Apple's music-creation and audio editing application, Soundtrack. It's important to note that these specialized markers should always be added only to the Timeline. None of these markers, if added to clips, will carry over into other applications. Markers are also searchable within a sequence, as we shall see.

Using In and Out Points

Another method of working with media without DV Start/Stop Detect is to open the original master clip into the Viewer and mark your shots with In and Out points.

1. If you have placed any markers in *Temple*, delete them as we did before so that you have only the long clip.

2. Next open *Temple* into the Viewer by double-clicking on it or dragging it into the Viewer.

3. Mark an In point at the beginning of the clip with the **I** key.

4. Play through the clip or scrub through it until you find the last frame of the first shot. Use the **Left** and **Right** arrow keys to find the frame at 10;15.

5. Mark an Out point with the **O** key.

Your Viewer will look like Figure 3.10. Notice the Out point mark in the upper right corner of the picture, indicating that the playhead is at the Out point.

6. To make this shot a subclip, press **Command-U** or choose **Modify>Make Subclip.**

7. The clip will immediately appear in the Browser with its name highlighted, ready to be renamed.

8. Type in a name for the clip.

9. Switch back to Viewer (**Command-1** above the QWERTY keyboard, not on the keypad), and you're ready to mark new In and Out points to the master clip to make the next subclip.

Although making a subclip does not create a separate QuickTime file, the subclip is treated as a separate piece of media, even though in reality it's not. There are several advantages of working with subclips. One is that it's easy to scrub the clip, running the mouse along the length of the media. Another is that it prevents you from inadvertently extending one shot into the adjacent shot during a transition as we shall see in Lesson 8.

Note

Removing Subclip Limits: Creating a subclip limits the available media to the length of the shot. If you ever need the rest of the captured material within the original shot, select the clip or clips in either the Browser or the Timeline and use **Modify>Remove Subclip Limits**. You will then be able to open the shot in the Viewer and access the whole length of the clip, which is still on your hard drive.

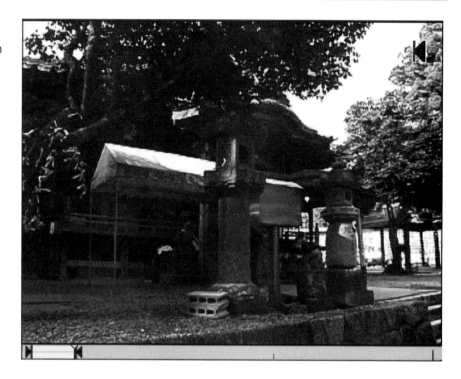

3.10 Viewer with In and Out Points Marked

Slicing Your Clips

All of these methods described so far have been based on creating sub-clips. You can also work by making clips and turning them into master clips so that they can be renamed.

Slice 1

3.11 Clearing In and Out Points in the Viewer

There are a few different ways to do this. Let's do this first in the Viewer:

1. Open *Temple* from the Browser into the Viewer.

2. It will probably have an In and Out point marked. We need to clear those.

3. Right-click on the scrubber bar at the bottom of the Viewer to evoke a shortcut menu, and select Clear In and Out. This will—surprise, surprise—clear the In and Out points (see Figure 3.11). You can also use the keyboard shortcut **Option-X**.

4. Let's begin with the second shot in *Temple*. Find the shot change at 10;16.

5. Mark an In point by pressing the **I** key.

6. Press the **spacebar** to play *Temple*. Use the Left and Right arrow keys to find the end of the shot, the last frame of the thatched hut at 18;29.

7. Mark an Out point with the **O** key.

8. Create a new bin in the (**Command-B**) and name it *Clips*.

9. Drag the marked clip of *Temple* from the Viewer and drop it into the Clips bin. Do not rename this clip; this would rename *Temple*. The new clip still has an affiliate clip relationship to the master clip.

10. Go back to the Viewer and repeat the process, marking new In and Out points for each shot and dragging each into the *Clips* bin in turn.

You still cannot rename the clips because they are still affiliate clips. However, the next feature gets around this problem.

11. Select all of the clips you've created in the *Clips* bin by marquee-dragging through them or by double-clicking on the bin to open it and then using **Command-A** to **Select All**.

12. With the clips selected from the **Modify** menu, go to **Modify>Make Master Clip**.

This will turn all of the clips into master clips, allowing you to rename them and organize your material.

Slice 2

The second Slice method is in the Timeline. This is where you really are slicing with a digital razor blade.

1. Open *Temple* from the Browser into the Viewer.

It will probably have an In and Out point marked. We need to clear those.

2. Right-click on the scrubber bar at the bottom of the Viewer to select **Clear In and Out**, or use the shortcut **Option-X**.

3. If it's not already open, open the empty Timeline by double-clicking on *Sequence 1* in the Browser.

4. Drag *Temple* into it, dropping the clip on V1.

✎ Tip
Clearing from the Browser Only: You can clear the In and Out points for a clip that's been opened from the Browser; you can't, however, clear the In and Out from a clip that's been opened from the Timeline. A clip that's in a Timeline must by definition have an In and Out point, a start and end frame, even if it's the first and last frame of the clip.

✎ Tip
Edit Points: A note on the place where edit points occur. The shot change between edits takes place between the frames. That is, you see one frame, and the next frame you see is the first frame of a different shot. So when you're marking In and Out points, you should know where the shot change is taking place. If you mark the In point for a frame that you're looking at in the Viewer, that will be the first frame of the new clip. The edit will take place in the space before that frame. If you mark the frame you're looking at as an Out point, that will be the last frame in the clip, and the edit will take place after that frame.

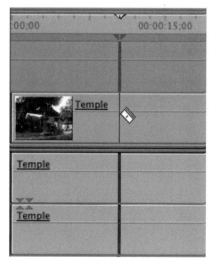

3.12   Blade Tool in the Timeline

✎ *Tip*
Keyboard Shortcut: In addition to using the Blade tool, you can move the playhead to where you want to make the cut and press the keyboard shortcut Control-V. This will cut the clip right at the playhead.

When you place a clip in the Timeline, the playhead automatically jumps to the end of the clip, ready for you to place another clip in position. In this case, we don't want it to do that.

5. Click in the Timeline window to make it active (or use **Command-3**), and press the **Home** key to take you back to the beginning of the Timeline.

6. To make it easier to work in the Timeline, press **Shift-Z**, which is **Fit to Window**, to fit the contents of the Timeline into the window.

7. Press the **spacebar** to play *Temple*. The video plays in the Canvas.

8. Use the **spacebar** to stop and the **Left** and **Right** arrow keys to find the start of the shot of the glass-fronted hut at 00:00:10;16.

9. Make sure Snapping is turned on. Check the indicator in the upper right corner of the Timeline window. We saw this at the section on the Timeline in Lesson 2 on page 32. Toggle it on and off with the **N** key.

10. Select the Blade tool from the Tools palette, or call it up with the **B** key, and move it along the Timeline to the playhead line.

As you move along the clip in the Timeline, your cursor will show the Blade tool, rather than the Selector (see Figure 3.12). You'll see dark triangles at the top and bottom of the playhead line indicating that the cursor is at the playhead.

11. Click with the Blade tool to cut the clip at the playhead.

This will cut the video and audio on the clip as though you were cutting it with a knife or a razor blade, which is what used to be done to cut film and audiotape, and even videotape when it was first edited. This is the digital equivalent for the same process.

12. Go to the end of the shot, using the **Left** and **Right** arrow keys to find the first frame of the next shot.

13. Click the Blade tool again or use the keyboard shortcut **Control-V**.

14. Now that you've made one cut, find the next shot. Its first frame starts with the quick zoom at 00:00:19;00. Again, use **Control-V** or the Blade tool to cut the shot.

15. Go through the Timeline and slice more clips by using **Control-V** to cut at the first frame of every new shot (see Figure 3.13).

16. After you've cut out the clips you want from the long shot in the Timeline, go to the Browser and select *Sequence 1*.

17. From the **Modify** menu, select **Modify>Make Sequence Clips Independent**.

18. If you've been using the Blade tool, you need to switch back to the standard Selection tool. To switch to it, you can click on the tool at the top of the Tools palette or press the **A** key. Think A for Arrow.

19. Drag the clips into a bin in the Browser.

These clips are all master clips and can be renamed, reedited, and organized. They will have the same master/affiliate relationship as a captured clip, an imported clip, or a subclip.

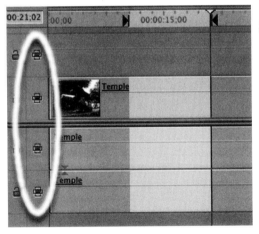

These *Temple* shots come into the Browser with In and Out points marked, and if you open the clips, you'll find that each contains all of the video that's in the original master shot called *Temple*. The upside of this is obvious. Because a sliced clip is a copy of the master clip, you can now access any shot in the reel from inside any sliced clip.

3.14 In and Out Marked in the Timeline with Auto Select Functions

3.13 Cut Clips in the Timeline

\Note
Edit Points Redux: We talked about where the cut takes place when you're editing, that the In point cuts the space before the frame you're looking at, and the Out point cuts after the frame you're looking at. The Blade always cuts on the gap in front of the frame you're seeing in the Canvas. So to get the last frame of *Temple* when slicing in the Timeline, you have to be looking at the first frame of the shot after it. If you press Control-V on the last frame of the memorials shot, the thatched hut shot will have one frame of the memorials at its head.

That's the upside; the downside is scrubbing. The master clip is made up of a long length of material, perhaps even a whole reel of film or a roll of videotape, although I would advise against this. It's now difficult to scrub in the Viewer because even a tiny movement will move the playhead a long way up and down the scrubber bar.

Slice 3

With the Slice 2 method, you're cutting the pieces you want to keep and moving them into the Browser. Let's look at another method that works almost exclusively in the Timeline. Here we'll cut away the pieces we don't want to use and leave behind in the Timeline the shots that contain the good material.

🐾 *Note* _____
Browser and Timeline Clips:
Now may be a good time to explain the relationship between the clips in the Browser and the clips in the Timeline. Quite simply, there isn't one—no direct, linked relationship, anyway. They are separate, distinct items. They may be copies of each other, but they are separate clips that share the same media. So in the first Slice method, when you mark up the master clip with In and Out points, you are marking one clip and making copies of it in the *Clips* bin. When you drag the master clip from the Browser and place it in a Timeline, you are placing a copy of the master clip. So when you razor-blade and ripple-delete the clip in the Timeline, you are not in any way affecting the master clip that remains untouched in your Browser.

1. Begin by deleting everything in *Sequence 1*. **Command-A** will Select All, and the **Delete** key will remove everything.

2. Make sure there aren't any In and Out points marked in the master clip *Temple*, and bring a fresh copy into the sequence by dragging it into the Timeline.

3. Press the **Home** key to return to the start of the sequence.

4. Play forward until you reach the beginning of the second shot at 00:00:10;16. We want to remove the second shot from the sequence, because we don't need it.

5. Mark an In point in the sequence by pressing the **I** key.

6. Play forward through the second shot and through the zoom at the beginning of the third shot, until about 00:00:21;02. We will cut out everything from the first frame of the second shot up to and including the frame where the playhead is parked just as we mark In and Out points in the Viewer.

7. Press the **O** key to enter an Out point in the Timeline, which should look like Figure 3.14.

Notice the highlighted area in the tracks. This is the Auto Select function in Final Cut. Tracks can have their selections toggled on and off with the buttons circled on the left in Figure 3.14. This allows you to select some tracks while not selecting others.

8. Now that we have the area we want selected, press **Shift-Delete** to execute a ripple-delete, removing that section of the video. You can also use the **Forward Delete** key on an extended keyboard to do this.

It is critical that nothing is selected in the sequence when you use this technique. Anything that is selected (e.g., clip, audio, title) will be ripple-deleted instead of the marked In and Out section. The simplest way to avoid this is to press **Command-Shift-A** to Deselect All, the opposite of **Command-A**, Select All. This drops anything that's been selected. A good habit to get into before you execute this technique is to always make sure the Timeline is the active window and press **Command-Shift-A**, or if you really like the menus, use **Edit>Deselect All**.

This method of cutting away the bad material in the Timeline is a fast and efficient way to edit material. You end up with the shots you want to keep in the Timeline. If you do want to organize and rename your material again, choosing **Modify>Make Sequence Clips Independent** will separate the clips in the Timeline from their master/affiliate relationship. Now you can pull them into bins and rename them if you wish. I'd use this method for working on something like a news story, where fast turnaround and quick cutting is necessary, and you're not concerned with storage, organization, or logging your material carefully.

Slicing, whether in the Viewer or the Timeline, has the advantage of quickly and easily accessing all of your material while still cutting it up into shots for editing. It has a couple of disadvantages, however: the problem of not being able to scrub easily in the Viewer when the shot is very long, and the problem of transitions, in which you might accidentally extend the transition into another shot, appearing as a flash on the screen. This cannot happen with properly made subclips.

Range Clipping

Another technique for slicing or making subclips is to use the **Range** tool in the Timeline. Some people prefer this method because it offers a visual display of the In and Out points as you work. Let's try this.

3.15 Range Tool

> ❦ *Tip*
> ***Auto Select Shortcuts.*** There is a collection of keyboard shortcuts using the keypad of the extended keyboard to toggle off and on the Auto Select functions. Command-1, -2, -3, -4, and so on will toggle tracks V1, V2, V3, V4, and so on. Option-1, -2, -3, -4, and so on will toggle audio tracks A1, A2, A3, A4, and so on. Option-clicking on the Auto Select button for a video track will toggle soloing for just that one track. Option-clicking on the Auto Select for an audio track will do the same there.

1. Again, make sure there are no In and Out points in the master clip *Temple* before dragging it into an empty *Sequence 1*.

2. Select the Range tool from the tools. It's under the second icon from the top. You can also call it up by pressing **GGG** (the letter **G** three times) (see Figure 3.15).

3. Position the playhead in the Timeline where you want the clip selection to begin.

4. With the Range tool, stroke one section of the clip (see Figure 3.16).

As you stroke the clip to make the selection, the Canvas will give you a two-up display that shows you the start and end frames as well as the timecode in the Timeline (see Figure 3.17).

3.16 Range Tool in the Timeline

3.17 Range Selection Two-Up Display in the Canvas

5. Grab the selection from the Timeline and drag it to the Browser, where it can be changed into a master clip if you wish.

Organizing the Clips

Once you have your material diced up, you should spend some time putting it away so you can find it again. There are no firm rules about this, and I find that each project tends to dictate its own organizational structure. Usually I begin with one bin that holds all of the master shots. These are usually pretty big chunks of video: 10, 20, 30 minutes, usually not smaller. From the master shots, clips are separated into bins. Keeping the master shots has the advantage that you can go back to the material in bulk to look through it again. As the project nears completion, I like to do this to see if I overlooked or discarded anything, which can be useful in light of the way the material gets cut together.

The separate bins can be organized in a variety of ways. Narrative projects tend to have material broken down into scene bins, with sub-bins for different types of shots or characters, depending on how complex the scene is. Documentary projects tend to break the material down into subject matter: a bin for all of the forest shots, another for logging scenes, another for road work, another for weather, another for all of the interviews, another for sound, another for narration tracks, another for music, another for graphics. As I said, there are no hard-and-fast rules on how material is organized.

The real trick is to break down your material into enough bins so that your material is organized, but not so many bins that it becomes difficult to find material. As you move clips into bins, add notes—lots of them. The more information you include on the clips, the easier it will be to find them.

Cutting up your shots and organizing them into bins is critical to working efficiently, particularly for long-form work, projects longer than 20 minutes or so. The longer the project, the more tapes you have, the more sequences, the more complex everything becomes. Having your material well organized is crucial. Fortunately, FCE provides ways to help you, such as the comments and logging information that we saw in the previous lesson.

Final Cut's search tool is called the Finder. To search for something in a project, use the same keyboard shortcut as the Desktop Finder: **Command-F**. This brings up the **Find** window (see Figure 3.18). The first pop-up menu lets you search:

- The open project
- All open projects
- The *Effects* tab

3.18 Find Dialog Box

It searches anything tabbed into the Browser.

The second pop-up menu selects **All Media** or a choice of **Used** or **Unused Media**, and the third pop-up menu lets you replace or add to existing results. The two pop-ups at the bottom define parameters. The left one sets where it's going to look. Unless you have a pretty good idea where the information is (e.g., if you're looking for a specific type of file), just leave it on the default Any Column. The right pop-up menu lets you limit the search parameters to speed up the process by limiting the number of results.

If you click the **Find All** button rather than the default **Find Next**, the requested clips appear in a new Browser window (see Figure 3.19).

3.19 Finder Results Window

Note the two buttons at the bottom, which let you:

- Show a selected item in the regular Browser bins
- Remove selected items from a project

An important point to understand about this Finder is that all of the items it locates are directly related to the items in the Browser. Unlike FCE's usual behavior where clips in sequences and bins can be copies of each other, here the found clips are directly linked to the clips in the Browser. Highlight a clip here, and it's highlighted in the Browser. Delete a clip here, and it's deleted from the Browser.

Look before You Cut

However you work your video into clips or subclips, you're really looking through your material. You should watch for relationships, shots that can easily be cut together. Getting familiar with the material is an important part of the editing process, learning what you have to work with and looking for cutting points.

✏️ *Tip*
Using Find to Keep Track.
Because FCE doesn't keep track of shots that are taken from the Browser and put in a sequence, the Find window is one way to do this. By selecting the Unused pop-up menu, you can find the material. You can then use the check mark in the Good column to mark the unused clips. Unfortunately, Find searches only media, not subclips, so if any part of a piece of media is used, even one subclip, then all of the subclips based on the same media are considered used.

✏️ *Tip*
Other Searches. The search engine isn't only for finding shots. You can search for anything in FCE. You might want to find a filter or a transition. You can search for those as well.

While looking through the material in the Timeline, some editors even like to roughly cut up the shots into sequences as they sort through the pictures. As they come to groups of shots that work together, some editors put them together in sequences.

Look through the master shot *Temple*. It's quite short, but it shows a few shots that have obvious relationships. The same woman, in the white woolen hat, appears in four of them:

- In the third shot, as she bows before an incense bowl
- The shot from behind her that looks a little blue, in which she is walking up the stairs
- Another, in quick succession to the previous one, also from behind as she goes up the steps
- In medium shot from the side as she bows and prays

These shots can obviously be cut together to make a little sequence. You might want to put in a cutaway between the shot of her bowing at the bowl and her from behind walking up the steps or at the top of the steps already. From either of those two shots, a direct cut to her bowing would work without problem.

Searching for these relationships between shots is critical as you look through your material. Some editors like to immediately create small sequences and group them together, not finely honed, but roughly laid out, so that first important impression is preserved. You may not use it in your final project, but assembling related shots quickly into a sequence is an efficient way to make notes about your material. We'll look at assembling material into sequences in our next lesson.

You can have multiple sequences open at the same time. Timelines normally tab together into one Timeline window, but you can pull the timelines apart so that you have two sequences open on the screen at the same time. You can pull shots from one sequence into another. By doing this, you're copying the shot from one sequence into the new sequence.

Summary

In this lesson, we've covered using DV Start/Stop Detect and working with markers, creating subclips, and slicing up our clips, as well as organizing our material so that we can work efficiently. In the next lesson, we'll look at more precise ways of editing sequences, moving your clips into the Timeline, and trimming them with some advanced editing tools. Next we're going to look at putting our shots together in a sequence.

Lesson 4

Editing Basics: Placing Your Shots

Now that you've marked up your material in Final Cut Express, we're ready to put them into the Timeline. FCE has several different ways, usually three or four, to do most of the editing functions. You can edit directly into the Timeline with the mouse, in the Viewer with buttons, or with keyboard shortcuts, which is probably the most efficient way to edit in most instances.

Loading the Lesson

If you haven't already moved the *Media* and *Projects* folders onto your computer, you should do so now as at the beginning of Lesson 2.

Let's begin by opening the *Projects* folder on your hard drive and double-clicking the project file, *Lesson 4*, to launch the application.

As in Lesson 2, before the project finishes loading, you'll be greeted with the **Reconnect** dialog box.

1. Click on the **Reconnect** button in the Offline Files dialog (see Figure 4.1). Do not click Continue.

2. In the next window that comes up, check the box to specify the drive where your media is located (see Figure 4.2).

3. Click the **Search** button.

4. FCE will find one of the items. The computer will now search through your hard drives looking for the QuickTime file called *Food*. If it's the correct item, make sure it's selected and click the **Choose** button in the dialog box (see Figure 4.3). If it doesn't find it, use the **Locate** button to find it manually. It should find the rest of the files as well.

5. All of the files should then have been moved to the bottom of the Reconnect Files dialog box. Click the **Connect** button to reconnect the files (see Figure 4.4).

You will have to do this for each of the projects from this book that you open. If one of the lesson projects you're working on ever gets corrupted, you should retrieve a fresh copy from your DVD, move it to your hard drive, and reconnect it as we have just done.

4.1   Offline Files
          Dialog

4.2   Reconnect Files
          Dialog Box

4.3 Reconnect Files Dialog Box

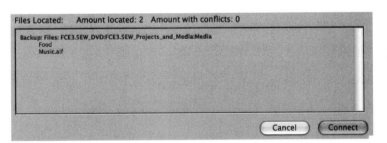

4.4 Items Ready to be Reconnected

4.5 Dragging into the Timeline

Setting Up the Project

Inside the Browser of your copy of *Lesson 4*, you'll see an empty *Sequence 1*. In the Browser there is also an audio file called *Music.aif* and the master clip, *Food*, together with a bin called *Clips*. Open the *Clips* bin and you'll see that the shots from *Food* have been cut up into subclips.

Working with the Clips

To start, let's look at where we're coming from and the material we have to work with:

1. The empty *Sequence 1* should already be open; if it is not, double-click on it.

2. Open the *Clips* bin and double click on the shot called *Food1*, which is 6;01 long, six seconds and one frame.

3. Play the shot. Let it pan from left to right across the trays of food, let the pan end, give it a beat, and then stop.

4. Enter an Out point by pressing the **O** key or the Out point button in the Viewer.

This will probably be around 4;12, about four and one-half seconds long.

4.6   Edit Overlay

Try it a few times until you get the pacing of the movement down. You might find that the more times you try it, the more you're shaving off the shot. Perhaps you'll feel that the front needs to be shortened as well. Instead of beginning right at the start of the shot, enter an In point just before the camera pans right. When you have it the way you want it, you're ready to move it into the Timeline.

There are four ways to get material from the Viewer to the Timeline:

1. Drag it there. Grab the image from the Viewer and pull it directly into the Timeline, dropping it onto V1 as shown in Figure 4.5.

2. Drag the clip from the Viewer to the Canvas, and the visual dialog box called the Edit Overlay (see Figure 4.6) immediately appears. Drop the clip on Overwrite.

3. Use the Overwrite keyboard shortcut, **F10** (see the Note called "Dashboard and Exposé").

4. If you added the Editing Workshop buttons (see the Note called "Edit Buttons"), you can click on the red Overwrite button as in Figure 4.7.

✎ *Tip*
Dashboard and Exposé: If your keyboard shortcuts don't work properly, see the section on Dashboard and Exposé in the Lesson 1 section on Optimizing Your System.

4.7   Editing Workshop
      Button in the Canvas

Which way you execute the edit is a question of personal preference. Many people prefer to drag to the Timeline. It can be easy when you're unpracticed to drop the clip into the wrong track or to do an Insert instead of an Overwrite when you drag to the Timeline. I prefer the accuracy and exactness of dragging to Overwrite or using the keyboard shortcut.

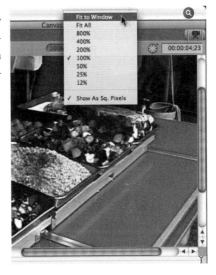

4.8   Fit to Window

✏️*Tip*
Edit Buttons: Although there are
no edit buttons in the Canvas, you
can make your own buttons for the
primary edit functions that we'll be
looking at in this chapter. I have created a button list for these functions
that you can use. You'll find it in the
Extras folder of the DVD. In addition
to the edit functions, a couple of
other buttons are useful, which
appear over the Browser.

To load the buttons, right-click in one
of the coffee-bean button holders
and choose Load Main Button Bars
from the shortcut menu. Navigate to
the Extras folder on the DVD and
select Editing Workshop Button Bar
to add the buttons to the windows.

Overwrite

Let's look at the Edit Overlay (see Figure 4.7). It offers seven different
editing options. The most commonly used is the **Overwrite** command.

4.9   Patch Panel

4.10   Patch Panel
with Stereo
Music Only

1. Drag the clip from the Viewer until the box marked Overwrite
    highlights.

2. Drop the clip.

It will overwrite whatever is in the Timeline beginning at the point at
which the playhead is parked. When you drag a clip onto the Edit Overlay or use a keyboard shortcut to execute an edit, the clip is placed in the
Timeline on the designated destination tracks, in this case V1 and A1/A2.
These are the default destination tracks set in the patch panel at the head
of the Timeline (see Figure 4.9).

The number of tracks and the types available as destination tracks are controlled by what is loaded in the Viewer. For instance, if you have a still image in the Viewer, only one destination track for video will be available. Similarly, if you have a piece of stereo music loaded in the Viewer, only two tracks of audio will be available as destinations and no video tracks, as in Figure 4.10.

4.11   In Point Mark in the Timeline

So that we can look at the functionality offered in the Edit Overlay, let's quickly drag a few shots into the Timeline to see how they work.

1. If you haven't already done so, drag *Food1* from the Viewer and drop it on Overwrite.

2. Select clips *Food2* and *Food3* in the Browser and drag them directly to the Overwrite box in the Edit Overlay.

The clips will appear in the Timeline following *Food1* in their bin order. Every time you place a clip in the Timeline, the playhead automatically leaps to the end of the clip, ready for the next edit event.

Insert

If Overwrite is the most commonly used of the Edit Overlay features, then the next most used must be **Insert**. This is where a nonlinear editing system shows its power.

1. Move the playhead to the edit between *Food1* and *Food2*.

Tip

Dropped Frames: One of the most common causes of dropped frames, especially for FCE users with slower computers, is that their viewing window is not fit to the video. If you look at your DV video in a small frame while the material is set to full size, you're expecting the computer to display only a portion of the video while playing it back. If this doesn't produce dropped frames on playback, it will at the very least show as stuttering video on your computer monitor. You can always tell if the image is too large for the viewing window when you see scroll bars on the sides, as in Figure 4.8. To correct this, select Fit to Window from the Viewer's Zoom pop-up menu, the left of the two pop-up menus at the top of the Canvas, or use the keyboard shortcut Shift-Z. Shift-Z is also used in the Timeline to fit the contents into the window.

Tip

Timeline In Point: You can also define the In point in the Timeline to be a different point from the playhead. Go to the Canvas or the Timeline window and press the I key to mark an In point (see Figure 4.11). This will be the In point for the next edit, and when you drag the clip from the Viewer to the Canvas or press F10, the clip will drop at the marked In point and not at the playhead's current position.

4.12   Snap Markings

As you move the playhead onto the edit point, it should snap strongly to the join and display on the tracks the marks in Figure 4.12. If you don't see the snap marks, **Snapping** is turned off.

2.   Press the **N** key. Try it several times, toggling the Snapping function on and off.

The **N** key may become one of your most often used keys in Final Cut Express. You'll probably be changing from one mode to the other often.

Now with Snapping on, you should have the playhead parked between the clips.

3.   Grab *Food5* directly from the Browser and drag it to the Canvas, call-ing up the Edit Overlay.

4.   Drop it on Overwrite to see what happens.

5.   *Food5* wipes out all of *Food2* and some of *Food3*.

6.   Quickly undo that with **Command-Z**.

7.   This time, instead of dragging *Food5* onto Overwrite, drag it onto Insert.

Immediately the Timeline rearranges itself. *Food5* drops into the Time-line, appears between *Food1* and *Food2*, and pushes everything farther down in the Timeline, as shown in Figure 4.13.

Insert will move everything down the track regardless of a clip's position. So if you insert into the middle of the clip, the clip will be cut, and every-

4.13 The Insert Edit

thing on all of the tracks will be pushed out of the way. This applies to all tracks, including music or narration, which you may not want to cut.

Track locks are useful in these circumstances. For instance, to prevent an insert from slicing into a music track, lock the track or tracks. All of the other tracks will move, but the locked tracks will remain stationary.

Let's try this and see what happens:

1. Undo the Insert edit that you did when moving *Food5* into the Timeline.

2. In the Browser is an audio track called *Music.aif*. Grab the icon and drag it directly into the Timeline and place it on tracks A3/A4. Make sure you have a downward-pointing arrow when you place it on the tracks.

It takes up two tracks of audio because a stereo pair has left and right channels, one channel of audio on each track.

3. Move the playhead back between *Food1* and *Food2* again.

4. Execute the Insert edit with *Food5*. Or use the keyboard shortcut **F9**. Or, if you've added the Editing Workshop buttons, use the yellow Insert button.

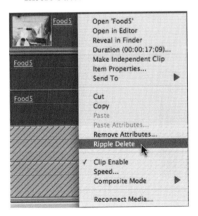

4.15 Shortcut Menu Ripple-Delete

> **Tip**
> **Select an Edit:** A useful keyboard shortcut is the V key, which selects the nearest edit point and moves the playhead to it.

4.14 Track Locks

Immediately you'll notice that not only is the video being inserted into the sequence, but the music track is also being cut with the insert.

5. Undo that edit with **Command-Z**.

6. Click on the track locks (see Figure 4.14) at the head of each track. Remember that you need to lock or unlock both tracks of a stereo pair.

7. Redo the Insert edit, and you'll see that although the video moves to accommodate the clip, the music tracks do not.

Before we go any further, let's undo the Insert edit and remove the audio on A3/A4, bringing the Timeline back to just three clips, *Food1*, *Food2*, and *Food3*.

You can also remove the inserted shot by right-clicking on it and using the shortcut menu to do a ripple-delete (see Figure 4.15), or ripple-delete with **Shift-Delete**. You can also ripple-delete using the **Forward Delete** key on an extended keyboard, which is sometimes marked as **Del**.

Alternative Overwrite and Insert

Overwrite and Insert are the primary functions in the Edit Overlay, but let's look at another way to do them. Drag *Food5* directly from the Browser to the Timeline. As you drag it onto the edit point between *Food1* and *Food2*, a little arrow appears, indicating how the edit will be performed. If the arrow is pointing downward as in Figure 4.16, the edit will overwrite. If the little arrow is pointing to the right as in Figure 4.17, you will be doing an insert edit, which will ripple the sequence, pushing the other material in the Timeline out of the way. Notice as you do this how the two-up display in the Canvas changes. In Figure 4.18 the video is being overwritten, beginning at the end of *Food1* and wiping out all of *Food2* and most of *Food3*. In Figure 4.19 the shot is being inserted between *Food1* and *Food2*.

⭐ Tip

Keyboard Shortcuts: As usual in FCE, there are keyboard shortcuts for locking and unlocking tracks. To lock a video track, press F4 and the track number. To lock an audio track, press F5 and the track number. If you want to lock all of the video tracks, press Shift-F4; for all of the audio tracks, Shift-F5. These key commands are toggles: unlocked tracks will lock, and locked tracks will unlock. Sometimes it's handy to lock all of the video or audio tracks except one. Use Option-click on the lock, and that track will remain unlocked while all of the other tracks of that type, video or audio, will lock. Press Option-click on the track again to unlock everything.

4.16 Overwrite Arrow

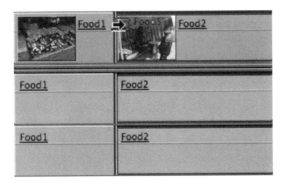

4.17   Insert Arrow

You'll notice also as you work in the application that in addition to the arrow indicators, the clip colors change. In Overwrite, the track color changes to the highlighted brown color. In Insert, the track has an outline box.

4.18   Overwrite Two-Up Canvas Display

The point at which the arrows switch from Insert to Overwrite is indicated by the faint line running horizontally through the clip about one-third of the way from the top. When you drop the clip, if the cursor is in the upper third, the edit will be an Insert. If it's in the lower two-thirds, the edit will be an Overwrite. It's the faint horizontal line you see running through the clips in Figures 4.16 and 4.17.

Replace

We'll skip Overwrite with Transition and Insert with Transition for the next lesson and look at:

- Replace
- Fit to Fill
- Superimpose

Replace is remarkably sophisticated in the way it works. It will replace a clip in the Timeline with another clip either from the Viewer or dragged from the Browser to the Canvas. The trick to understanding how Replace

4.19 Insert Two-Up Canvas Display

works is to understand that it works precisely from the point at which the playhead is positioned.

Let's do a Replace edit:

1. Start with your base three shots in the Timeline: *Food1*, *Food2*, and *Food3*.

2. Place the playhead at the edit point between *Food1* and *Food2* so that we're at the beginning of *Food2*.

3. Open *Food5* into the Viewer and make sure the playhead there is close to the beginning of the clip.

4. Drag it into Replace in the Canvas, or use the keyboard shortcut **F11**. *Food5* will immediately replace *Food2* in the Timeline. If you have loaded the Editing Workshop buttons, you can also use the blue Replace button.

The Viewer and the Canvas will show the same frame because Final Cut has taken the frame that was in the Viewer and placed it in exactly the same frame position as the shot it's replacing in the Timeline. It has extended the shot forward and backward from that point to exactly fill the duration of the shot it's replacing.

Take a look at the clips in Figure 4.20. The clip in the Timeline, *Food2*, has the playhead parked toward the end of the shot. I want to replace it with the clip *Food5*. In the Viewer, *Food5* has the playhead parked near the beginning of the shot. The current position of the playhead in *Food5* is indicated. I won't be able to replace *Food2* with *Food5* even though the new clip is much longer than the clip it's replacing. Why? Because FCE calculates the Replace edit from the position of the playhead. There just aren't enough frames in front of the current position of the playhead in *Food5* in the Viewer to replace all of the frames in front of the current position of the playhead in *Food2* in the sequence.

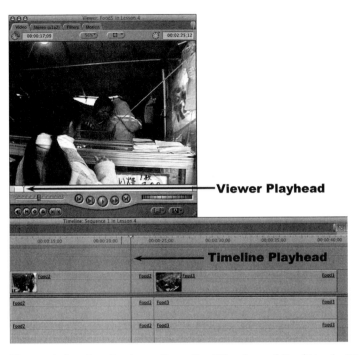

4.20   One Clip Trying to
       Replace Another

Viewer Playhead

Timeline Playhead

If you tried to do a Replace edit to *Food5* in place of *Food2* in the Timeline, you would get an "Insufficient content for edit" error message.

4.21   Ins and
       Outs in the
       Timeline

Fit to Fill

Fit to Fill functions similarly to Replace except that it's never hampered
by lack of media. Fit to Fill adjusts the speed of the clip to match the area
it needs to occupy. This is a great tool for putting in still images or titles
that you want to be a specific length. Because they aren't real video, Final
Cut will produce the images very quickly and accurately. It's a little more
problematic when using it with video where it can raise some problems.

> ✎ *Tip*
> **Alternative Replace:** Another
> way to do a replace function is to
> use Overwrite after first defining the
> limits of the shot you want to
> replace. That's easy to do in FCE.
> With the playhead parked over the
> shot, press the X key. This sets In and
> Out points on the Timeline that are
> exactly the length of the clip, as in
> Figure 4.21. If you now do an Over-
> write edit, it will replace the shot in
> the Timeline. What gets selected and
> highlighted in the Timeline is con-
> trolled by the Auto Select buttons at
> the head of the tracks.

1. To see how this functions, delete everything that you may already have in the Timeline and make sure the playhead is at the beginning of the Timeline.

2. Grab *Food4*, *Food5*, and *Food6* and drag them to Overwrite in the Edit Overlay to move them into the Timeline.

3. Move the playhead in the Timeline so that it's sitting over *Food5*, the middle of the three clips in the Timeline. Open the clip *Food1* into the Viewer.

4. Press **Option-X** to clear any In and Out points that might be marked on the clip.

You can see by the duration in the upper left corner of the Viewer that *Food1* is quite a bit shorter than *Food5*. Food1 is 6:01, while *Food5* is 17:09.

5. Drag the *Food1* clip from the Viewer to the Edit Overlay and drop it on the Fit to Fill box. Or use the keyboard shortcut **Shift-F11**. Or if you have the Editing Workshop buttons loaded, click the green Fit to Fill button.

The clip will immediately drop into the Timeline, and unless it is exactly the same size as the clip it's replacing, a colored render line will appear at the top of the Timeline—red if your system is not capable of playing back a speed change in real time and green if it is. The red or green render line indicates that the section of the Timeline needs to be rendered at some point before output. If the line is red, the clip will have to be rendered immediately to be viewed; if it's green, you will have real-time preview. This section needs to be rendered because of the speed change to *Food1*, which is now in slow motion to accommodate the Fit to Fill edit. The clip in the sequence shows the speed change, in this case, 35 percent of real speed (see Figure 4.22). You will also see a green line at the top of the audio portion of the clip, indicating that it too, because the sound is also slowed down, will need to be rendered before outputting.

4.22 Slow-Motion Clip in the Timeline

But the 35 percent shown in the Timeline is not quite true. Let's check the speed.

Select the clip *Food1* in the Timeline and press **Command-J**, which calls up the **Speed** dialog box (see Figure 4.23).

In this case, the speed is 34.68 percent. The real problem with speed changes is that it is difficult to create smooth motion, particularly at odd speeds such as 34.68 percent. At full-size, interlaced DV, you can get some nasty stuttering effects, particularly if the clips are speeded up. It's better if you want to do slow or fast motion to use simple multiples: 50, 150, 25, or 200 percent. These are much easier to calculate and generally produce better results. Fit to Fill calculates an absolute number and, as you can see, usually a bizarre one.

4.23   Speed Dialog Box

Modify>Speed (**Command-J**) is where all clip speed changes are made. It is unfortunately not possible to ramp speed up or down so that it accelerates and decelerates. Frame blending can help, but it will slow down render time. The default is to have Frame Blending turned on. With Frame Blending off, FCE merely duplicates or drops frames as necessary to make up the right speed. For slow motion, you usually want to have Frame Blending turned on, but for clips being speeded up, it works better to have it switched off.

If you're slowing down the material, there is another way to do a Fit and Fill that will usually produce better results. With the playhead in the Timeline at the start of the clip, use the **F** key to match back to a new copy of the clip, and then mark an In point. Execute the speed change, say, to 50 percent, and drag the clip to Replace. The slomo will be the duration of the clip it's replacing without rippling the sequence (see the tip *Changing to Slow Motion*).

Superimpose

Superimpose is used primarily to place titles on the track above the video. It again works a bit like Replace. The clip you're superimposing takes its duration from the clip you're placing it above. Drag the clip on Superimpose, and it will be placed above the clip that the playhead is sitting on.

1. Let's ripple-delete the Fit to Fill shot, the middle of the three in the Timeline, so that we're left with only *Food4* and *Food6*.

2. Place the playhead somewhere over the middle of *Food6*.

> ✎ *Tip*
> ### Changing to Slow Motion.
>
> When a speed change is done in a sequence, a Ripple edit is performed (i.e., the contents of the Timeline shift, based on the new length of the clip). This is usually good, but sometimes you just don't want that to happen. If you're speeding up the material, the easiest way is to go to the head of the clip and use Command-Shift-F to match back to a new copy of the clip. This is not the clip in the Browser, which you can match-frame to with the F key, but a new copy of the media called up from your hard drive. Mark an In point and press Command-J to call up the Speed Change dialog. Change the speed to, say, 200 percent and then Overwrite back into the Timeline, cutting away what's left of the clip that you don't need.

★ *Tip*
Superimpose: There is often some misunderstanding about the term superimpose. In FCE it is used to mean placing a clip on the track above the current destination track. It does not mean what many people expect, that the superimposed image will appear partially transparent and that the underlying image will still be visible beneath it.

3. Drag *Food5* from the Browser to the Canvas and drop it on the Superimpose box, or use the keyboard shortcut F12. Or if you have the Editing Workshop buttons loaded, click the purple Superimpose button in the Canvas.

The clip appears in the Timeline above the clip on the destination track, above *Food6* in this case, as in Figure 4.24. Notice where the audio track has gone onto A3 and A4, the tracks below the destination tracks.

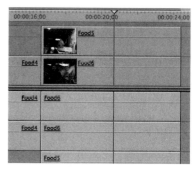

4.24   Superimpose

★ *Tip*
Different In Point: If you want to superimpose at some point other than right over a clip, you can do this by entering an In point in the Timeline. Go to the Canvas or the Timeline window and press the I key to mark an In point. This will be the In point for the next edit, and when you drag the clip from Viewer to Canvas to Superimpose, the clip will drop at the marked In point and not at the playhead's current position.

Summary

In this lesson you've learned how to use the editing tools that moved clips into the Timeline:

- Overwrite
- Insert
- Fit to Fill
- Replace
- Superimpose

We used drag and drop to the Canvas Edit Overlay, the keyboard shortcuts for each, as well as the Editing Workshop buttons. Now that we've looked at how to edit your shots and at the editing tools available in FCE, we'll look at putting a sequence together using these shots.

Lesson 5

Editing Basics: Building Your Sequence

Now that you've cut up your material in Final Cut Express, we're ready to begin putting it all together. There is no right way to edit a scene or a sequence or even a whole film or video; there are only bad ways, good ways, and better ways.

Loading the Lesson

Let's begin by opening the *Projects* folder on your hard drive and double-clicking the project file, *Lesson 5*, to launch the application.

As in Lesson 2, before the project finishes loading, you may be greeted with the Reconnect dialog box. Follow the steps in the previous lessons to reconnect:

1. Click on the **Reconnect** button in the Offline Files dialog.

2. In the next window that comes up, check the box to specify the drive where your media is located.

3. Click the **Search** button.

4. FCE will find one of the items. If it's the correct item, make sure it's selected and click the **Choose** button in the dialog box. If it doesn't

find it, use the **Locate** button to find it manually. It should find the rest of the files as well.

Making the Sequence

Inside the Browser of your copy of *Lesson 5*, you'll see four sequences:

- Food Sequence
- Rough Cut
- Sequence 1
- Slip & Slide

In the Browser there is also the master clip, *Food*, together with the *Clips* bin as in the previous lesson. *Sequence 1* is empty, and we'll look at *Slip & Slide* later in the lesson. *Rough Cut* is the first part of the edited sequence made up for you. Before we begin though, take a quick look at *Food Sequence*. This is where we're going.

Now that we've gone through the principal means of going from Viewer to Canvas, let's edit our sequence together into the Timeline, and then look at how to trim, adjust, and rearrange our clips. To start we'll edit together a quickly paced sequence of shots. I like to begin by looking at the material I'm going to use for the sequence. Open the master clip *Food* in the Viewer and look through the material the way it was shot.

Let's start working with the subclips that have already been prepared for you:

1. Double-click on *Food1* in the Browser to open it into the Viewer.
2. Scrub through to the point where the camera starts moving from left to right.
3. Find the beginning of the movement and mark the In point.
4. Now find the end of the movement and mark the Out point. We can leave the shots a little loose at this stage.

Marking Edit Points. Many editors like to mark their Out points on the fly. This allows you to judge the pace of the shot and of the sequence, to do it almost tactilely, to feel the rhythm of the shot. After a few tries you'll probably find you're hitting the Out point consistently on the same frame. If you're not, perhaps it isn't the right shot to be using, or perhaps you should look again at the pace the sequence is imposing on you. It's possible the shot doesn't work where it is.

Marking the In point is a little different because often you want to mark the edit point before an action begins, but judging how far in front of the action to begin on the fly is difficult. Some editors like to mark the In point while the video is playing backward. By playing it backward, you see where the action begins, and you get to judge the pace of how far before the action you want the edit to occur.

5. After you've marked the In and Out points, drag the clip to Overwrite or press **F10**.

I'm not sure which part of the second shot, *Food2*, I'll use at this stage. I'll probably use something, so I'll cut a long piece.

6. Open *Food2* into the Viewer and take the shot from just before the zoom starts and let it run almost to the end, including the part with the hands turning the skewers.

7. Again Overwrite to the Timeline.

Food3 is a little more complex. I want to use more than one part of the shot.

8. Start by marking the In point at the beginning of the shot.

9. Mark the Out point just before the short zoom out.

10. Overwrite the clip.

Ins and Outs

By putting the shot in the Timeline, I made a copy of the shot that's currently loaded in the Viewer. So now I can set new In and Out points for the clip that's still in the Viewer without affecting what I've already done to the shot in the sequence.

1. Set a new In point in the Viewer just before the pan left begins.

2. Let the shot carry over to the steaming kettle, until about the 8;18 mark.

3. Add an Out point and add that to the Timeline.

4. Take a third section from that clip, from just before the camera tilts up until shortly before the shot ends and add that to the Timeline.

Food4 might fit nicely before the close-up of the steaming tray.

5. Position the Timeline playhead between *Food2* and *Food3* in sequence.

6. Mark an In point at the beginning of *Food4* and an Out point just before the pan to the right, around 2;28.

7. Drag the clip to Insert or use the shortcut F9.

We might be able to get another piece out of *Food4*.

8. Mark an In point around 5;15, just at the beginning of the static portion of the shot of the man hunched over his soup.

9. Mark an Out point just before the camera pans left around 9;09.

10. Move the playhead in the Timeline in front of the first portion of *Food4*, to the edit point that separates *Food2* and *Food4*.

11. Execute an Insert edit to move the shot from the Viewer into the Timeline.

Bookends

Let's look at *Food5*. It's the most human part of the material, the little girl at the food stall. My thought is to use it as bookends: the little girl at the beginning of the sequence and at the end.

✦ Tip

Timecode Location: To go to a specific timecode point in either the Canvas, the Viewer, or the Timeline, tap out the number on your keypad. (In the case of working with *Food6*, type in 316 and press Return.) The playhead will immediately move to that point.

1. Make the first part of the shot one clip, basically until after she hands the vendor her money. Mark an In point near the beginning of the shot and an Out point around 6;12.

2. Make sure the playhead is at the start of the Timeline, then drag to Insert or **F9**.

3. Make the second part of *Food5* begin shortly before the vendor reaches for the biscuit, around 7;27. Mark an In point there and let it go until just before the end.

4. Move the playhead to the end of the Timeline with the **End** key.

5. Drag the second half of *Food5* from the Viewer to Overwrite, or press **F10**.

We want *Food6* to go just before the last shot.

6. Open *Food6* in the Viewer and play it.

7. Set the In point near the beginning.

8. Set the Out point before the second move with the biscuits, around 3;16.

9. In the Timeline, the playhead is probably at the end of the material. Use the **Up** arrow to move backward one edit.

10. Now drag the clip from Viewer to Insert, or use **F9**.

Food5	Food1	Food2	Food4	Food4	Food3	Food3	Food3	Food6	Food5
Food5	Food1	Food2	Food4	Food4	Food3	Food3	Food3	Food6	Food5

5.1   Timeline after First Cuts

The duration of this little sequence should be about 45 seconds, depending on how tightly you cut the shots. Looking through the clips, it obvious the sequence needs to be tightened up, as well as have the order rearranged. Your Timeline should look like Figure 5.1. The sequence called *Rough Cut* is made up of the edits up to this point for you to use if you wish.

Rearranging the Sequence

FCE has several tools for refining your edit, fine-tuning, and rearranging the sequence. Let's look at some of those, working with the shots that we have edited together into the Timeline.

Swap Edit

There are three pieces of *Food3* in the sequence. Let's begin by moving *Food1*, which is now the second shot in sequence, between the first two pieces of *Food3* in the Timeline. This is called a *Swap edit*.

1. Grab the *Food1* shot and pull it along the Timeline to where you want to place it.
2. Make sure the head of *Food1* snaps to the edit point between the first two cuts of *Food3*.
3. When you get it where you want it to go, before you release the mouse, hold down the **Option** key.

The cursor will change into a downward hooked arrow on the clip (see Figure 5.2). You'll also see a number displayed. This tells you how far in the sequence you have moved the clip.

> ✯ *Tip*
>
> Swap Edit Limit: The Swap Edit function that lets you move clips will only work on one clip at a time. Unfortunately, you can't grab a couple of clips or a small section of clips and do the same thing. It also works best if you have Snapping turned on to avoid slicing off a little bit of a shot by accident.

4. With the **Option** key down and the clip at the edit point, release the mouse to drop the clip between the two shots.

5.2 Swap Edit Arrow in the Timeline

If you look at the Timeline, you'll see that you've done an insert edit as well as a ripple-delete. You've removed the clip from one point on the timeline, placed it somewhere else in the Timeline, and pushed everything out of the way to make room for it. Figure 5.3 shows the sequence after the Swap edit. This is a great hidden tool that I often use.

5.3 After Using Swap Edit

✎*Tip*

Gaps and Syncing: FCE defines a gap as a space in the Timeline that extends across all tracks. So if you have a music track on A3 and A4, for instance, FCE will not see the space between the shots on the video tracks as a gap. This is where the ability to lock tracks really helps. If you lock those music tracks, you can then close the gap. Or use Option-click to lock all other tracks, and again you can close the gap. There are several ways to close a gap: Right-click in the gap and from the shortcut menu choose Close Gap. With the playhead over the gap, press Control-G.

Click on the gap to select it and then press the Delete key.

Ripple Cut and Paste Insert

Although you can only move one shot at a time when you do a Swap, there is a handy way to move groups of clips. Look at the two pieces of *Food4* followed by the first part of *Food3*. These three shots should be moved together right after *Food5* at the head of the Timeline. This would make them the second, third, and fourth shots in the sequence. I could just move *Food2* after them, but let me show you a way to move groups of clips.

1. Start by selecting the clips. It's simplest to marquee-drag through them, or select the first clip and **Shift**-select the third clip.

2. Next, cut them out, not with the usual **Command-X**, but with **Shift-X**.

Using **Command-X** would create what's called a **Lift** edit but leave a gap in the sequence. Sometimes you do want to do this, but in this instance we use **Shift-X**, which performs a **Ripple Cut** instead of the simple Lift. This not only cuts the clips out of the Timeline but also closes the gap the missing clips leave behind.

3. Now move the playhead to the edit at the end of *Food5*, between *Food5* and *Food2*. This is where you want to place the clips. Press **Shift-V**, which will paste the clips as a Paste Insert edit. **Command-V** would also paste but as an Overwrite edit.

Your Timeline should be laid out something like Figure 5.4.

5.4 Timeline after Paste Insert

Let's look through the sequence again. It's getting better, but there are still a few edits I don't like and quite a few shots that need trimming. We'll get to trimming in a moment, but let's rearrange a few more shots.

Add Edits

In the first shot, I like the way the camera moves around the girl at the beginning, and I like the way she hands over her money with her fingers splayed out. I'd like to lengthen the effect of this scene by basically making it take more time than it actually did. I'd like to move *Food2* right into the middle of that first shot. I know *Food2* is too long; we'll get to trimming it shortly.

1. Scrub or play through the beginning of the Timeline to find the point just after the camera moves around the girl and the vendor picks up the bag, around 2;15 into the sequence.

2. Make sure nothing is selected in the sequence and use **Control-V** to slice the clip in the sequence.

3. Play or scrub forward in the Timeline to find the point just before the vendor reaches his hand out for the money, around 2;21.

4. Press **Control-V** again. You have now isolated a short section to cut out.

5. Ripple-delete it either by right-clicking to call up the shortcut menu or by selecting it and pressing **Shift-Delete**.

Instead of using the Add Edit function with **Control-V**, you could also have done this by marking an In and Out point in the Timeline as we did in the previous lesson and ripple-deleting the short section. While the keyboard shortcut is more efficient, you can also make an add edit with the Blade tool.

Range Clipping

Another way to do this would be to use the Range tool (**GGG**), which we saw in the previous lesson. You can use this feature to select a portion of the clip to ripple-delete (see Figure 5.5). You may have to switch off Snapping to make such a short edit. While you're dragging with the Range tool, you'll see a two-up display in the Canvas showing you the start and end points of the edit (see Figure 5.6). The timecode display in the Canvas is that of the clip, beginning from the clip's start time of 00:00:00;00.

Tip
Moving the Playhead: Shift-Left or Right-arrow will move the playhead forward or backward in one-second increments.

5.5 Range Tool Selection in the Timeline

5.6 Two-up Canvas Display

5.7 Food Sequence Beginning

Moving More Clips

Obviously the sequence now has a jump cut. So let's take *Food2*, which we moved earlier and should now be the sixth shot in the sequence, and do a Swap edit.

Jump Cuts. The sequence as we've laid it out so far has the most obvious form of jump cut, which is any abrupt edit that jars the viewer. This is generally considered bad editing. The most common cause is placing side-by-side shots, such as the two halves of *Food5*, that are very similar but not the same. You get this disconcerting little jump, as if you blacked out for a fraction of a second. It suddenly pulls the viewers out from the content of the video as they say to themselves, or perhaps even out loud, "What was that?" You can also get a jump cut if you put together two very different shots, such as the shot of a long street with the small figure of a person in the distance, cutting to a tight close-up. It's disorienting because the viewer has no reference that the close-up belongs to the person seen in the far distance in the previous shot. These are jump cuts. The general rule is to avoid them if you can. Or use them so often that it becomes your style. Then it's art.

1. Drag and then hold the **Option** key to drop *Food2* between the two halves of *Food5* at the beginning of the sequence.

The beginning of the Timeline should look like Figure 5.7.

As you go through the sequence, you'll see another jump cut between two parts of *Food3*. The camera pans right from the cooking tray to the steaming kettle and then in a separate shot tilts up from the kettle to the cook. I would remove the first of these shots, taking out the pan. I've seen that cooking tray already, but the kettle and the chef are new.

The arrangement is almost right, but there is a problem with the very last shot that I don't care for. Just after the vendor puts the biscuit in the bag, the camera jiggles. I'd like to remove this. So let's do this in the Timeline.

2. Scrub or play through *Food5*, the last shot in the sequence, to the frame when the biscuit just disappears into the bag behind the counter.

3. Use **I** to mark the In point in the Timeline.

Right after this the camera is jostled.

4. Move further down to where the vendor is about to reach forward with the bag, just before his hands separate.

5. Mark the Out point with the **O** key and ripple-delete the middle portion.

Now we have the same problem we had in the first shot. This time we're going to move *Food3* from its earlier position. This is the shot of the tilt from kettle to cook.

6. Drag and then add the **Option** key before you drop it between the two halves of *Food5* that you just split.

If you look through the sequence, you'll see that the shots are in the order we want, but we still need to tighten it up, trimming the shots to make them faster-paced.

5.8   Scaling Slider and Tabbed Slider

Storyboarding

Another way to lay out your sequences is by building storyboards in bins. Some editors like to do this. In Large or Medium Icon mode, you can:

- Trim and set the clips
- Set the Poster frame
- Arrange the layout order of the shots in the Browser

To set the Poster frame of a clip when you're in Icon view, either:

- Open the clip into the Viewer, find the frame, and use **Mark>Set Poster** Frame (**Control-P**), or
- Press **Control-Shift** while you click on the icon in the bin. This will let you scrub the clip. Hold down the two modifier keys and release the mouse over the clip where you want to set the Poster frame.

Storyboarding is a fast, easy way to move the shot order around, to try different arrangements and sequences. Although you can't play the clips back as a sequence, you can make a quick arrangement of shots in your bin. Then marquee through the shots and drag them into the Timeline (see Figure 5.9).

The shots will appear in the sequence in the order they are in the bin. Notice that the shots in the Timeline in Figure 5.9 follow the bin order as they are laid out, left to right, top to bottom. Be careful with the row heights: clips that are placed higher up in the bin will appear earlier.

> **Tip**
>
> **Timeline Scaling:** You can change the scale of the Timeline to zoom in and out with the tabbed slider at the bottom of the window. Pulling either end of the tab will change the scale of the Timeline window. At the bottom left is a little slider that will adjust the scale (see Figure 5.8).
>
> My favorite is to use the keyboard shortcuts Option −= (think Option −+) to zoom in and Option − (that's Option-minus) to zoom out. What's nice about using the keyboard shortcuts is that it leaves the playhead centered in the Timeline as you zoom in and out. Just be careful a clip isn't selected in the Timeline, because the scaling will take place around that rather than around the playhead. You can use Command-+ and Command-− to scale in other windows, but Option-+ and − will always scale the Timeline even if the Viewer or the Canvas is the active window.

5.9 Storyboarded Bin and Shots in the Timeline

5.10 The Tools

The Trim Tools

The trim tools—**Roll** and **Ripple**, **Slip** and **Slide**—are among the tools shown in Figure 5.10. The trim tools are clustered in the fourth and fifth buttons. The first two trim tools, Ripple and Roll, change the duration of clips, and the second two, Slip and Slide, leave the clip duration intact.

A *Ripple* edit moves an edit point up and down the Timeline by pushing or pulling all of the material on the track, shortening or lengthening the whole sequence. In a Ripple edit, only one clip changes duration, getting longer or shorter. Everything else that comes after it in the track adjusts to accommodate it. In Figure 5.11 the edit is rippled to the left, and everything after it moves left to accompany it, just as in a ripple delete.

A *Roll* edit moves an edit point up and down the Timeline between two adjacent shots. Only those two shots have their durations changed. One gets longer, and the adjacent shot gets shorter to accommodate it. The overall length of the track remains unchanged. In Figure 5.12 the edit point can be moved either left or right.

A *Slip* edit changes the In and Out points of a single clip. The duration of the clip remains the same, and all of the clips around it remain the same. Only the In and Out of the slipped clip change. If more frames are added on the front, the same amount are cut off the end, and vice versa: if some are added to the end, an equal amount are taken off the beginning.

In Figure 5.13 the contents of the shot change by changing In and Out points, but neither its position in the Timeline nor either of the adjacent shots are affected.

5.11 Ripple Edit Left

5.12 Roll Edit Directions

5.13 Slip Edit Direction

5.14 Slide Edit Directions

A *Slide* edit moves a clip forward or backward along the Timeline. The clip itself, its duration, and its In and Out points remain unchanged. Only its position on the Timeline, earlier or later, shortens and lengthens the adjacent shots as it slides up and down the track. In Figure 5.14 the shot *Food6* can slide up and down the Timeline. The shot doesn't change, only the two adjacent shots.

The Ripple Tool

We're first going to work with the Ripple tool. Press the fourth button and extend the pop-out to select the tool as in Figure 5.15. You can also call it up by pressing **RR**; that's the **R** key twice. Let's use it on some of the shots we want to work on. Start with the edit between shots *Food4* and *Food3*. Take the tool and place it near the edit. Notice that it changes direction as you move it across the edit as in Figures 5.16 and 5.17.

When the tool is on the right side, it will ripple the second shot; when it's on the left side, it will ripple the first shot. In this case, we want to ripple the second shot. The edit almost works, but it can perhaps be a little improved by tightening up. The little pause at the beginning of *Food3* before the ladle moves makes the edit look awkward. You can ripple right in the Timeline. As you grab the clip, you will get a small two-up display in the Canvas.

A word of caution about rippling: If you're working with material that's cut to narration or music, rippling will easily upset the timing of the sequence, because it's pulling and pushing the entire track and its sync sound. So what's working for you at this moment in the edit may be ruin-

5.15 The Ripple Tool

5.16 Ripple Tool Right

5.17 Ripple Tool Left

5.18 The Roll Tool

5.19 The Roll Tool in the Timeline

⭐*Tip*

Ripple and Roll Shortcuts: You can also use the Ripple and Roll tools incrementally with keyboard shortcuts in the Timeline. Select the edit point by moving the playhead over it and pressing the V key. Now, by using the U key, you can toggle through Ripple Right, Ripple Left, and Roll. Whichever edit you have selected, you can now move incrementally with the left bracket [and the right bracket]. Each tap will move the edit one frame left or right in the direction the bracket is pointed. Shift-[and Shift-] will move the edit whatever duration you have set for Multi-Frame Trimming in your User Preferences, which we'll look at in the next lesson. This also works if you select a clip in the Timeline and choose either the Slip or Slide tool.

ing something else further down the timeline. In these cases, the Roll tool may work better for you.

The Roll Tool

The Roll tool is also under the fourth button in the Tools, shown in Figure 5.18. It can be evoked with the **R** key. It is controlled similarly to Ripple and can be used in the Timeline as in Figure 5.19.

The Roll tool acts on both shots, extending one shot while shortening the other. Although the Ripple tool changes the overall length of the sequence by moving everything up and down the line, the Roll tool only affects the two adjacent shots.

Using Roll and Ripple, tighten up some of the shots in the sequence. I rippled the zoom into the skewers in *Food2* until all you see are the hands turning over the sticks on the grill.

Extend Edit

Final Cut's **Extend Edit** is another nice way to perform a Roll edit. It's a simple way to move an edit point, even one with a transition.

1. Select an edit by clicking on it or by using the **V** key.

2. Move the playhead in the Timeline to where you want to move the edit. Press **E** or select **Sequence>Extend Edit**.

If the selection is dimmed in the menu or you hear a system warning, it's because you don't have enough media to perform the Extend edit.

3. Undo that edit when you're done.

The Slip Tool

Let's look at Slip and Slide next. Slip works in the Timeline and the Viewer, whereas Slide works in the Timeline only. They do pretty much what their names imply. Slip is one of my favorite tools, although I'm not very keen on the display in Final Cut Express. You can select the Slip tool from the fifth button in the Tools, as shown in Figure 5.20, or call it with the **S** key.

I've created the *Slip & Slide Sequence* to help explain these two tools. Open the sequence by double-clicking it in the Browser. Use the Slip tool to grab the middle clip in the sequence. Move the clip from side to side, and you'll see the display in Figure 5.21. What you're doing is slipping the media for the clip up and down its length. The overall duration of the clip remains unchanged, but the section of media for that duration is adjusted.

The Canvas again shows you a two-up display. This is showing you the first and the last frames of the video. The shot in the sequence begins at 3;00 and ends at 4;29, a two-second shot. By slipping the clip 10 frames as we see in the figure, the shot will now start at 2;20, 10 frames earlier, and end at 4;19, keeping the same duration. It starts earlier so it will end earlier. If the shot slipped in the other direction it would start later in time but also end later.

5.20   The Slip Tool

The two-up display will help you from slipping the clip too far into some unwanted material. If you're working without subclipping your material as we discussed in the last lesson, you can see if you're slipping into the next shot.

5.21   The Slip Tool in the Timeline

It is also possible to slip in the Viewer, which can be especially beneficial when you're adjusting a clip before you bring it into the Timeline.

1. To slip in the Viewer, double-click the clip to load it into the Viewer.

2. Hold down the **Shift** key as you grab either the In point or the Out point and drag. This way you will drag both points together and maintain a constant duration.

This is *slipping*, and what you see in the display (see Figure 5.22) is the start frame in the Viewer and the end frame in the Canvas. It doesn't matter which end you grab to pull; the display is always the same: start in the Viewer, end in the Canvas.

5.22   Slipping in the Viewer with the Canvas Display

Slide Tool - ss

5.23 The Slide Tool

The Slide Tool

Let's look at the last trimming tool, the Slide tool, also in the fifth Tools button (see Figure 5.23). The Slide tool can be brought out with **SS** (**S** twice). Like the Slip tool, it also works in the Timeline, although not in the Viewer. The Slide tool doesn't change anything in the clip you're working on; it grabs the clip and pulls it forward or backward along the Timeline, wiping out material on one side and extending the material on the other side, as shown in Figure 5.24.

5.24 The Slide Tool in the Timeline

Notice that you're not only moving the clip but also affecting the two adjacent clips, which is why they're highlighted with boxes.

The Canvas display (see Figure 5.25) is unlike other two-up displays. You don't see the clip you're moving at all. What are displayed are the two adjacent shots:

- On the left, the end of the shot in front of the one you're moving
- On the right, the beginning of the shot after the one you're moving

5.25 The Slide Tool Canvas Display

In these figures, by moving the second clip, *Food1*, earlier in time, the first shot *Food5* is being shortened by 20 frames, and the last shot *Food4* is being lengthened by 20 frames.

You are limited in how far you can slide a clip by the amount of media available in the adjacent shots. If you move to the end of the available media, the film sprocket overlay will appear in the two-up display.

How Long Is Long Enough? A static shot, either close-up or medium shot, needs to be on the screen a much shorter time than a long shot in which the audience is following a movement. A shot that has been seen before, a repeat, can be on the screen quite briefly for the audience to get the information. Though there is no hard-and-fast rule, generally shots without dialog remain on the screen no more than six to eight seconds on television with its small screen. In feature films, shots can be held for quite a bit longer because the viewer's eye has a lot more traveling to do to take in the full scope of the image. This is probably why movies seem much slower on the television screen than they do in the theater. While a close-up can be on the screen quite briefly, a long shot will often contain a great deal of information and needs to be held longer so viewers have time for their eyes to rove around it. You can often hold a moving shot such as a pan longer because the audience is basically looking at two shots, one at the beginning and the other at the end. If the movement is well shot—a fairly brisk move, no more than about five seconds—you can also cut it quite tightly. All you need to show is a brief glimpse of the static shot, the movement, and then cut out as soon as the camera settles at the end of the move.

Look at your finished sequence. It should look something like the sequence called *Food* in the Browser. I still wouldn't be very happy with the piece, principally because the audio is so abrupt and choppy, marking each cut. Work would need to be done to smooth out the sound, perhaps extend sound from a single clip, or add some constant underlying sound from somewhere else. But that's a topic for another lesson.

Summary

In this lesson we've learned how to assemble our sequence and trim our shots using:

- Swap
- Ripple Cut
- Paste Insert
- Storyboarding
- Ripple
- Roll
- Extend
- Slip
- Slide

Now that you know the basic tools of editing with Final Cut Express, you'll probably want to start trying these techniques out on your material. To do this we'll have to capture your video, and bring it onto your hard drive from your tape. But before we start capturing, we need to set up your User Preferences and your System Settings, which we'll do next, and then in Lesson 7 we'll look at capturing your video.

Lesson 6

Setting Up Your Application Preferences

Digital video editing is divided into three phases:

1.   Getting your material into the computer

2.   Editing it, which is the fun part

3.   Getting it back out of your computer

This lesson is about setting up your computer so it's ready for the first part, getting your material into your computer. Before you capture your material, you have to set up your application correctly. In Final Cut Express HD 3.5, as in most video editing programs, that means setting up your preferences, several choices for video and audio and system settings.

After setting preferences, we'll go into capturing your media. These fundamentals are absolutely necessary for FCE to function properly. Set it up right, get your material into your project properly, and you're halfway home. You cannot overestimate how important this is.

Setting Up a New Project

There is no Lesson 6 project on the accompanying DVD, so let's begin by creating a new project. Start by double-clicking the Final Cut Express

87

✎ *Tip*
Adding Items to the Dock:

Remember that you can add any application to the Dock by dragging the application icon there. After you've launched an application, you can also add it permanently to the Dock by mousing down on the icon and from the shortcut menu selecting Keep in Dock.

icon in the Applications folder. Or better yet, if you've created a Dock alias for FCE, click on the icon in the Dock.

FCE will launch the last project that was open. If a previous project does open, close the Browser, which will close the project.

1. Go up to **File>New Project (Command-Shift-N)**.

You get a new project called **Untitled Project**, with the empty sequence in the Browser called *Sequence 1*.

Because FCE uses your project name to create folders that organize your material inside designated folders such as the *Capture Scratch* and *Render* folders, it's a good idea to give your project a name right away. At this stage you can't save the project because there's nothing to save. However, you can use **Save Project As** to save it with a name. FCE will use that name to create files in designated places on your hard drive.

2. Give the project a name and save it inside your *Documents* folder.

User Preferences

Final Cut Express has three separate preferences settings:

- **User Preferences**, which sets up how you want to work with the application
- **System Settings**, which sets preferences that control your computer
- **Easy Setup**, which is for audio/video preferences and deals with how you get your material in and out of your computer

The first is the **User Preferences**. To access these go up to the **Final Cut Express HD** menu and select **User Preferences (Option-Q)**.

As soon as you open **User Preferences**, you see the pane in Figure 6.1.

General Preferences

This is the **General Preferences** panel. The User Preferences may seem daunting because it's made up of four tabbed windows. We'll work through it, starting with General, the first window. Fortunately, most of the items here can be left at their default setting.

The first item you should change is the Levels of Undo, which defaults to 10 actions, which is the same default used when Final Cut was first introduced in 1999, when we could run the application on a PowerMac

User Preferences

General \ Editing \ Timeline Options \ Render Control \

Levels of Undo: [10] actions   ☐ Prompt for settings on New Project
List Recent Clips: [10] entries   ☐ Prompt for settings on New Sequence

Real-time Audio Mixing: [8] tracks   ☑ Report dropped frames during playback
Audio Playback Quality: [Low (faster) ⬍] ☑ Abort capture on dropped frames
☐ Limit real-time video to: [20] MB/s ☑ Do not show A/V Device Warning on launch

☑ Show Tooltips
☑ Bring all windows to the front on activation
☑ Open last project on application launch   Browser Text Size: [Small ⬍]
┌ ☑ Autosave Vault ─────────────────┐   ┌ ☑ Auto Render ──────────────────┐
│ Save a copy every: [30] minutes │   │ Start Render after: [45] minutes │
│ Keep at most: [40] copies per project │ Render: [Open Sequences ⬍] │
│ Maximum of: [25] projects   │   │ ☑ Render RT Segments   │
└──────────────────────────────────┘   └─────────────────────────────────┘

6.1   User Preferences General Tab

300MHz G3 using OS 8.5 with 128MB of RAM. You should increase the number to 32, which is as high as it will go.

For **List of Recent Clips**, 10 seems like a good number. This is the number of clips retained for the pop-up at the bottom of the **Viewer** (see Figure 6.2). The limit is 20.

Real-time Audio Mixing determines how many tracks the application will try to play back in real time before it requires rendering. This is no guarantee that it will be able to do it, but it will try. The default is fine, although if you're mixing a lot of tracks, most computers and hard drives can support more tracks, so then you should raise the number to something like 24.

The default setting for the **Audio Playback Quality** pop-up menu is Low. It's fine to work in Low; it will allow a greater number of real-time tracks for playback. When you're outputting to tape, exporting, or doing an audio mixdown, these are automatically done at High quality. You don't need to reset this. Changing this item will also reduce the number of audio tracks that you can preview without rendering.

The **Limit real-time video** option is of little value in FCE. It's holdover from Final Cut Pro, where you can work with very high data rate video. It's best to simply leave it unchecked. Neither DV nor HDV, the two formats FCE works with, exceeds 20MB/per second of data.

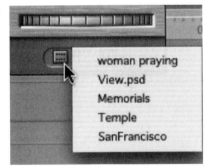

6.2   Recent Clips in Pop-Up Menu

The next two items, **Show Tooltips** and **Bring all windows to the front on activation** should probably be left checked. The third item here is new to this version of FCE. I usually leave the **Open last project on application launch** checked on as well. Most single users will probably find it easiest for the application to work this way. In schools, however, or other multiuser environments, I would strongly suggest that this item be unchecked so that either you manually open the project you're working on, or open a blank project when you launch the application. It helps prevent people from capturing material into the wrong location.

In the lower left of this panel are the **Autosave Vault** preferences. Autosaving saves your project incrementally with a date and time stamp. Here you can assign how often you want the project saved, how many copies to keep, and how many projects you want to be held. Saving a project to disk can take a moment or two. The larger the project gets, the greater the number of clips and sequences, and the longer the save will take. So interrupting your workflow by setting the **Save a copy** box too small might be counterproductive.

I find the default of 30 minutes a good number. You probably won't lose too much if the application does crash, plus you'll save a couple of days' worth of work in the vault. If you make the save time too quick—say 10 minutes or less—you may want to increase the copies per project that are saved. The saved files can be called up from the *Autosave Vault* folder from the **File** menu by selecting **Restore Project**. You'll be given a dialog that offers you a list of time-stamped copies of that project (see Figure 6.3).

6.3 Restore Project Dialog Box

You can save up to 100 copies of each project, with a maximum of 100 projects. It works on a first-in/first-out basis. The oldest project saved is dumped into the **Trash** as new autosaves are added. Because it's not deleted from your hard drive, you can still retrieve an autosaved project from the Trash if you haven't emptied it.

On the right side of the General preferences panel is a list of checkboxes. The default settings for the first five are probably best left the way they are. It's probably wise to leave **Report dropped frames during playback** checked on, as well as **Abort capture on dropped frames**. You may find that FCE is giving dropped frame warnings immediately when a capture begins. If this is happening, you might try switching this feature off and seeing if you can capture your material cleanly. Also, if it aborts 55 minutes into a one-hour capture, you've lost everything and have to start all over again. The most common cause of dropped frames can be traced to two things: (1) your media drive not being fast enough for digital video, and (2) your computer trying to do too many things at the same time.

You can set the Browser Text pop-up to Small, Medium, or Large. If your eyes are good, I'd use Small. The Medium and Large settings use too much Browser space and also increase the size of the text in the Timeline clips, which makes it difficult to see clip names of short shots.

The **Auto Render** settings allow you to set a time for which the application will start rendering material based on your settings when your computer is idle. It's great to find all of your rendering done when you come back from lunch or after you leave your computer on overnight.

That's it for the first window of Preferences. Open the next tab, Editing preferences, which is new to this version of FCE (Figure 6.4).

▶ *Tip*
Restoring Project: When you restore a project, the application first gives you a warning. The project then opens with the project name, and when you save it, it saves in the location of the original project. You can also use Revert Project, which, as in other applications, will take you back to the last saved state. Note that neither Restore nor Revert will bring back arrangements. These are in your preferences and will not be restored.

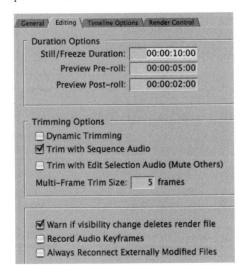

6.4   Editing
        Preferences Panel

Editing Preferences

Editing preferences is where you define your personal preferences for how you work with the application.

Still Image Duration sets the length of imported single-frame graphics and freeze frames made in FCE. You can change them once they're in FCE, but they'll appear at this length in the Browser. The default setting of 10 seconds seems long to me, so I usually set it to 5 seconds, a reasonable length for most stills or graphics from applications such as Photoshop. If you're doing training or other videos that require many full-screen graphics, leaving it at 10 seconds might be better for you. Although stills and freeze frames have a default duration of 10 seconds, they're actually two minutes and 10 seconds long when they're imported. The duration can be changed to any length you want.

You have to set the maximum duration for the still inside the Browser before it is placed inside a sequence. After that, the still cannot be extended beyond its designated duration unless you use the Fit to Edit edit function, which we looked at in Lesson 4. It can be made shorter, but not longer. There is also a sequence time limit of four hours that you cannot exceed.

In the previous lesson we talked about playing around the current time. If you hit the **Play Around** button or use the keyboard shortcut \, playback will begin a defined amount of time before the playhead and play for a defined amount of time past it. You define those times here. The default Preview preroll is five seconds, a traditional preroll time for VTR machines. The default Preview postroll is two seconds. Five seconds for a preroll always feels long to me, so I set it to three seconds. I leave the postroll at two seconds. When we get to use this feature, you can play with it and see what feels right for you.

In the Trimming Option section, I would leave this at the default. It can be changed at a later time when you're using the Trim Edit window.

Multi-Frame Trim Size sets the number of frames that can be trimmed in the Trim Edit window or the Timeline. Five is the default, which seems fine to me, but after you've worked with the tools you might prefer to pick a different value that suits you better. We'll look at items such as multiframe trimming in closer detail in later lessons.

The next two items I would leave as they are. The visibility warning is useful, and can also be turned off when it comes up. The **Record Audio Keyframes** checkbox lets you adjust and record audio levels in real time while you control the levels of a clip in the Viewer. It's a feature that we'll look at in Lesson 10 on page 166, although it has limited use in FCE because you can't really mix tracks with it in the application. The last of these three items, **Always Reconnect Externally Modified Files**, I would check on, because it's a useful function if you edit images like still files in an application such as Photoshop or Photoshop Elements.

Timeline Options

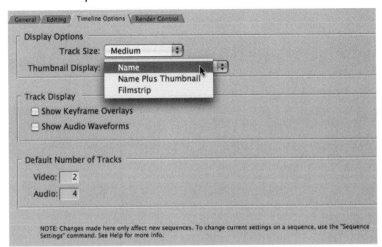

6.5   Timeline Options Tab

The next tab, **Timeline Options**, is where you define your personal preferences for your sequence timeline layout. You can set:

- The track size
- The default number of tracks a new Timeline opens with
- Thumbnail display style

The style the tracks are displayed in: **Name**, **Name Plus Thumbnail**, or **Filmstrip** (Figures 6.6 to 6.8).

6.6   Name

6.7   Name Plus Thumbnail Style

6.8   Filmstrip Style

★ *Tip*
Filmstrip: Although Filmstrip style may look like the best way to edit, it is very taxing on any computer. Using Filmstrip style on anything but the fastest computer will make the application work very slowly.

I leave the two checkboxes, **Show Keyframe Overlays** and **Show Audio Waveforms**, off. They're more conveniently toggled on and off in the **Timeline** as needed.

As the warning at the bottom indicates, all of these settings in Timeline Options affect only new sequences. Existing sequences will not be affected. To change the Timeline Options of an existing sequence, you'll have to open the sequence and use **Sequence>Settings** (**Command-zero**) and change them there, or use the triangle pop-up in the lower left of the Timeline window that we saw in the last Lesson 2 in Figure 2.30.

Render Control

The **Render Control** panel (Figure 6.9) allows you to change the render quality of your material from the default high-resolution to quite low-resolution rendering at low frame rates. The advantage of this is that low-resolution material will render out much more quickly than full DV or HDV resolution settings. Here you can also set to render Filters or just motion as well as adding in **Motion Blur** and **Frame Blending**. These last two, which produce better results, will slow down rendering considerably. Render Control for individual sequences, which is where you're more likely to need it, can also be accessed from **Sequence>Settings**. Be careful with changing these settings. See the lesson on outputting, in the last lesson on page 324 for the problems this potentially creates.

6.9   Render Control

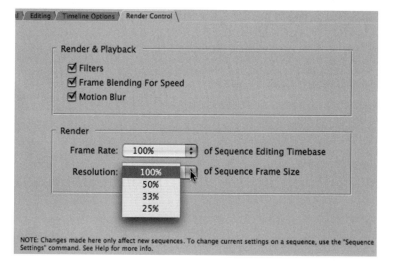

System Settings

Systems Settings (Shift-Q) has several important function controls, especially in the first panel.

Scratch Disks

The first panel in the tabbed window is **Scratch Disks** (see Figure 6.10). This is perhaps the most important of all the preference panels. Let's look at the bottom portion of the panel first. The locations of **Waveform Cache**, **Thumbnail Cache**, and **Autosave Vault** all default to the drive that you set when you first launched the application, which should be your media drive and is probably where you should leave them.

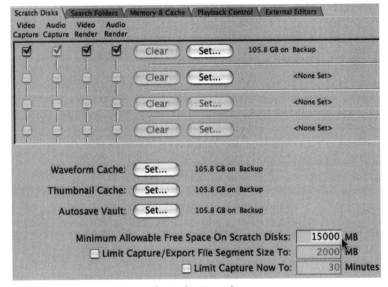

6.10   Scratch Disks Panel

Minimum Allowable Free Space on Scratch Disks defaults to a low number, much lower than it should be. Most people feel that at this setting the hard drive will fragment heavily and slow down. Some go so far as to say that you should leave 25 percent of your drive free. For large drives, this seems a bit excessive. Experienced users recommend 10 percent or at least 10GB. If you have a single partition larger than 100GB, I would suggest setting this number to at least 10GB to 15GB, or 10,000MB to 15,000MB.

Unless you have a particular reason, you should leave **Limit Capture/Export Segment Size To** as well as **Limit Capture Now To**

Tip

Scratch Disk Preferences: FCE's preferences are system based, a separate set of preferences for each user. They are not project based. Unfortunately, there is no way to have the Scratch Disks change with whatever the open project is. However, inside the Capture Scratch folder, the capture material is segregated into separate folders based on the project name. So when you open a project and go to capture, whatever you capture goes into a folder that keeps its material separate from that of other projects.

unchecked. This feature limits the size of segments FCE can capture or export. There isn't any particular reason to limit it.

Let's get back to the main body of the **Scratch Disks** panel. Here you assign scratch disks for your captured material and for your render files. Normally you set your project's video, audio, and render files in the same location. By default, FCE assigns separate render folders for audio and video. When you click the **Set** button, a navigation window allows you to select the location for these files. Usually I go to the media drive I want to use for a project and select the drive itself.

Selecting the drive will create some folders. There will be a folder called *Final Cut Express Documents*, inside of which will be folders called *Capture Scratch*, *Render Files*, and *Audio Render Files*. As you capture your video material, it is stored in *Capture Scratch*. The next time you want to set a scratch disk, do not select the *Capture Scratch* folder; select the drive or partition. Selecting the folder rather than the drive will make another *Capture Scratch* folder inside the current one.

⭐Tip _____
Scratch Disk Warning: A scratch disk warning appears if you start the application with the assigned scratch disk unmounted. The warning dialog in Figure 6.11 appears, giving you a chance to either Quit, mount drive and Check Again, or Reset the scratch disks to an available partition or disk. If the scratch disk with your media is missing, the items in your Browser as well as your render files will go offline. So it may be worth reconnecting that missing drive rather than reassigning the scratch disk to another location.

If you have more than one hard drive or partition, you can set multiple locations in the Scratch Disks panel. In FCE you can set up to 12 drives or partitions. The application automatically switches from one partition to another as they fill.

6.11 Missing Disks Warning

Search Folders

The second panel, **Search Folders** (see Figure 6.12), is new to FCE. Here you can set what drives or folders you want FCE to search for when looking to reconnect material. If you have large drives, or many of them, you can set the search locations here. It will let the application reconnect automatically and also improve search and reconnect speed.

Memory & Cache

The next panel, **Memory & Cache** (see Figure 6.13), allows you to control the amount of memory used by the application. Normally the default values are fine. If you want to work in other applications (e.g., if you have an application such as Adobe After Effects that you would like to render in the background while you work in FCE), then you can lower the application RAM to allow some for the other application to work with.

6.12 Search Folder Panel

6.13 Memory & Cache Panel

Also if you're working with a lot of large images in a sequence, you might want to set the **Still Cache** memory allocation higher. If you're working with a lot of stills, adding more physical RAM to your computer might also be a good idea.

6.14 Playback Control Panel

Thumbnail Cache (Disk) and **(RAM)** values are relatively small. I'd keep them at the default values unless you like to work in the Browser with lots of bins in Icon view or like to keep thumbnails open in List view. If you do, you may want to raise these values from the default. Make sure you have extra RAM available. Some people make these numbers quite high, 30MB or more. I don't use icons much, so I leave it low.

Playback Control

Playback Control (see Figure 6.14) is best left at its default settings. As with **Timeline Options**, these settings are best changed for individual sequences and can easily be done with the handy **RT** pop-up in the upper left corner of the Timeline window that we saw in Lesson 2.

Video Quality can be set to **High**, **Medium**, or **Low**. The lower the settings, the poorer the image quality, but the greater the real-time playback capabilities. These settings affect only playback quality and do not change your render quality at all.

Two new items introduced in this version are the checkbox for Beep when playing unrendered audio and the Record quality pop-up at the bottom. The first lets you switch off the beeping sound you get with unrendered material, like material captured in iMovie or MP3 audio files. Switching it off lets you ignore the warning, which you obviously can't otherwise.

The Record quality pop-up, which, unlike the video quality and frame rate controls, does not appear in the Timeline RT pop-up, lets you record to tape at reduced level for a quick preview copy without having to render out your material. It's a useful added feature to FCE.

External Editors

The last panel is the **External Editors** tab. Here you can define which applications are used to work on different types of files outside of FCE (see Figure 6.15).

This allows you to launch an application to alter a clip in either the Browser or the Timeline. Select a clip and right-click for the shortcut menu choice Open in Editor (see Figure 6.16).

Tip ————— **Remember:** Using Filmstrip in your sequences will require considerably more system overhead and a larger Thumbnail Cache size.

6.15 External Editors Panel

This will launch the application that you specify in this preferences panel. After you edit the clip—such as a still image in Photoshop—those changes will be reflected in FCE.

You can set **External Editors** for stills, video, and audio. The default setting for audio is Soundtrack. Be aware, though, that if you set the QuickTime Player as your editor for video files, when you select **Open in Editor** for the audio portion of a sync sound clip, FCE will open the QuickTime Player, not Soundtrack. FCE thinks of the audio track as part of a single video clip and so uses the QT Player. Single audio files, even if the creator type is QuickTime, will still open with the specified audio editor.

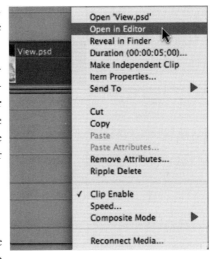

6.16 Open in Editor

Easy Setup

From the **Final Cut Express** HD menu, select **Easy Setup**, or use the keyboard shortcut **Control-Q**. When you open Easy Setup, it brings up the panel in Figure 6.17.

6.17 Easy Setup Dialog Box

🐾 *Note*

Changes in Photoshop: Sometimes changes made to a file in Photoshop, particularly to the layer structure and opacity, will cause the file to appear to be offline. Select Reconnect and navigate to the Photoshop file on your hard drive. If the dialog does not come up and the file still appears to be offline, select the item in the Browser, and from the shortcut menu choose Reconnect Media.

The default setting is DV NTSC, based on standard DV with an audio sampling rate of 48kHz. If you check the **Show All** box in the upper right corner from the pop-up you can select any of the 21 setups available, nine for NTSC and nine for PAL, and three for HDV. These are the same options that we saw in the Lesson 1 when we first started up the application.

The trick to **Easy Setup** is to base it on the specifications used in your camera. If you're working with an audio sampling rate of 32kHz, choose one of those presets. If you work in anamorphic, sometimes called widescreen or 16:9, choose one of those settings. If your camera or deck needs to use FireWire Basic instead of the standard FireWire, choose that. Check the Apple Final Cut Express web site's qualification page at *http://www.apple.com/finalcutexpress/qualification.html.*

All Canon cameras and some Panasonic and JVC cameras need FireWire Basic, but all Sony devices work with standard FireWire, also called iLink and IEEE1394. You should check with your camcorder manual to see its specifications.

NTSC versus PAL. NTSC, which some ways say stands for Never Twice the Same Color, is actually the now-defunct National Television Standards Committee, which established the format used by television broadcasting in the United States. All of North America and Japan use this format as well. Europe and most of the rest of the world use PAL, for Phase Alternating Lines, which refers to the way color is handled. PAL uses a frame rate of 25fps and a DV frame size of 720×576 (720 pixels wide and 576 pixels tall). NTSC has a standard frame rate fixed at 29.97fps, not, as many think, a more manageable 30fps. The NTSC DV frame size is 720×480.

Notice there is no difference in HD and HDV between PAL and NTSC frame sizes, just in their frame rates, 1080i50 (for 25fps) and 1080i60 (for 30fps, or 29.97). Unfortunately, FCE only supports 720p at the North American frame rate of 30fps (really 29.97). The HD frame sizes are 1,920×1,080 (compressed to 1,440×1,080 in HDV), and 1,280×720.

One setting that is not apparent in FCE is the ability to work with progressive, noninterlaced material, either 30p (actually 29.97fps), the NTSC standard; 25p, the PAL standard; or 24p. You can work in these formats in FCE, but you have to make each sequence you work on render material without fields. To do this after you've made your new sequence in NTSC or PAL:

1.   Select the sequence in the Browser.

2.   Right-click on it and from the shortcut menu choose **Item Properties**.

3.   In the Item Properties window, right-click in the **Field Dominance** value box (Figure 6.18) and choose **None**.

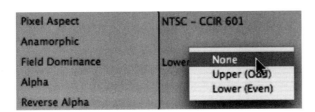

6.18   Field Dominance>None

This works for material that's been shot at 29.97fps or 25fps. Material that was shot with a camera such as a DVX100a using 24p normal 3:2 pulldown can be edited this way in FCE. Material shot using 24p advanced pulldown cannot be edited in FCE. Nor can HDV material shot using 720p at 24fps, which is not currently supported in FCE either.

If you are using a DV converter box, or using your camera in digital passthrough mode, to capture from analog material, choose one of the DV Converter options. This is for use with a noncontrollable device, a device that will not provide the machine with any timecode, which is what the application is looking for when it captures DV material. There is no device control with HDV material, and the camera or deck has to be controlled from the device and not from inside FCE.

The settings you choose here are for both your capturing and your sequences. The two need to match. Be careful that you don't use one setting to capture and then later change the settings for other material. Any sequences you create after changing the settings will reflect the new settings and will not work properly with material captured using the original settings.

> **What is anamorphic anyway?** Anamorphic is a 16:9 widescreen video that is compressed, squeezed horizontally into the standard 4:3 frame. Though widescreen televisions are only slowly being introduced in the United States, and usually as HD televisions, they have been fairly common throughout Japan and Europe for some time. Consequently, Japanese manufacturers have included this capability in many DV camcorders for quite a few years. The camera squeezes the pixels anamorphically (so that everything looks squashed, as though it's tall and narrow) to fit into a 4:3 frame and then unsqueezes them for playback on a widescreen TV.

Note

Canon Cameras and FireWire Drives: Because of the way FireWire Basic works, it does not play well with external FireWire drives. This has caused problems for many users, particularly those using Canon cameras as a capture device. One drive manufacturer, LaCie, has gone so far as to say that they do not support the use of their FireWire drives with Canon cameras while they are on the same bus. All Macs only have one FireWire bus, so additional hardware is needed. In a desktop tower computer, an inexpensive card can be added to give an additional FireWire bus. The PowerBooks and MacBook Pros have a cardbus slot that can be used for this as well. This is a real problem for iMac users, who don't have these options. Their usual recourse is to capture to the internal system drive and then move the media to the external drive. Or to capture from a cheap Sony camera or other device that uses the full FireWire device control protocol.

The problem is that many people want to do 16:9 but don't have the equipment to do it properly. To monitor it, you need a widescreen monitor or one that can switch between 4:3 and 16:9. FCE will output the correct 16:9 display if the presets are correct, but you won't see it correctly without the right monitor. You will not see a letterboxed version. Some fairly expensive decks will take a 16:9 image and output it as letterboxed 4:3. You can also place your 16:9 material in a 4:3 sequence and force it to render out the whole piece as letterboxed 4:3.

Most DV camcorders will flag 16:9 material as such, and tell the software that the material is anamorphic. The camera and the application will, in most cases, read this regardless of whether you use the 16:9 setup. If it doesn't do this, you will have to set it manually in the clip's Item Properties panel by checking in the Anamorphic line item. If you are shooting true 16:9 (i.e., with an anamorphic lens or with 16:9 CCDs) the correct setup has to be used to force FCE to treat it as widescreen material, even though it doesn't get the DV flag from the camera. Even true 16:9 CCDs will squeeze the image to conform to the 4:3 frame size specification of the DV format.

6.19 Final Cut Express User Data Folder Contents

Preferences Folder

If you have problems with FCE, one of the first remedies anyone will suggest is to trash your *Preferences* file. If there is a problem with your system, it's often your FCE preferences that are corrupt. To delete them, go into your user home folder, **Command-Option-H** from the Finder. Go to your *Library*, choose *Preferences*, and find the file *com.apple.finalcutexpress.plist*. This file should be deleted. In the same folder, find the *Final Cut User Data folder* (see Figure 6.19).

Inside you can find four or five items, including two or three folders (*Custom Settings*, *Button Bars*, and *Plugins*). The other items should be your *Final Cut Express 3.5 Prefs*, *Final Cut Express Obj Cache* and *Final Cut Express Prof Cache*. If you do need to trash your preferences, the only files you should remove from the folder are the three document files: the 3.5 Prefs and the two Cache files. You should do this with the application closed.

Summary

With this lesson, you have learned how to set up your system so that you are ready to capture. Doing this right is critical to the next step, getting your media onto your hard drive and into your project.

☞ Tip
Mixing Settings: Do not try to mix settings. If you shot your video in 32kHz, do not think that by capturing in 48kHz your material will become 48kHz. All that will happen will be that your audio is liable to drift out of sync.

Lesson 7

Getting Material into Final Cut Express HD

Now that we've set up our preferences and gotten everything ready, we can begin bringing our own material into the application. The process is called capturing and is used to do a file transfer of the digital data on your camera tape to put that binary information that makes up your video and audio and other data onto your computer hard drive.

Capture

To begin, go to **File>Capture** (**Command-8**). This brings up the **Capture** window (see Figure 7.1).

The window is divided in two. On the left is a Viewer like the standard FCE Viewer, but this is a viewer for your tape deck or camera. The control buttons—**J**, **K**, **L**, **I**, and **O** keys and spacebar—work the same as in the FCE Viewer except that they control your deck or camera through the FireWire cable.

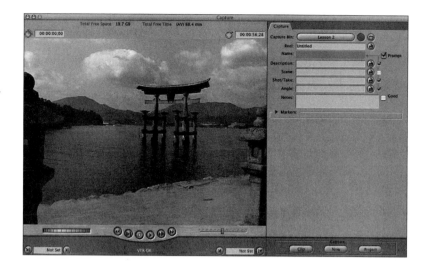

7.1   Capture Window

The Timecode in the upper right of the Viewer portion of the Capture window is your current timecode on your tape, and the Duration on the upper left is the duration you set with your In and Out points as you mark the tape (see Figure 7.2). Notice the displays at the top of the window that tell you how much available drive space you have on the designated scratch disk and how many minutes of video you can store on it.

In addition to your keyboard shortcuts for **Mark In** and **Mark Out**, you also have buttons and timecode displays at the bottom of the Viewer for these functions (see Figure 7.3).

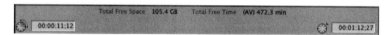

7.2   Current Time and Duration Displays in the

7.3   Capture Viewer Controls

The two inner buttons mark the In and Out points: **In** on the left, **Out** on the right. The timecode on the left is the In point, and the timecode on the right is the Out point. Of the buttons on the far outside, the left one will take the tape deck to the assigned In point, and the far right one to the assigned Out point, or you can use the keyboard shortcuts **Shift-I** to go to the In point and **Shift-O** to go to the Out point.

In the right half of the Capture window is the panel where you add information that is used to organize your media (see Figure 7.4). At the top of this panel is a button that has the project name. The button to the far right of the name will add a bin to the Browser and designate it the capture bin. Clicking the button again will add a new bin inside the previously designated bin. Using the button to the left, right next to the bin name, will take the capture bin up one level. If you click it enough times it will go right up to the Browser level. There is, however, no button to take you back down through the hierarchy. The button with the project name will take you to the designated capture bin and open it.

Creating a capture bin means that any material that you capture will be added directly to that designated bin. The bin appears in the Browser with a clapperboard icon on it when in Icon view or next to the bin's name when in List view.

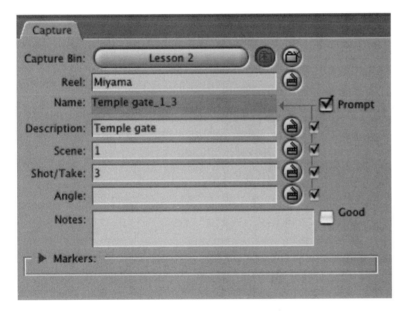

7.4   Capture Panel

You can also select a capture bin directly in the Browser with a shortcut menu. Right-click on a bin, and from the shortcut menu choose **Set Capture Bin** (see Figure 7.5).

7.5   Set Capture Bin

One critical piece of information in the Capture panel is the **Reel** name or number. This is really referencing the videotapes you shot, though it uses the film term reel. It is extremely important that reel or tape numbers be properly assigned. Every reel should have a separate number or name.

The number should be written on the tape, and that number should be put in the Capture window. This number is actually attached to the QuickTime file when it's captured and is important for FCE being able to recapture material should you ever need to. This is so important that when the application is in Capture mode, it will auto-detect when the reel in your camera or deck has been ejected and a new reel inserted and will put up a warning message. The little clapperboard next to the reel name to the right can be clicked to increment it numerically.

In the Capture panel you can enter information about your clips before you capture them. You can't enter a name for the clip in the Name area of the Capture window, but you can give the clips names by combining Description, Scene and Shot/Take number, or other information. You probably want to keep these as short as you can. They can be combined through the checkboxes, next to the tiny clapperboard icons, into creating the name for the clip. It's important that some information be added into the clip name, otherwise the media file on your hard drive will be called *Untitled*, which is not very useful.

At the bottom of the Naming portion of the panel is an area where you can add notes about a clip or the section of material that you're capturing. This can be useful for organizing and searching through your material while you're editing.

> **★ Tip**
> **Angle:** The Angle function that you see in Figure 7.4 is a holdover from Final Cut Pro and serves no function in Final Cut Express. It's used to designate angles in multicamera editing, a feature that is only available in FCP.

Below the Naming portion of the window is a box that you can twirl open with a disclosure triangle. This box allows you to add and name markers (see Figure 7.6). We'll look at markers more closely Lesson 3, but here markers are a way of letting you add more information about a clip, keyed to a specific point somewhere inside the material. Once the clip has been captured, markers will appear attached to the clip, where they can be accessed from the Browser, as we'll see in the next lesson.

7.6   Markers Window

Strategies for Capturing

There are three strategies for capturing DV material, and you choose the one you want to use with the buttons at the bottom of the **Capture** window (see Figure 7.7). The options you have are:

- **Now**
- **Clip**
- **Project**

7.7   Capture Buttons

Capture Now

This is the simplest way to work, but it gives you least control. It also requires that your material be properly shot, preferably without timecode breaks. Breaks in the timecode can cause havoc with any capture, particularly if you use **Capture Now**. FCE captures around timecode breaks, but it should be avoided if at all possible, because it will still lose audio/video synchronization if it comes across a section of unstable video or a section of tape with no video at all, even if timecode is present.

FCE handles the capture around timecode breaks automatically, albeit slowly. If there is a break on the tape but the timecode continues getting higher, a new clip will start at the break, but the same reel number will be maintained. If the timecode resets to zero at the break, which is what most commonly happens on consumer cameras, the reel number will be changed and incremented as well as making a new clip. This will treat each portion of the tape where the timecode resets to zero as a separate tape. Avoid having breaks in your timecode if you can. It will make your life easier.

Capturing large chunks of video with the Now function is a common work strategy. To use Now, you should name the material you're about to capture a name as described previously, then put the deck in play and click the **Now** button. A capture screen comes up and begins recording as soon as it's checked your drives and found a video signal from your camera or deck.

If you are working with a non-controllable device using the **DV Converter** preset, **Now** is the only capture choice available to you. I would recommend that, if possible, you dub your analog material to DV tape and then use the tape—properly reel-numbered—as your master. Dubbing allows you to easily access the material again if you ever need to recapture.

⭐ *Tip*
Monitoring: When capturing, audio should be monitored through external speakers connected to the camcorder or deck you're playing back from. You will not be able to hear the sound through the computer's speaker while the Capture window is open or during capturing itself. See the sections "Monitors" and "Speakers" in Lesson 1 beginning on page 5.

FCE records the clip on your designated scratch disk until one of three events occur:

- It runs out of hard drive space.
- It hits your preference time limit.
- You hit the **Escape** key and stop the process.

If the capture stops because of the time limit, the deck also stops.

After your capture is complete, if you did not name the video prior to capturing, it appears as a clip called *Untitled* inside the Browser or designated capture bin. Whenever a clip is captured, it is saved inside the *Capture Scratch* folder on the drive you selected in your Preferences. Inside *Capture Scratch* there will be a folder with the project's name, one folder for each project.

Your captured material is stored inside that folder. Your clip will be in that project's folder with the same name *Untitled* or the name you gave it. It's always a good idea to name the clip before you click the Now button, so it will appear in the Browser and in your *Capture Scratch* folder with the name you assigned. If you capture a clip using Now and you decide you don't want to use it, you'll have to go into your *Capture Scratch* folder, dig it out, and throw it into the Trash to get it off your hard drive and retrieve that drive space.

Using Capture Now, you can bring all of your video material into your computer for editing into smaller subclips rather than using your deck to select clips. As we've seen FCE has a wonderful tool for those working with DV material, the ability to automatically mark up shot changes with DV Start/Stop Shot Detect and then break them up into separate clips. We looked at this beginning on page 38 in Lesson 3.

If you don't want to prestripe the tape, you then just have to be careful when you shoot. After you shut off the camera to change batteries or play back your tape to review what you shot, for instance, not simply stop it after a shot, it's a good idea to back up the tape just a second to get back into the area of timecoded material. This is why it's always a good idea when shooting to let the camera run for a few moments after the action you're shooting is complete, before you stop the recording. That way you will have that moment or two of unnecessary material to back up into.

Any timecode break is liable to cause a sudden loss of audio-video sync when you capture across it. So if you do have a tape with timecode breaks in it, one of the simplest ways to get around the problem is to dub the tape. By dubbing it from one deck or one camera to another, the video and audio portion of the tape is actually cloned exactly as it was on the original, while the recording deck is creating new, unbroken timecode. Unfortunately this often means that you lose the ability to work with DV Start/Stop Detect.

Aside from shooting carefully, or prestriping the tape, another way around the problem is to use the Clip method to capture material between the timecode breaks.

Timecode Breaks. Timecode breaks or control track breaks have been the bane of video editors since tape machines were invented. Many editors have cursed many a cameraperson for failing to keep good timecode on the tapes. These days, most consumer and prosumer cameras are designed to generate frame-accurate timecode, and that's the way tape should be delivered. FireWire uses the timecode recorded on tape when the video was shot to find your clips and control the deck during capture. This timecode information is passed to the application and remains with the clip throughout the editing process.

There are several ways to ensure that there are no breaks in your DV timecode. The simplest way, which I recommend for beginners and students in particular, is to prestripe your tapes (i.e., record black and timecode on your tape before you shoot). You can do this in any camera or VCR: (1) connect a video signal into the recording device; (2) put it in VCR mode if you're using a camera; and (3) press the Record button. With some cameras you may not be able to do this and will have to put it into camera mode; just put a lens cap on it or point it at a wall and put it into record. Now whenever you shoot, your tape will have timecode written on it. The camera will then read the timecode and start writing from whatever it reads. No breaks.

Clip

7.8   Prompt Checkbox

7.9   Clip Name Window

7.10   Duplicate Item Filename
       Dialog Box

Another option in the Capture window is the **Clip** button. This requires that you enter In and Out points for where you want the capture to begin and where it should end. In the Clip method, you mark up the section of video you want to capture and then press the Clip button. This is a controlled form of Capture Now.

1. Mark an In point near the beginning of the reel and then an Out point near the end.

2. Click **Clip**.

If you have checked the Prompt box in Figure 7.8, you will get a dialog box asking to confirm the name (see Figure 7.9). If you didn't name the clip in the Capture panel, you'll have to enter one now. Notice the little clapperboard to the right of the name box. This lets you increment the name numerically.

3. Click the **OK** button and let the deck and the computer do their thing.

If you enter a clip name that already exists in the project's scratch folder, you'll get the dialog box in Figure 7.10 asking you to rename the clip, skip capture, or abort it. If the clip is not active in your project, or mistakenly got captured into the scratch folder, you'll also get an option to Overwrite the existing clip.

During capture you will get a large black window and, at the bottom, information about what's happening, such as in Figure 7.11, which shows that the deck is *Cueing* source material, the clip that's being captured, the duration, and how much more to capture off that reel. When capture begins, you'll see the image in the Capture window, and the display in the bottom will change to the **Now Capturing** message in Figure 7.12.

Do not be dismayed that the quality of the video in the Capture window seems poor and stuttering. A computer monitor cannot display a full-screen interlaced image with full motion at full resolution during capture.

> **Note**
> **Preroll and Postroll:** Camcorders and decks cannot start and stop instantly. They require some time to get up to speed and to stop after they're playing. This is called preroll and postroll. This is a fixed preset in FCE of three seconds. So when you mark In and Out points to capture a clip, you need to make sure that your marked In point is no earlier than 03;00 from the beginning of the tape or from the last timecode break and that the Out point is no closer than three seconds to the end of the video material. In reality most cameras will need a bit more than three seconds of preroll, so I'd set 04;00 as the minimum. Most cameras don't need as much as three seconds of postroll and usually stop within one second. Still it's better to be safe if you can than lose a long capture because the camera ran out of timecode during postroll.

> Capture Project – CUEING SOURCE MATERIAL
> Capturing File: Temple gate_1_3 (00:00:23:27) – Item 1 of 1
> Remaining to capture on Untitled: 00:00:23:27

7.11 Cueing source material message

Capture Project – NOW CAPTURING (press 'ESC' to abort)
Capturing File: Temple gate_1_3 (00:00:23:27) – Item 1 of 1
Remaining to capture on Untitled: 00:00:23:27

**7.12 Now Capturing
message**

After you've captured your material, you are ready to edit. Close the Capture window before you start, however. You should not try to play video while Capture is open. So shut it down before you begin editing.

Once you've captured your material, it appears in the Browser. If you switch to List view, each clip will have a duration but with no In or Out points defined. Capturing only sets the media limit, and FCE assumes you will want to edit the material further, so no In or Out points are designated. The clip has the *de facto* In and Out points marked by the limits of the media; they're not displayed in the Browser in the In and Out columns.

Project Capture

**7.13 Browser
with Offline
Clips**

> **Tip**
> **Renaming Clips:** If you have to rename the clip because the name you've chosen is already used (as in Figure 7.10), the original incorrect name you assigned will appear in the Browser. This may mean that you have two clips in the Browser with the same name. The actual media file name will be correct, but the one in the Browser will not be. It's a good idea, if you do rename a clip in the warning dialog box, to immediately rename the clip in the Browser to match the media file name you gave the clip before capture.

**7.14 Browser with
Offline Clips**

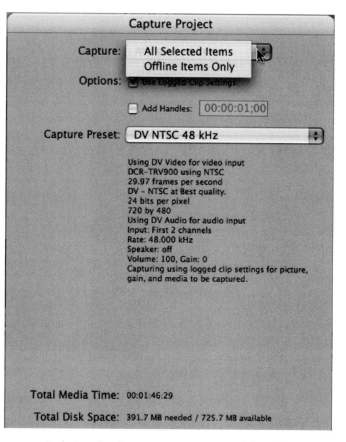

7.15 Capture Project
Dialog Box

Project capture is designed to let you recapture material for old projects to reconstruct them. To do this, reopen the project. If the material is not available, you will get the Reconnect dialog box we've seen at the beginning of the earlier lessons. Click the **OK** button and let the project open.

All of the media will probably appear offline, with the Browser displaying clips with red slash marks through them (see Figure 7.13) and the words Media Offline across a glaringly red Canvas (see Figure 7.14). You could at this point evoke the Capture window and press the Project button. This will bring up the dialog box in Figure 7.15.

Normally the pop-up at the top would display only **All Items**, but if some of the clips are available to you while others are offline, then you'll get the choice of picking **All Items**, **Offline Items Only**, or **Selected Items**.

Notice the box that allows you to **Add Handles**. This will set the computer to capture a designated amount of material beyond the In and Out points defined in your clips. You can select any of the available Capture Presets, and the window will display what your selected settings are. At the bottom you get an indication of the hard drive requirements for Total

Media Time and Total Disk Space. Check that you have enough drive space for the capture. Also look closely at the media time to make sure it looks about right, that you're capturing all the media you need but not too much.

When you click **OK**, you'll get a window telling you what tapes will be required for the project capture and how much will be captured off each tape. Load the first reel and click Continue. FCE will prompt you whenever a reel change is required.

If you capture with handles, the clips will come into the Browser with your designated In and Out points marked already, not the usual **Not Set** indication, and if you open the clip into the Viewer, you'll see that there is the extra media beyond the marked In and Out points.

It's important to understand the way project capture works. It works best if you've captured your material using the Clip method (i.e., selected the portions of the video you want to use and captured them as separate clips). But if you haven't, you can still use the **Project** button to trim down your material to just what you need, provided you had cut up your material into subclips, which we looked at in Lesson 3. If you have, this is how you do it:

1. Start by reopening your project file with the missing material that needs to be recaptured.

2. Delete everything except the sequence or clips you need to recapture. You'll probably get the warning message in Figure 7.16. Click **OK** and push on.

3. Select the sequences, and from the **Modify** menu choose **Make Sequence Clips Independent**. This will separate the edited clips from the long masters you may have captured.

4. Start up the Capture window, and click the Project button.

One or more of the clips you have selected are Master clips. By deleting them you will break their relationship to any clip or item affiliated with them. Do you want to continue?

Cancel   OK

7.16 Master Clip Delete Warning

The application will now recapture only those clips that it needs to reconstitute your sequence. It will not capture any of the clips that you didn't use and that you deleted from your project, nor all the rest of the material that is not part of your sequence. If you captured whole reels of tape or large chunks, FCE would want to recapture all of the pieces that use even a very small portion of your clips. So if you originally captured a 60-minute reel and used only 10 seconds of it, the application would still want to capture the entire 60 minutes just to get that 10 seconds it needed to reconstitute your sequence. That's why you need to make the clips into subclips first and then use the **Make Sequence Clips Independent** function.

Project capture does not work with HDV material; it works only for the DV material. When your HDV material is captured, it is converted to the Apple Intermediate Codec during capture, and the timecode information is lost. This does not happen with DV material. The timecode information is retained for each media clip, even though it is not displayed within the application.

When a project is complete, you should separately back up imported audio and graphics files. You should also be aware that tracks recorded using the **Voice Over** tool are not able to be recaptured because they have no useful timecode. It's a good idea to build an *Import* bin that contains audio files, still images, graphics files, and your voice-over tracks. The **Source** column in the Browser or the clip's Item Properties will let you find the file path to where the media such as stills and voice-overs are stored. These should be backed up separately if you want to re-create the project at a later time. It may be simplest to burn this data material onto a CD or DVD for storage.

Importing Files

In addition to capture material, you can also import material into FCE. QuickTime movies should be converted outside of FCE into the format you're working with in the application, either DV or HDV. FCE does not directly accept MPEG-2, DV Stream, MPEG-4, or other types of Quick-Time or AVI that are not in the correct formats the applications work with. FCE also allows you to import sound files, still images, and more.

There are a couple of different ways to import material. You could use **Command-I** to import a single item or groups of items from one folder, or the **File** menu under **Import>Folder** to bring a folder full of clips or other material. Another way is to move the Canvas to the left, grabbing it with the bar at the top and sliding it out of the way to access your Desktop. You can drag and drop folders and files from anywhere on your drives directly into the Browser. This is the simplest, quickest way to bring lots of material into your project.

You can also right-click in the Browser window and choose **Import>Files** or **Folder** from the shortcut menu.

Importing Music

Importing music either from a CD or in other formats (such as MP3) is slightly different from importing video. FCE can work with audio CD files, but they do raise some problems. Audio CDs use an audio sample rate of 44.1kHz. This is not the sampling rate used by the DV format, which uses either 32kHz or, most commonly, 48kHz. MP3s should also be converted to the AIFF format while being resampled and having their compression removed. Although FCE can deal with resampling the audio while it plays it back, it doesn't do it very well, and it requires processor power, which may limit your ability to do real-time effects or to play back video or multiple tracks of audio without dropping frames (i.e., the audio or video stuttering). To avoid this, I always recommend resampling the audio to the correct sampling rate you want to use before importing it into FCE. There are several different ways to do this.

I think that the best way to do this is to use the QuickTime Pro Player. The standard QT player will not be sufficient, but by upgrading to the pro version you will get the ability to change files into several different formats. You can also do basic video and audio editing in the QT Pro Player. It's a great value and can easily be purchased from Apple at *www.apple.com/quicktime*.

To resample the audio of a CD track or an MP3 file, drag the track(s) from the CD onto the QuickTime icon that is probably in your **Dock** (see Figure 7.17). This will launch the QT Pro Player and open the files into it.

1. Once the files are open, choose **File>Export** (**Command-E**).

2. From the **Export** pop-up menu, select **Sound to AIFF** (see Figure 7.18).

3. Click on the **Options** button, make sure **Sound** is checked on, and then click the **Settings** button as in Figure 7.19.

4. In the Settings panel, choose the correct settings: Linear PCM for Format, Stereo LR for Channels, and either 48,000Hz, which is most commonly used in DV, or 32,000Hz, if that's the setting the rest of your material uses (see Figure 7.20). Set the other items as in the figure.

5. Give the new file a name, such as *SongName48k*, and save it onto your media drive.

➤ Tip

Item-Level Rendering: We'll look at rendering in greater detail later, but FCE has a feature that is worth mentioning here. There are render settings in the application that include the ability to render audio at the item level. This means that you can render a piece of audio, such as an MP3 file or a piece of 44.1kHz CD music, into the correct sampling rate as a separate item. If you place an audio clip in the Timeline and render it out, that render file will stay with the clip wherever you place that audio in your Timeline. It will remain fully rendered to the correct settings. It will have a blue indicator bar on the clip to tell you it's been rendered as an item and will not need to be re-rendered. Unfortunately, as of this time, item-level rendering of MP3 audio files does not produce the best quality and should be avoided.

7.17 QuickTime Icon

The file will be copied from the audio CD onto your hard drive, converted and resampled to the correct sampling rate. This is the file you should import into and work with in FCE.

7.18 Export>Sound to AIFF

7.19 Export>Sound to AIFF

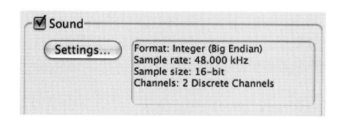

7.20 Sound Settings Dialog Box

Another way to do this if the QuickTime Pro Player is not available to you is to use iTunes. To do this you have to set up your iTunes preferences.

7.21 iTunes Importing Preferences

1. Under the **iTunes** menu, go to **Preferences**, select **Advanced**, and go to the **Importing** tab (see Figure 7.21).
2. From the **Import Using** pop-up menu, select **AIFF Encoder**.
3. From the second pop-up menu, select **Custom**.
4. Set the sampling rate to 48,000Hz or whatever sampling rate you're working with.
5. Set the **Channels** to **Stereo** and the **Sample Size** to **16-bit**, as in Figure 7.22.

Now you're ready to import the music.

7.22 iTunes Custom Settings

7.23 iTunes Window

7.24 Show Song File

6. In the **iTunes** window, **Command**-click on one of the checked track boxes. This will deselect all of the tracks.

7. Check the tracks you want, and click the **Import** button in the lower right corner of the window (see Figure 7.23).

iTunes will copy the track from the CD to your iTunes library, which can be a labyrinthine place to find a track. You want to find the track because you want to move it from your iTunes library, which is on the internal system drive of your computer, onto your media drive. The simplest way to find the track is to right-click on the track in your iTunes library and from the contextual menu choose **Show Song File** (see Figure 7.24). This will open a Finder window for the folder that holds the file and select the file for you. Copy it, or by holding down the **Command** key, move it to your media drive, and you're ready to import it into FCE.

Summary

With these two lessons, you have completed the process of correctly setting up your system and the application and gone through the capture process. We are now ready to take you into some of the more advanced features in Final Cut Express, starting with transitions. When you want to smooth out cuts or to change between scenes, you might want to use transitions. That's what we're going to look at in the next lesson: transitions, how they work, and how to use them.

Lesson 8

Adding Transitions

Transitions can add life to a sequence, ease a difficult edit into something smoother, or give you a way to mark a change of time or place. The traditional grammar of film that audiences still accept is that dissolves denote small changes, and a fade to black followed by a fade from black mark a greater passage of time. With the introduction of digital effects, every imaginable movement or contortion of the image to replace one with another quickly became possible—and was quickly applied everywhere, seemingly randomly, to every possible edit. They can be hideously inappropriate, garish, and ugly, but to each his own taste. Transitions can be used effectively, or they can look terribly hackneyed. Final Cut Express gives you the option to do either or anything in between.

Let's look at the transitions FCE has to offer. There are quite a few of them, 60 to be exact, although there is redundancy in the transitions. Some people seem to think that just because Apple put all those transitions in there, you have to use them all. Remember that most movies use only cuts and the occasional dissolve. Most film and television programs are cuts only, with a fade in at the beginning and a fade out at the commercial breaks.

There are also many third-party transitions and effects that can be purchased online from plug-in providers such as CGM Online, CHV effects, Joe's Filters, and many others. A quick Google search will find them for you. Any transitions or effects created using Apple's FXScript code base will work in Final Cut Express HD 3.5.

119

8.1   Effects Window

In this lesson we'll look at adding transitions, controlling them, and using their parameters you can adjust to change the look of your transitions.

Loading the Lesson

Let's begin by loading the material you need on the hard drive of your computer, if you have not done so already.

1. Open the hybrid DVD. From the folder called *Hybrid DVD-ROM Contents*, drag the *Media* folder from the DVD to your media drive. This contains the media needed for this project.

2. You may also want to drag the folder called *Transitions* from the DVD onto your media drive. This contains samples of each of the 60 transitions available in Final Cut Express HD.

3. Also make sure your have the *Projects* folder on your system hard drive.

4. Eject the DVD and launch the *Lesson 8* project from the *Projects* folder on your hard drive.

5. Once again, you may have to go through the reconnect process as in the previous "Loading the Lesson" on page 14 in Lesson 2. You will first get the Offline Files window. Click the **Reconnect** button.

Inside your copy of the project *Lesson 8* you'll find in the Browser:

- An empty sequence called *Sequence 1*
- The sequence called *Transitions* that has a few shots laid out in it waiting for transitions
- The master clip *Village*
- The bin called *Clips*
- A still image called *Gradient.pct*, which we'll use later

To see the basic settings for each of the 60 FCE transitions, use **File>Import>Folder** to bring into the application the *Transitions* folder you copied onto your hard drive. The folder contains bins with all of the transitions grouped in the same fashion they are in the application.

Applying Transitions

In the Browser, usually behind the project window, is a tab called *Effects*. If you open it, you see a window with a group of folders—sorry, bins—as in Figure 8.1. You'll notice more than transitions in this window. For the moment, we're going to concentrate on the *Video Transitions* bin.

One of the bins in the Effects window is *Favorites*. We'll look at *Favorites* later in the lesson. Here is where you can park your special transitions and effects. It's probably empty now.

Double-click on *Video Transitions* to open the bin. It should look like Figure 8.2. The *Video Transitions* window shows yet more bins, and these bins contain the available transitions grouped into categories. I'd be very surprised if anyone has ever used them all in earnest on real projects, not just playing with them to try them out. The *Transitions* bin you imported contains previews of each of the transitions available in FCE. We're going to try out some of them in this lesson.

The default transition in FCE is the Cross Dissolve with a default duration of one second. In the bins in the Effects window and in the menus, you may see some transitions highlighted in bold. These are real-time capable transitions, if your system is fast enough to support them. If your system isn't fast enough, very few will be in bold.

There are several different ways to apply a transition in Final Cut Express:

- Drag the transition you want from the Effects panel of the Browser, and drop it on an edit point.

- Select the edit point. (Remember, **V** will select the nearest edit point.) Then use the **Effects>Video Transitions** menu and choose one.

- Select the edit point, and apply the default transition with the keyboard shortcut **Command-T**.

- Select the edit point, and by right-clicking on the edit point, call up the default transition from the shortcut menu.

There are a couple of other ways that we skipped in the last lesson, using the two items in the Edit Overlay:

- Insert with Transition
- Overwrite with Transition

The default transition will appear in your sequence when you select Insert with Transition (**Shift-F9**) or Overwrite with Transition (**Shift-F10**).

Checking the Media

Let's begin by opening *Sequence 1* if it's not already open.

1. Select the three clips in the *Clips* bin and drag them directly to the sequence.

8.2   Video Transitions
       Window

2. It might be helpful to use **Shift-Z** (Fit to Window) if the clips appear too small in the Timeline.

8.3 Transition Error

Remember that these are all subclips, and so each shot you just placed in the timeline contains the full extent of the media for that clip on the hard drive. Or at least so Final Cut Express thinks.

8.4 Insufficient Content Error

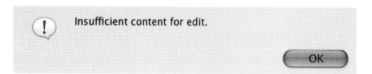

Let's try putting a transition onto the sequence we've laid out.

3. Grab the *Cross Dissolve* transition from the *Dissolve* bin and drag it onto the edit point between *Village1* and *Village2*.

You see that this isn't possible because you get the transition drag icon with a small X, as shown in Figure 8.3. If you try to perform the edit by using the keyboard shortcut **Command-T**, you'll get the error message in Figure 8.4. Why is this happening? The answer is simple. There isn't enough media in either clip beyond the edit point to perform the transition. The shots must overlap; frames from both shots must appear on the screen simultaneously. For a one-second transition, both shots have to have one second of media that overlaps with the other shot. These frames come partly from inside the clip and partly from media beyond the edit point. The extra video frames, those beyond the edit point separating the two shots, are called *handles*.

1. Double-click *Village1* in the Timeline to open it into the Viewer.

2. Go to the end of the shot. Use **Shift-O** to take you to the Out point.

If Overlays are switched on in the View pop-up as they normally are, you'll see the telltale film sprocket hole indicator on the right edge of the frame (see Figure 8.5).

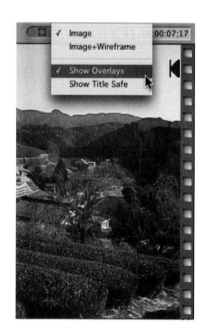

8.5 Film Sprocket Overlay in the Viewer

This overlay tells you that you're right at the end of the available media for that shot. There needs to be extra media available to create the overlap for the transition, as shown in Figure 8.6.

The pale shot on the left has to overlap the dark shot on the right by half the length of the transition, and vice versa. If that media does not exist, you can't do the transition. FCE usually assumes as a default that the transition takes place centered on the marked edit point, not that it ends at the edit point. Therefore, to execute the default one-second transition, you need at least half a second, 15 frames, of available media after the Out point on the outgoing shot and 15 frames in front of the In point of the incoming shot. In this case there is nothing, hence the error messages when you try to execute the transition. Unless you think of it ahead of time—and many times you don't—you'll have to deal with it when you're fine-tuning your edit. Often you'd rather not deal with transitions while you're laying out your sequence, leaving them until you've laid out the shot order.

If you know you have extra media in the original clip, you can always go back to extend the media. If this option is available, it's easy to do in FCE. Select **Remove Subclip Limits** from the **Modify** menu.

However, in this case, extending the media will push it into another shot, producing a flash frame during the transition, something to be avoided. This is one of the benefits of subclipping. It prevents you from going beyond the shot when you're laying in a transition.

To be able to put in transitions, we'll have to trim the Out point of *Village1* and the In point of *Village2*. We could do this by dragging the ends of the shots to make them shorter, but that would leave a hole in the Timeline. Instead, we'll use the Ripple tool to shorten the shots.

8.6   Overlapping Video

8.5   Ripple Tool in the Timeline

1. Select the Ripple tool from the Tools palette, or use the keyboard shortcut **RR**.

2. With the Ripple tool, click just to the left of the edit point between *Village1* and *Village2*, as in Figure 8.7.

3. With Ripple active, type in **−15** for 15 frames. Notice the display that appears in the middle of the Timeline window (see Figure 8.8). Press the **Return** key.

8.6   Ripple Value in the Timeline

We know this is the navigation shortcut for going backward half a second. Because we're in the Ripple tool, we're rippling it backward one-half second.

4. Click on the right side of the edit point at the start of *Village2*. Remember that you can use the **U** key to toggle from rippling one side, to roll edit, and to ripple the other side of an edit point.

5. This time type **+15** and press **Return** to ripple the edit point half a second.

We've now rippled *Village2's* In point by half a second, half a second off the end of the first shot, and half a second off the beginning of the second. So we have removed a half second of material from both clips, leaving this as handles, so that there is enough room for the transition.

Over these three shots laid in the Timeline, if I ripple the Ins and Outs on both edits in the Timeline, taking 15 frames off the end and the beginning of each shot, I reduce the overall duration by two seconds. This will substantially change the timing of my sequence. If you plan to use transitions between shots, it's best to allow for the extra material within the shot before you lay it in the Timeline.

6. Once you've rippled the edits, go to the edit point in the sequence between *Village1* and *Village2* and apply the transition.

Transition Alignment

If you drag a transition from the *Transitions* bin to an edit point, it does not need to be dragged only to the center-line. It can also be dragged to the Out clip so that the transition ends at the edit point (the A side) or to the In clip so the transition begins at the start of the clip (the B side). This can be done only if there is sufficient material for this type of transition.

After you've applied a transition, if you double-click on the transition in the Timeline, it will open into the Viewer. Make sure you click on the transition area as in Figure 8.9, not on the edit point that divides the two shots. Here you can see how the video overlaps and why extra material—handles—are needed on either side of the edit point to create the effect (see Figure 8.10). We'll look at this in more detail in the next lesson.

8.7   Transition in the Timeline

Once it's in the Timeline, the transition displays in one of three ways, depending on how it was placed. Figure 8.9 shows the center position; the other two appear as in Figures 8.11 and 8.12.

Making the transition to start or end on edit is useful if you have media available on only one side of the edit point, if you have a title or other clip on a track without any material adjacent to it, and at the beginning or end of your program.

Notice the sloping line indicators showing the type of alignment in each case. The last two transitions can be only half-second dissolves. When we

Note

Handles on One Side: If you only have video available for the transition overlap on one side of the edit, you should not try to execute the transition from the menu or with Command-T. These methods will usually execute the default Center on Edit transition. If one of the shots does not have enough material to do the transition, you'll get a one-frame transition. Just be careful, because it may seem that a transition has been entered into your sequence when there isn't anything there of value.

8.10   Clips Overlapping in the Transition Editor

8.11   End on Edit transition

8.12   Start on Edit transition

rippled the sequence by 15 frames on each side of the edit point, only enough media was made available for a half-second Start or End on Edit transition. If the transition is to end on the edit point with the default duration, the incoming shot has to be extended one whole second underneath the outgoing shot to accommodate it. Similarly, if you wanted to start the transition on the edit point with the default duraction, the outgoing shot has to extend one second into the incoming shot, one second beyond the start of the edit point. If we made these changes, then we could also easily change the type of transition alignment with the shortcut menu on the transition alignment with the shortcut menu on the transition in the Timeline (see Figure 8.13).

8.13 Transition Alignment Shortcut Menu

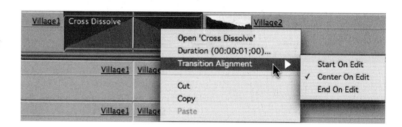

Using the Edit Overlay

Let's back up a bit to see another way to use the Canvas Edit Overlay to create transitions.

1. Delete everything in the Timeline.

2. Open *Village1* from the Browser into the Viewer.

Because this will be the first shot in the Timeline, I won't need to shorten the front of the clip.

3. Press the **End** key to take you to the end of the shot.

4. Press **Shift-left** arrow to move the playhead backward by one second.

5. Press **O** to enter the Out point and drag to the Edit Overlay Overwrite box, or press **F10** to overwrite it into the Timeline.

6. Open *Village2* in the Viewer from the Browser.

This clip we should shorten on both ends.

7. Go to the beginning of the clip and press **Shift-right** arrow to move forward by one second, and enter an In point.

8. Then go to the end of the clip and enter an Out point one second before the end (press **Shift-left arrow**, and then press **O**).

9. Drag *Village2* from the Viewer to Overwrite with Transition—not to Overwrite. Or use the keyboard shortcut **Shift-F10**.

The clip immediately drops into the Timeline after the first clip. The default transition has been added at the beginning of the clip, as well as a default audio crossfade. Adding the audio crossfade is a bonus that enhances the edit and helps smooth the transition (see Figure 8.14). If you use the shortcut menu to create a transition in the Timeline, this will also add the audio crossfade.

8.14 Transition with Audio Crossfade

Rendering

Before we look at controlling our transitions, let's look at rendering, which will also apply to the work we do with animation and effects in later lessons. Rendering is creating media for a section of your sequence that doesn't exist on your hard drive. Sometimes your computer is fast enough to do this on the fly, just with its processor power and RAM, but other times it's not, and then a small QuickTime file has to be created on your hard drive so you can play back the sequence. This is called a **render file**.

Let's begin by adding a transition to your sequence.

1. Double-click the *Transitions* sequence to open it into the Timeline window.

2. Click on the edit point between *Village1* and *Village2* to select it, or move the playhead to it and press the **V** key.

3. From the **Effects** menu, select **Video Transitions>3D Simulation>Cube Spin**.

With the transition applied in the sequence, you may have encountered for the first time the need for rendering. After you've entered a transition, you'll see that the narrow bar at the top of the Timeline has changed color from the normal midgray. The bar inside the circled area in Figure 8.15

will have changed to red, green, yellow, or orange, depending on the type of transition you applied, your system capabilities, and your RT settings. If you are working with a system with no real-time capabilities, then a bright red line will appear over the transition, indicating that a portion of the sequence needs to be rendered.

8.15   Render Indicator

8.16   Unrendered Warning

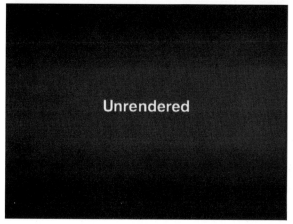

Rendering means that the application has to create media for which none exists. Most of the two shots are on your hard drive, but not for the 30 frames that make up this one-second cross-dissolve, during which one shot is changing into the other. The material of one shot mixed together with another is not on your hard drive. All you have done is give the computer instructions to create that media. If you try to play across that part of the timeline with a non–real-time system, the Canvas will momentarily display the message in Figure 8.16.

Real-Time Preview

FCE's real-time preview can be seen only in the Canvas and only when the external viewing is switched off. It will not send a real-time DV signal out the FireWire cable. So you have a choice: either monitor through FireWire but not in real time, or monitor on your desktop screen.

So if you think you have real-time capabilities and you're still seeing a red line in your sequence, it's probably because you have external viewing turned on. You can switch it off from the **View** menu by going down at the bottom to the **Video Out**. Here you can select either **Canvas Playback** or **Apple FireWire**.

Remember, this is real-time preview only. As soon as you revert to viewing your video externally or you want to output your material to tape, all those items that were in real time on your desktop a moment ago now have to be rendered out.

If you have your RT settings, which we saw in Lesson 2 on page 34, on Unlimited RT, you may get a yellow or an orange bar. The yellow bar indicates that playback is a proxy only; that is, if you've created a complex setting for your transition, only the default will be visible in real time. Orange indicates that you will likely get dropped frames when playing through this area. If you do play through, you may get the dropped frame warning message in Figure 8.17. If you switch this warning off in the lower left corner, you can then work in Unlimited RT without hindrance but with the occasional frame drop. To turn on the dropped frame warning, you'll have to go back to your User Preferences and switch it back on in the first tab.

8.17 Unlimited RT Dropped Frame Warning

8.18 Sequence>Render Selection

FCE has the ability to do what's called **Dynamic RT**, which means that it will automatically, dynamically adjust the resolution of the image to preserve real-time playback. You'll see this when material with complex effects suddenly changes quality during playback. We'll see this more and more as our effects get more complex in the next lessons. Dynamic RT depends on the speed of the computer and the settings you use. With Safe RT, the render function will kick in if playback cannot be supported without dropped frames. With Unlimited RT, you can get playback with dropped frames, so a sort of stuttering real-time playback of complex effects. With Dynamic, Unlimited RT, it will pretty much play through anything one way or the other. If the effect is too complex, or the computer less capable, you reach a point of diminishing returns, the point where it's just grabbing a few frames here and there for playback, and although it's real-time, it's hardly viewable, at which point it's better to use **Option-P**, I think.

Render Commands

FCE's render commands are extremely flexible, if perhaps a bit confusing. What gets rendered is controlled by a complex combination of settings in the **Sequence** menu under **Render Selection**, **Render All**, and **Render Only**.

To render a selection like a transition, you have to select it. You can click on the transition to select it. If you want to render a section of your Timeline, you can mark In and Out points in the Timeline and that area, controlled by the Auto Select buttons will be your render selection.

The **Render Selection** menu (see Figure 8.18) controls rendering of a selection, either a clip, clips, or a segment of the Timeline marked with In and Out points. Normally only the red Needs Render bar is checked for both video and audio. If you want to force a render on any of the other available items, select it. It will remain checked in the menu. Whenever you give the **Render Selection** command (see Table 8.1), those checked items would be included in the render.

Table 8.1   Render Commands

Command	Shortcut
Render All	Option-R
Render Selection	Command-R
Render Audio Selection	Control-Option-R
Render Proxy	Command-Option-P
Render Preview	Control-R
Mixdown Audio	Command-Option-R

Digital Cinema Desktop: In addition to using the Canvas or FireWire for playback, you may also have the option for Digital Cinema Desktop playback. This allows you to see your video full screen on your computer. This feature will only appear in your View menu if your computer has an AGP graphics card installed. It will not work with a PCI graphics card.

The **Render All** menu (see Figure 8.19) gives you the same list except that many more items are checked by default. The **Render Only** menu (see Figure 8.20) is similar. It allows you to render selected items without changing the settings in **Render** and **Render All**. Note the inclusion in the **Render Only** menu of **Mixdown** for audio. This allows you to render out a mixed audio file of all your tracks, allowing easier playback. This is particularly important when outputting to tape.

8.19 Sequence>Render All

8.20 Sequence>Render Only

FCE has the ability to render audio at **Item Level**. This allows you to render a piece of sound, such as an MP3 file or a piece of 441kHz CD music, into the correct sampling rate as a separate item. Wherever you place that audio in your Timeline, it will be fully rendered to the correct settings. It will have a blue indictor bar on it to tell you it's been rendered as an item and will not need to be re-rendered. To render an audio selection, use the keyboard shortcut **Control-Option-R**.

The **Render Proxy** and **Render Preview** shortcuts allow you to force a render of material that is in proxy mode or real-time playback, which would not normally be rendered if you use **Render Selection**. You can render a selection that is proxy or real-time with the shortcuts or from the **Render Only** submenu.

Render Control

Normally, FCE will render to full resolution, but it is possible to adjust your render settings. Render settings are in the **Render Control** tab (see Figure 8.21) in **Sequence Settings**, which can be called up from the **Sequence** menu or with the keyboard shortcut **Command-0 (zero)**. Here you can set what you want to render, as well as control your render quality with the **Frame Rate** and **Resolution** pop-up menus. Setting these two pop-up menus to lower numbers will greatly speed up your rendering process.

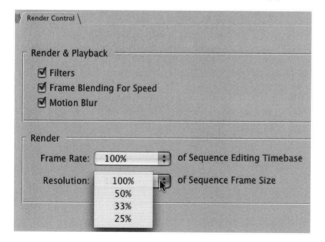

8.21   Render Control

In FCE you can switch between render settings at any time, which means that you can have material in various render resolutions throughout your sequence simultaneously. This can be a useful feature, because it allows you to render complex material at lower resolution to speed up your workflow and to switch to full resolution for easier material. The feature does create one substantial problem, which we shall look at in the lesson on Outputting, Lesson 19 on page 324.

Name	Date Modified
Sequence 5-FIN-0000000b	Today, 7:41 AM
Sequence 5-FIN-0000000a	Today, 7:41 AM
Sequence 5-FIN-00000007	Today, 7:40 AM
Sequence 5-FIN-00000006	Today, 6:55 AM
Sequence 5-FIN-00000001	Today, 5:16 AM
Sequence 5-FIN-00000005	Today, 5:06 AM
Sequence 5-FIN-00000004	Today, 4:53 AM
Sequence 5-FIN-00000003	Today, 4:02 AM
Sequence 5-FIN-00000002	Today, 3:46 AM
Sequence 3-FIN-00000008	Yesterday, 9:49 PM
Sequence 3-FIN-00000007	Yesterday, 7:16 PM
Sequence 3-FIN-00000006	Yesterday, 7:16 PM
Sequence 1-FIN-00000015	Yesterday, 7:15 PM
Sequence 1-FIN-00000014	Yesterday, 7:15 PM
Sequence 1-FIN-00000011	Yesterday, 5:38 PM
Sequence 1-FIN-00000010	Yesterday, 5:38 PM
Sequence 1-FIN-0000000f	Yesterday, 3:51 PM
Sequence 1-FIN-00000008	Yesterday, 2:43 PM

8.22 Render Files in List View

Render Management

Render files are stored in the *Render Files* folder and the *Audio Render Files* folder of your designated scratch disk. The renders are stored in separate folders based on the project name, one folder for each project. FCE keeps track of the renders required for the output of each sequence. It keeps all of the renders it generates for each session so that you can step back through those 32 levels of undo and not lose your renders. As you keep rendering and changing and re-rendering, FCE holds onto all of those renders it creates while the application is open. When you quit the application, it dumps any render files it no longer needs to play back any of the sequences in the project. It will hold onto any renders it needs for playback. All of these render files will start to pile up after a while. If you delete a project, its render files won't go with it. They'll just sit on your hard drive taking up space in the folder with the project's name.

❧ *Tip*
Playing the Red: By using Option-P, you can still play through a red transition without leaving the sequence, not in real time but in slow motion. This is a good way to see if the transition will play smoothly, if there are any unforeseen flash frames or other unpleasant hiccups in the effect. The faster your system, the faster it will play through the transition. More complex effects that we will see later will only play slowly, even on the fastest computers. What's good is that FCE caches the playback so that the first time you play back using Option-P, it might take quite a while, but the next time the playback will be considerably faster. This applies only to using Option-P. Regular play with the spacebar will still produce the unrendered message. You can also scrub through a transition by switching Snapping off and mousing down in the Timeline Ruler, slowly moving the playhead through the transition area.

It's a good idea to weed out the old files in your render folders, video more than audio because the files are much larger. Sometimes it might be as simple as discarding an old project folder, throwing out all the renders associated with it. Sometimes, for long-form projects that go on for a long time, managing your render files requires you to go in and dig out these old files. The simplest way to do this is to open up the Render Files folder for that project and switch the window to List view as in Figure 8.22. List view will show you not only the file names, which are pretty meaningless, but also the date modified. By clicking on the **Date Modified** column, you can sort the renders by when they where created, giving you a clue about which ones are worth keeping and which aren't.

8.23   Render Files and Preview Window

If you're uncertain, select the render file and switch to **Column** view, where you can use the preview window to look at the little QuickTime file that the render generates (see Figure 8.23). Move the files you think you don't need into the trash and run the project. If the project needs some of the render files, you'll get the **Reconnect** dialog box. That will give you a chance to move the missing items back into the *Render Files* folder.

8.24   Lengthening a Transition in the Timeline

8.25 Rolling the Transition Edit Point

Controlling Transitions

Once you've played back your transition with **Option-P** a couple of times or rendered it and looked at it, you may discover that it isn't quite the way you'd want it to be. You may want to shorten or lengthen it or shift the actual edit point. Assuming you have material available for this, it is easiest to do in the Timeline. To change the duration of the transition, grab one end of it and pull, as in Figure 8.24. It's a good idea to switch Snapping off (toggle with the **N** key) before you do this, because it's easy to snap the transition down to nothing. As you pull the transition, a little window displays the amount of change as well as the new duration of the transition. If you have an audio crossfade as well as a transition, that will also change with your action. While you're dragging the transition end, you'll get the two-up display in the Canvas that shows you the frames at the edit point.

You can also reposition the edit point in the center of the transition. Move the Selector to the center of the edit, and it will change to the Roll tool, allowing you to move the edit point, together with the transition along the Timeline, left and right as desired (see Figure 8.25). You can also ripple either shot, but to do that you have to call up the Ripple tool (**RR**) and pull either shot left or right, shortening or lengthening the sequence while not affecting the transition (see Figure 8.26). Again, the two-up display in the Canvas will show you the frames you're working on.

8.26 Rippling the Transition Edit Point

Transition in the Viewer

Final Cut gives you another way to fine-tune the transition in the Viewer (see Figure 8.27). I've replaced the Cube Spin transition with the Swing transition. To do that, select the transition in the Timeline, and from the menus choose **Effects>Video Transitions>3D Simulation>Swing**.

Double-click on the transition in the Timeline window to open it into the Viewer. The Viewer displays the transition as a separate track sitting between the two clips as if they are overlapping on two video tracks.

8.27 Swing Controls in the Viewer

8.28 Alignment Buttons

The Viewer allows you to control the transition. Some of the transitions, such as Swing in Figure 8.27, have quite a few controls. At the top in the center is a small group of buttons (see Figure 8.28) that lets you align where the transition will occur. By default the transition is placed in the Center on Edit position between the two clips, shown by the middle button. Using the left button moves the transition so that it begins at the edit point. The right button moves the transition so that it ends at the edit point.

Here you can fine-tune the effect, to shorten or lengthen it as needed. As in the Timeline, you can do this by dragging either end of the transition. The Canvas displays the end and start frames for the two shots. By grabbing the center of the transition, you evoke the Roll tool, which allows you to drag the transition forward and backward along the clips, provided that media is available.

8.29 Rippling a Clip in Viewer

You can also Ripple edit the end of either and outgoing or incoming clip by pulling it (see Figure 8.29). You don't have to call up the Ripple tool. By moving the cursor into position, it will change to the appropriate tool. As with all Ripple edits, you are changing the duration of the tracks involved and may be pulling the alignment of clips on different tracks out of kilter.

Notice the two sliders in the Viewer, one for Start and the other for End, each with percentage boxes adjacent. The transition starts at 0 percent completed and ends at 100 percent completed. You can adjust these sliders so that the effect will pop in at more than zero to start or suddenly finish before the transition reaches completion. In most transitions, this produces a rather ugly effect. There is also a small arrow button to the right of the End slider. This will swap the effect for you, usually reversing the direction. Below that is a small circle with a red cross in it. This is the **Parameters Reset** button. This is useful for more complex transitions. Note that the **Reset** button does not reset the Start and End sliders, nor the arrow, only the other parameters.

Using Transitions

Now that we know how to add and trim transitions, let's look at the transitions themselves. To change the transition:

- Drag the new transition from the transitions folder in the Effects window and drop it on the existing transition in the timeline *or*

- Select the transition in the Timeline by clicking on it and then select a new choice from the **Effects>Video Transitions** menu.

I'm not going to go through each of the transitions, although I would like to highlight a few of them because they will show you how the controls work in some of the other changeable transitions. To see all of the transitions, look at the individual QuickTime movies in the *Transitions* folder on the DVD. Many of the transitions have lots of variables, such as colored borders and the direction in which a motion transition such as Swing occurs.

> ✈ *Tip*
> **Navigating the Viewer:** The grab handle in the upper right corner lets you pull a transition from the Viewer onto an edit point in the Timeline. This is useful if you've opened the editor directly from the *Transitions* bin, or if you want to apply the same transition to another edit point. This is the only way you can grab the transition. There is also a pop-up menu for recent clips in the Viewer. This is handy sometimes, because you can't access all of the standard features like the Generators and other tabs when you have a transition open in the Viewer.

Page Peel

Page Peel (see Figure 8.30) is often overused, but sometimes it really is the right effect, especially for wedding videos. This is also the first introduction to FCE's **Well**.

8.30 Page Peel

Apply the transition from **Video Transitions>Page Peel>Page Peel** and then double-click on it to open it into the Viewer (see Figure 8.31). The **Direction** dial changes the angle at which the page peels back. The default is −30 and pulls the lower-right corner toward the upper center of the image.

8.31 Page Peel Controls

The **Radius** slider sets the tightness of the peel. A small number will make it peel very tightly, and a high number will make the turn of the page quite loose.

The **Highlight** slider puts a gleam of light on the back of the turning page. The farther to the left you move the Highlight slider, the more muted the shine becomes. There is no control of the width of the highlight area.

If you uncheck the **Peel** checkbox, the image will not only peel back but also curl in on itself. With a tight **Radius** you'll get the image rolling up like it's a scroll.

If you uncheck the **Peel** checkbox, the image will not only peel back but also curl in on itself.

One of Page Peel's interesting features is the **Well**, which lets you use another image as part of an effect. The Well, the indented filmstrip icon that controls the **Back** function, lets you map another image onto the back of the page peel. The default is to place the same image, flopped, on the back of the page, but you can use any image in your project.

To put a color on the back, as in Figure 8.30, use the **Generator** in the Viewer to create a color matte.

⚞ Note
Static Well: Unfortunately, the Well won't track an image or change if a video clip is used. The Well uses the In point of the video clip as its map. In the case of Page Peel, there is no movement on the backside of the page. Sorry.

8.32   Generators Button

8.33   Color Matte Controls Tab

8.34 System Color Picker

> ✎ *Tip*
>
>
>
> **Selecting Color:** Whenever you need to select a color from anywhere on your desktop, click on the color swatch to open the color picker. If you click on the magnifying glass next to the color swatch, you can move around anywhere on the computer desktop.

1. Open any clip into the Viewer, or call one up from the Recent Clips pop-up. The A with the Filmstrip icon in the lower-left corner evokes the Generators (see Figure 8.32).

2. Select **Matte>Color**.

3. Set the color in the Controls tab (Figure 8.33). Click on the swatch to access the system color picker (Figure 8.34).

Note the swatch tray at the bottom, which lets you move color selections from application to application, not just within FCE.

4. Switch back to the Video tab and drag the Color Matte from the Viewer into the Browser.

5. Reopen the Page Peel transition from the Timeline into the Viewer.

6. Pull the Color Matte from the Browser, and drop it into the Well, making it part of the transition.

Push Slide

The **Push Slide** transition (**Video Transitions>Slide>Push Slide**) is often used when making still slide shows where one image pushes the other out of the frame and replaces it. The controls (Figure 8.35) are pretty straightforward: an **Angle** dial and controls for adding a border.

Angle defaults to straight up, but you can set it to any angle you want. At –90 the incoming image will slide in from the right and push the outgoing image off the left side of the screen.

8.35 Push Slide Controls

The **Border** control can be quite useful. It not only helps in separating the images more clearly but also covers the black band that appears on the edge of some digitized images. This is normally in the blanking area under the television mask and not seen by the viewer. However, if the image is moved, as it is here and in other digital video effects, the black edge becomes visible. The Border will help disguise that or at least make it a feature.

Gradient Wipe

8.36 Gradient Wipe Controls

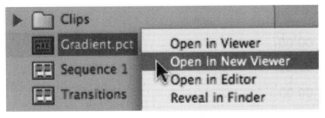

8.37 Open in New Viewer

The **Gradient Wipe** transition (**Video Transitions>Wipe>Gradient Wipe**) is a deceptively simple-looking filter with very few controls. Its real power lies in the Gradient Well (see Figure 8.36). In its default condition, it's nothing more than a simple wipe from left to right.

In the Browser is an image called *Gradient.pct*. To see what it looks like, rather than open it into the Viewer where the transition is already loaded, right-click on it and select **Open in New Viewer** (Figure 8.37). You'll see that it's a complex, grayscale checkerboard pattern. This is the basis of patterning in a gradient wipe. The image will be wiped on or off, based on the grayscale values of pattern image. The darkest parts of the pattern image will be where the incoming image will appear first, and the lightest parts will be where the image will appear last. In the gradient pattern we have, some of the outside boxes will appear first, as in Figure 8.38.

The lower-left to upper-right diagonal of the image will still be from the outgoing shot. There is no end to the variety of patterns you can get to manipulate this control. If you don't like a pattern, replace it with another. To really see the power of transition effects, you should look at what Michael Feerer has created with his Video Spices. Check them out at *www.pixelan.com*. They add an important tool to Final Cut's transitions. His patterns can be used not only inside his own transitions but also inside Gradient Wipe as well.

8.38 Gradient Wipe Pattern

8.39 Favorites Bin

I like the Gradient Wipe because it is so infinitely variable, and you can always find some way to make it look just a little different and just right for the effect you want. A trick I've used in the past is to use a grayscale frame of either the outgoing shot or the incoming shot as the image for the Well. It makes the transition like a slightly sharp-edged dissolve because the elements of the shot are affecting how the transition happens.

Favorites

Once you've started to make a few transitions that you like, maybe a special Page Peel with your logo on the back, or a Gradient Wipe with a particular pattern, you might want to save these in your *Favorites* bin in the Effects tab behind your Browser.

To see how to do this: open the *Dissolves* folder, which holds seven different types of dissolves.

1. Grab the Gradient Wipe we just created, and drag the transition with the Grab Handle over to drop it into the *Favorites* bin. You can also drag a transition directly from the Timeline into *Favorites*.

2. Open *Favorites* and switch it to List view as in Figure 8.39. Remember that **Shift-H** will toggle through the views.

3. In List view you can change the duration of the transition to your favorite length.

You could drag a cross-dissolve from the *Dissolves* bin and change its duration to a favorite length you want to keep.

You may notice that the transition in the *Favorites* bin is a duplicate. The usual behavior when moving items from one bin to another is that the item is relocated. But when moving an element to *Favorites*, a copy is created. You can put any transitions, video or audio, any effect, or even a generator into *Favorites*. You can rename the transition or effect to anything you want.

Note that although *8Frames*, which is an eight-frame dissolve, appears underlined, it is not the default transition. Only the standard cross-dissolve with the standard one-second duration can be the default.

Summary

That's it for transitions. Everybody has his or her favorites. Mine are fairly simple: mostly cross-dissolves and Gradient Wipes occasionally, or a Push Slide. Many I've never used. Many should probably never be used, and most you'll probably never see. Next we go on to advanced editing techniques with the trim edit window and splitting edits.

✎ *Note*

Saving Favorites: It's important to note that Favorites are saved as part of your FCE preferences. If you trash your *Preferences* file, as you may need to from time to time, your Favorites go with it. There is a simple solution to this. Drag the Favorites bin from the Effects panel and place it in your Browser. This is a copy of the Favorites bin in Effects and will remain with the project, even if the prefs are trashed. I keep a Favorites project and in it a bin with my favorite effects and filters, sometimes in stacks in separate folders. Whenever I want to access these effects, I open the Favorites project and drag the folder into the new project. I add new effects to it and occasionally I burn the project onto a CD as a backup.

Lesson 9

Advanced Editing: Trim Edit and Splitting Edits

Film and video are primarily visual media. Oddly enough, though, the moment an edit occurs is often driven as much by the sound as by the picture. So let's look at sound editing in Final Cut Express. How sound is used, where it comes in, and how long it lasts are key to good editing. With few exceptions, sound almost never cuts with the picture. Sometimes the sound comes first and then the picture; sometimes the picture leads the sound. The principal reason video and audio are so often cut separately is that we see and hear quite differently. We see in cuts. I look from one person to another, from one object to another, from the keyboard to the monitor. Though my head turns or my eyes travel across the room, I really only see the objects I'm interested in looking at. We hear, on the other hand, in fades. I walk into a room, the door closes behind me, and the sound of the other room fades away. As a car approaches, the sound gets louder. Screams, gunshots, and doors slamming being exceptions, our aural perception is based on smooth transitions from one to another. Sounds, especially background sounds such as the ambient noise in a room, generally need to overlap to smooth out the jarring abruptness of a hard cut.

To do this we'll use some advanced trimming tools. First we'll look at the Trim Edit window, and then we'll see a few different ways to do Split edits so that the sound and the picture do not cut in at the same point.

145

Setting Up the Project

This is going to sound familiar, but it's worth repeating. Begin by loading the material you need on the media hard drive of your computer:

1. Launch the *Lesson 9* project from the *Projects* folder on your hard drive.

2. Once again, you may have to go through the reconnect process as in the previous "Loading the Lesson" on page 15 in Lesson 2. You will first get the Offline Files window. Click the **Reconnect** button.

You'll find in the project's Browser an empty sequence called *Sequence 1* and a *Rough Cut* sequence that we'll look at during this lesson. There is also the master clip *Backstage* and the folder called *Clips*, which contains the subclips pulled from the master.

In this lesson we're going to look at backstage preparations for a Kabuki performance. Before beginning the lesson, it might be a good idea to look through the material, which is about three and one-half minutes long. You can start by double-clicking the shot *Backstage* to open it in the Viewer and then playing through the material.

The Trim Edit Window

Before we get into editing this material, we should look at FCE's Trim Edit window, which is a powerful tool for precisely editing your material and looking at edit points.

1. You open the Trim Edit window by double-clicking on an edit point or by moving the playhead to an edit point and using the menu **Sequence>Trim Edit** or the keyboard shortcut **Command-7**.

2. Let's bring a couple of shots into the Timeline. Select *Backstage01* and *Backstage02* in the *Clips* bin and drag them directly to Overwrite in the Canvas.

3. Double-click on the edit point between the shots in the Timeline. This will call up the window in Figure 9.1.

Notice the sprocket hole indicators on the inner edges of the frames. This overlay indicates that the clips are at the limits of their media, but we can still ripple this edit just as we did in Lesson 8 when we had to ripple the two shots to create room for a transition.

9.1   Trim Edit
       Window

The green bars over the frames in the Trim Edit window indicate what mode you're in. When a green bar appears over both sides, as in Figure 9.2, you're in Roll edit mode. By clicking on one side or the other, you can ripple either the outgoing shot (as in Figure 9.3) or the incoming shot (as in Figure 9.4). To get back to Roll edit, click on the space between the two frames.

9.2   Roll Edit Indicator
       in Trim Edit

You can toggle between the Ripple and Roll tools in the Trim Edit window with the **U** key. The way the **U** key cycles between Ripple Left, Ripple Right, and the Roll tool is also reflected in the way the edit point is selected in the Timeline (Figures 9.5 to 9.7).

9.3   Ripple Left
       Indicator in Trim
       Edit

You can ripple and roll the edit points by dragging them in either window. When you're in Ripple mode, the cursor will change to the Ripple tool, and when you're in Roll mode, the cursor automatically becomes the Roll tool.

9.4   Ripple Right
       Indicator in Trim
       Edit

9.5 Roll Edit Indicator in the Timeline

9.6 Ripple Left Indicator in the Timeline

9.7 Ripple Right Indicator in the Timeline

You can also use the little plus and minus buttons at the bottom of the window to make incremental edits on either side of the Trim Edit window. FCE allows you to move the edit point by one or five frames at a time. The five-frame value can be changed anywhere from 2 to 99 in the preferences in User Preferences in Multi-Frame Trim Size.

There's a lot of useful timecode information at the top of the Trim Edit window, information about where the A side ends and the B begins and the durations of the shot and their place in the Timeline.

9.8 Timecode Display at the Top of the Trim Edit Window

- The number to the far left is the duration of the outgoing shot, *Backstage01* in this case (*A* in Figure 9.8).
- The next timecode number is the Out point of the outgoing shot (*B* in Figure 9.8).
- The center number under the track indicator is the current time in the sequence (*C* in Figure 9.8).
- The next number displayed is the duration of the incoming shot (*D* in Figure 9.8).
- On the far right of the window, the number is the current In point of the incoming shot, *Backstage02* (*E* in Figure 9.8).

You can play either side of the Trim Edit window with the J, K, and L keys. The green bars at the top determine which side plays. If you're rippling the left side, that side will play; if you're rippling the right side, the incoming shot will play.

When you're in Roll mode, the green bar above both displays and the side that plays are determined by the position of the cursor. If the cursor is over the left or outgoing side, that side will play. If the cursor is over the right or incoming side, that side will play.

To trim an edit, you modify the In or Out point with the I and O keys. Your change will be reflected in the edit, either as a ripple or as a roll, in the Timeline.

The **spacebar** serves an interesting function in the Trim Edit window. It acts in looped Play-around mode. It will play around the edit point again and again so that you can view it repeatedly. The amount of Play-around—how much before the edit and how far after the edit—is controlled in User Preferences under Preview Pre-Roll and Preview Post-Roll.

The default is five seconds before the edit and two seconds after. I usually set it down to two or three seconds before and two after.

Final Cut Express has the ability to do **dynamic trimming** in the Trim Edit window. You'll see a little checkbox at the bottom of the window that activates this function, which can also be turned on in User Preferences. Dynamic trimming affects the control of the **J**, **K**, and **L** keys. Whenever you press the **K** key to pause, the edit will automatically execute. This will work in any edit mode: Roll, Ripple Left, or Ripple Right. As soon as you press the key to pause, the edit will be executed. It's pretty slick. Try using the **J**, **K**, and **L** keys to dynamically trim:

1. Switch to ripple mode on either side. (We can't do a Roll edit because there isn't any available media until the shots have been trimmed.)

2. Use the **J** and **L** keys to play forward and backward.

3. If you want to stop playback without doing an edit, don't press the **K** key, but rather use the **spacebar** to stop.

4. When you do want to do the ripple, simply press the **K** key and the edit will be done.

The Split Edit

A common method of editing is to first lay down the shots in scene order entirely as straight cuts. Look at the sequence called *Rough Cut*. This is the edited material cut as straight edits. What's most striking as you play it is how abruptly the audio changes at each shot. But audio and video seldom cut in parallel in a finished video, so you will have to offset them.

When audio and video have separate In and Out points that aren't at the same time, the edit is called a split edit (see Figure 9.9), J-cut (see Figure 9.10), or L-cut (see Figure 9.11). Whatever you call it, the effect is the same. There are many ways to create these edits, which I lump together as split edits.

> **❧ Note**
> **Moving Slowly in the Trim Window:** You can move forward slowly by holding down the K and L keys together. To move backward slowly, hold down the K and J keys together. To go forward one frame, hold down the K key and tap L. To go backward one frame, hold down the K key and tap J.

> **❧ Note**
> **Trim Edit Shortcut:** In the Trim Edit window, in addition to the trim buttons, you can use the keyboard shortcuts [and] to trim plus or minus one frame and Shift-[and Shift-] to trim plus or minus the multiframe trim size. As with the buttons, these will work on the fly while you're in looped Play-around mode.

9.9   Split Edit

9.10 J-cut

9.11 L-cut

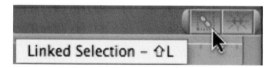

9.12 Linked Selection Button

In the Timeline

Many instructors tell you to perform these edits in the Viewer, but I think the Viewer is the least flexible place to create them. Let's set up a split edit inside the Timeline. It's a much more logical and effective place to perform this type of work.

In making split edits, particularly in the Timeline, you will be frequently linking and unlinking clips, switching off the link between synced video and audio. You can do this with the little switch in the upper-right corner of the Timeline window that toggles Linked Selection off and on (see Figure 9.12). When Linked Selection is turned on, the button is green; when it's off, the icon is black.

You might want to switch Linked Selection off if you want to move a lot of synced sound clips, splitting the audio and the video. But I don't think that's ever a good idea. I think Linked Selection should be maintained at all times and toggled on and off only as needed for individual clips. You might get away with leaving it off most of the time, but one day it will leap up and bite you hard. So for these lessons, let's leave Linked Selection turned on.

Before we begin working on the sequence, it is probably a good idea to duplicate the *Rough Cut* sequence. Select it and use **Edit>Duplicate** or the keyboard shortcut **Option-D**. This way you can also refer back to the original *Rough Cut* if you ever need to.

Start by double-clicking the copy of *Rough Cut* and looking at the Timeline.

The trick to smoothing out the audio for this type of sequence—or any sequence with abrupt sound changes at the edit points—is to overlap sounds and create sound beds that carry through other shots. Ideally, a wild track was shot on location, sometimes called *room tone* when it's the ambient sound indoors. This is a long section of continuous sound from the scene, a minute or more, which can be used as a bed to which the sync sound is added as needed. Here there is no wild track as such, but some of the shots are lengthy enough to have a similar effect.

Before we get started, we want to change the type of audio that's used in the sequence. Double-click on the first shot, *Backstage01*, to bring it into the Viewer. Notice at the top of the Viewer that there are two tabs for the two audio tracks Mono (a1) and Mono (a2). This is the default capture setting for FCE material. Unfortunately, it's more difficult to work with audio such as this because you have to adjust the two tracks separately. The best thing to do is to change your audio in the Timeline to a *stereo pair*. This is very simple to do.

1. Select everything in the Timeline, **Command-A**.

2. From the **Modify** menu, use **Stereo Pair** or the keyboard shortcut **Option-L**.

As soon as you do this, the clip that was in the Viewer will disappear. If you reopen it into the Viewer, you'll see that there is only one audio tab marked Stereo (a1a2), and each of the clips in the Timeline has little inward-pointing pairs of green triangles on each of the tracks. This indicates that these are grouped as stereo pairs. It's much easier to work with your audio when the tracks are stereo pairs, because both channels will move in unison.

▶ *Note*
The Cutaway. Any editor will tell you that cutaways are the most useful shots. You can never have too many, and you never seem to have enough. No editor will ever complain that you have shot too many cutaways. A cutaway shot shows a subsidiary action or reaction that you can use to bridge an edit, like the shot of the interviewer nodding in response to an answer. The cutaway allows you to bridge a portion of the interviewee's answer where the person has stumbled over the words or has digressed into something pointless. A wide shot that shows the whole scene can often be used as a cutaway. Make note of these useful shots as you're watching your material.

Making Split Edits

⭐️*Tip*

Toggling Linking: Option-clicking the audio (or video) edit point will turn off Linked Selection if LS is turned on. If Linked Selection is off, Option-clicking the edit point will turn it on.

1. Play through the first three or four shots in the *Rough Cut* copy sequence. The change between the first and second shot is quite noticeable, even more so between the second and third.

2. Hold down the **Option** key and select the audio portion of the second shot, *Backstage06*.

3. With the **Option** key still pressed, tap the **Down** Arrow key twice. This will move the stereo pair of audio down two tracks. This can be done with any tracks, video or audio, as long as there is nothing in the way, such as another clip.

4. Again holding down the **Option** key, drag the head of the audio edit point toward the beginning of the Timeline (see Figure 9.13). While you drag it, a small box will appear. It gives you a time duration change for the edit you are making. It may be helpful to toggle Snapping off with the **N** key.

5. Repeat the process on the other side of the audio. Holding down the **Option** key, drag out the audio so that your sequence looks like Figure 9.14.

You have now created two split edits for the clip *Backstage06*.

9.13 Dragging Audio to Create a Split Edit

9.14 Timeline after Making Split Edits

Adding Audio Transitions

We want the sound of the first shot, *Background01*, to fade out before it ends. The simplest way to do this is to apply an audio crossfade:

1. Select the edit point by clicking on it.

2. To add the audio transition, use either the menu **Effects>Audio Transitions>Cross Fade (+3dB)** or the keyboard shortcut **Command-Option-T**.

Because the audio is not butted against anything, the application will by default create an End on Edit transition, as shown in Figure 9.15.

9.15 Cross Fade Transition Applied

☆ *Tip*
Linear or Logarithmic: FCE has two crossfades, the default +3dB as well as a 0dB transition. The +3dB crossfade that FCE calls an equal power crossfade is generally preferred because it gives a logarithmic roll of sound, which is the way sound works. The 0dB crossfade is a linear fade. It will often produce an apparent dip in the audio level at the midpoint of the crossover from one track to the other.

9.16 Marking Split Audio In

9.17   Split Edit in the Viewer

In the Viewer

You can also create a split edit in the Viewer. Let's first set up a new sequence:

1.   Begin by opening *Sequence 1* again. You should have two shots *Backstage01* and *Backstage02* in it.

2.   Delete the second shot so that only *Backstage01* is left. Let's make a split edit with a clip from the Browser.

3.   Find the clip *Backstage06* in the *Clips* bin in the Browser.

4.   Double-click on it to open it into the Viewer. Because we want to use all of the audio, begin by marking a split audio In point at the beginning of the clip. With the playhead at the very start of the shot, either right-click and from the shortcut menu choose **Mark Split>Audio In** (see Figure 9.16) or use the keyboard shortcut **Command-Option-I**.

5.   Play through the clip until you find the In point for the edit at 4;10.

6.   Instead of pressing **I** to enter the In point, press **Control-I**.

Next we'll make the split edit for the Out point.

7.   Play forward until you get to the Out point at 9;18.

8.   Instead of pressing **O** to enter the Out point, press **Control-O**.

Note the markings in the Viewer scrubber bar and on screen in Figure 9.17 that indicate the split edit.

Viewer to Timeline

The simplest way to work with the split edit in the Viewer is to drag and drop to the Timeline.

1. Reset the destination tracks in your Timeline by pulling the a2 button down to A4 and the a1 button down to a3 in the patch panel at the head of the tracks as in Figure 9.18. Or use the keyboard short-cuts **F7-3** and **F8-4**.

2. Make sure Snapping is turned on. If it isn't, press the **N** to switch it on.

3. With the playhead at the end of the shot in the Timeline, drag the clip from the Viewer to the Timeline, as in Figure 9.19.

The edit will be performed as in Figure 9.20. This seems to be strange behavior on the part of the application, but it has always done this for some reason. When this happens, grab the clip and slide it to butt up against the first shot, as shown in Figure 9.21.

9.18 Setting Destination Tracks in the Patch Panel

9.19 Dragging a Split Edit to the Timeline

9.20 Displaced Split Edit in the Timeline

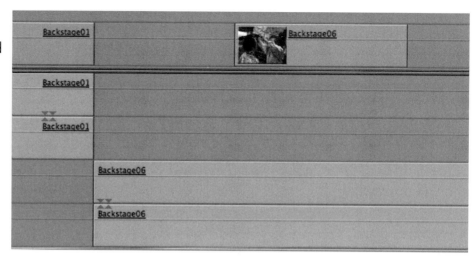

9.21 Correctly Placed Split Edit

Summary

In this lesson we've looked at working with the Trim Edit window and how to create split audio edits, in the Timeline and in the Viewer. We'll stop at this stage and pick up work on this sequence in the next lesson, where we look at how to adjust and control audio levels.

Lesson 10

Advanced Editing: Using Sound

We've started to work on the backstage sequence, and we've created a split edit in the Timeline and added an audio crossfade. Now we're going to adjust the sound levels for the sequence in the Viewer and in the Timeline.

Setting up the Project

From your hard drive, launch the *Lesson 10* project. Reconnect the media files if the Offline Files dialog appears. You'll find in the project's Browser an empty sequence called *Sequence 1*, which you can use to work with if you wish, and a couple of other sequences, *Rough Cut* and *Final*. There is also the master clip *Backstage* and the folder called *Clips*, which contains the subclips pulled from the master.

Look at the sequence called *Final*. The three and one-half minutes that is *Backstage* have been cut down to one minute and 23 seconds for the *Final* sequence. This is where we're going. Notice how the audio overlaps and the way it fades in and out.

Controlling Levels

You can control the audio levels for clips either in the Timeline or in the Viewer. It's easier and quicker in the Timeline, but the Viewer controls afford a great deal more precision.

In the Timeline

To work in the Timeline, let's start by duplicating the *Rough Cut* sequence as we did in the last lesson:

1. Select *Rough Cut* and press **Option-D** to duplicate it.

2. Then double-click the new *Rough Cut Copy* to open it.

To adjust the audio levels in the Timeline, you first need to turn on the **Clip Overlays** button in the lower-left corner of the Timeline window (see Figure 10.1) or use the keyboard shortcut **Option-W**. It's a good idea to leave the Clip Overlays turned off when you're not using them, because it's easy to accidentally shift the level line while just trying to grab a clip to move it.

When the Clip Overlays are turned on, a thin pink line appears through the middle of the audio portion of the clips. This is the audio level control for the clips. Notice also the thin black line that appears at the top of the video. This controls the opacity for the video portion.

10.1 Clip Overlay Button

Play the audio for the third shot in the sequence, *Backstage05*. It's pretty low and adds nothing to the soundtrack except to muddy it a bit. To eliminate the audio, you could select the audio portion of the clip with the Option key and delete it. However, if you ever decide you want that audio or if you move the clip to a place where the audio is needed, it's a bit of a nuisance to get it back.

10.2 Dragging the Level Line

10.3 Pen Tools

10.4   Adding a Keyframe

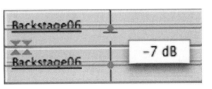

10.5   Lowering the Keyframe Level

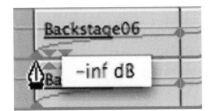

10.6   Fade-Out in the Timeline

A simpler way is to reduce the audio level to zero. With Clip Overlays turned on, move the cursor over the line. It will change to the Resizing tool. Grab the line and pull it down to the bottom of the clip as shown in Figure 10.2.

Fading Levels in the Timeline

You usually don't want to reduce the overall levels. More often you'll want to reduce the levels of portions of the sound, raise other portions, or fade in or out. For a simple fade, you could use the crossfade transition that we saw earlier, or you can do it by fading the level line. To do this you use the Pen tool. There are several available at the bottom of the Tools palette (see Figure 10.3). You can also call up the Pen tool with the **P** key.

Let's create a fade-in at the beginning of the second shot, *Backstage06*, which is on A3/A4.

1. Move the Pen over the pink level line in the clip. The cursor will change to a pen nib, allowing you to click on the line to create a point (see Figure 10.4). This adds a tiny diamond to the levels line called a keyframe.

2. Put a keyframe about one second from the beginning of the shot by clicking with the Pen tool on the level line.

3. As you move the cursor to the newly created keyframe, it will change into a crosshairs cursor. This lets you grab the keyframe and move it up or down. Pull the keyframe down to about –7dB as in

✎ Note

What Is a Keyframe? We'll be talking more about keyframes as we get farther into the book. A keyframe is a way of defining the values for a clip at a specific moment in time, a specific frame of video. Here we're dealing with audio levels. We're saying at this frame we want the sound to be at a particular level. By then going to a different point in the clip and altering the levels, we will have created another keyframe, defining the sound level at that particular frame. The computer will figure out how quickly it needs to change the levels to get from one setting to the other. The closer together the keyframes are, the more quickly the levels will change; the farther apart they are, the more gradually the change will take place.

Figure 10.5. Notice that because there are no other keyframes on the level line, the volume for the entire clip is reduced.

4. Take the Pen tool and grab the very left end of the level line. Pull it down to create a curved fade-up ramp (see Figure 10.6).

> **Note**
>
> **No Switching Necessary:** If you don't want to switch to the Pen tool from the standard Selector tool, as you move the cursor to the level line and it changes to the Resizing tool, hold down the Option key and the cursor will automatically change to the Pen tool. If you are working with the Pen tool and you want to switch to the straight-level line-moving Resizing tool, hold down the Command key.

We haven't finished with *Backstage06* yet. We still need to bring the sound up to full level as the shot is introduced and fade it out at the end.

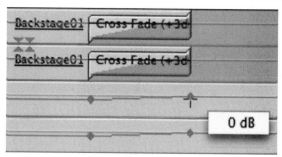

10.7   Ramping Up the Audio

10.8   Slow Fade-Out

5. To bring the level back up, add a keyframe at about the point where the crossfade begins on A1/A2.

6. Next, add another keyframe at about the point where the crossfade on V1 ends.

7. Push the level line back up to 0dB (see Figure 10.7). Because this is the last keyframe on the level line, everything after that point will come back up to full volume.

8. Finally, to finish *Backstage06*, we want to fade out the audio at the end. With the Pen tool, add a keyframe to the level line about two seconds before the end of the clip.

9. Go to the end of the clip, and pull the end of the line all the way down to create a slow fade-out as in Figure 10.8.

10. On A1/A2 it would be a good idea to add a crossfade transition between the silent *Backstage05* and the next shot, *Backstage04*. Select the edit point and press **Command-Option-T**.

10.9 Track Tools

10.10 Level Controls

Controlling Track Levels

10.11 Waveform in the Timeline

There may be occasions when you want to change the audio level for an entire track—say, of music—to give it a lower base level, especially CD music, which is often recorded and compressed at maximum audio levels, often too high for use with most digital video systems. You can do this by selecting the track you want with the Track tool, which is the first button in the third group in the Tools palette (see Figure 10.9).

You can select a single track, multiple tracks forward and backward, a single track forward and backward, or a whole track of audio and adjust its level globally. Select the items or the track with the Track tool (**T**). Once you have your track or clips selected, go to **Modify>Levels**, or use the keyboard shortcut **Command-Option-L**.

This command calls up a dialog box that allows you to adjust the audio levels of the clips (see Figure 10.10). The slider or the value box will change the gain setting for all of the clips selected. The Relative and Absolute pop-up menu sets how the gain is affected. Absolute will make the level you set affect all of the clips, eliminating any fades. Using the Relative setting will change the value of the levels relative to any current settings or fades. This global levels control works not only on audio but also on opacity on a title or on the video portion of a clip.

10.12 Timeline Options Pop-up Menu

Another way to change the audio level of more than one clip is to change its attributes. You can copy an audio clip by selecting it and pressing **Command-C**. Select the clips you want by marqueeing or **Command**-clicking, and choose **Paste Attributes** from the **Edit** menu or press **Option-V**. Then check the attributes you want to paste to the other clips' **Levels** or **Pan** values (see Figure 10.13).

10.13 Pasting Audio Attributes

Notice the Scale Attributes Over Time checkbox at the top. It defaults to the on position. If you have keyframed the levels in the copied clips, that keyframing will be distributed proportionately onto the pasted clip, based on the relative durations of the clips. If the copied clip is longer, the keyframing will be tightened up; if it is shorter, the keyframing will be spread out. If you want to paste the keyframes with the same duration as in the copied clip, uncheck **Scale Attributes Over Time**.

Note

Waveform in the Timeline. When you're working in the Timeline, it may be beneficial to turn on the waveform display in the Timeline window (see Figure 10.11). Do this by going to the Timeline Options pop-up menu by clicking the tiny triangle in the bottom left of the Timeline window (see Figure 10.12), and select Show Audio Waveforms, or use the keyboard shortcut Command-Option-W.

Because displaying the audio waveform in the Timeline takes a good deal of processing power (prereading the audio and then displaying it), the redraw ability and video playback capabilities of the computer are markedly slowed down. So it's a good idea to toggle the waveform display on and off as needed with that handy keyboard shortcut.

Tip

Changing a Range of Keyframes: You can also change the relative or absolute levels of a group of audio keyframes. Use the Range tool (GGG) to select the area that includes the audio keyframe (see Figure 10.14).

If you then apply the Levels function, it will raise or lower the relative or absolute values of the keyframes in the selected area.

Tip

Single-Track Audio: Often you record audio on a single audio channel. Many cameras do this when you plug in an external microphone; only one of the stereo channels gets used. It's worth deleting the empty track. If the audio is a stereo pair, first change it to Mono (a1)(a2) from the Modify menu. Then Option-click to select the track you don't need and delete it. You can center the audio for the remaining track if you need to by pressing Control-period. If you want to double the audio to fatten it, you can. Option-click on the remaining audio track to select it, then Option-shift drag it to the empty audio track to duplicate it. Select the video and two audio tracks and press Command-L to link them into a single clip.

More Fades

Before we look at how to control audio levels in the Viewer, let's do some more work on the *Rough Cut Copy* sequence.

Look at the fifth shot in the sequence *Backstage11*. We need to overlap its audio underneath the adjacent clips.

1. With the Option key pressed, select the audio portion of the clip. Still holding down the **Option** key, tap the **Down** arrow key twice to move the stereo pair onto A3/A4.

2. Holding down the **Option** key again, drag out the front and end of the audio portion of *Backstage11* so that it overlaps the adjacent clips as in Figure 10.15.

3. The next step is to add a fade out at the end of *Backstage04* on A1/A2. Select the edit point and use the keyboard shortcut **Command-Option-T** to put in the default audio transition.

10.14 Range Selection of Audio Keyframes

10.15 *Backstage11* Overlapping Clips

Backstage17, which immediately follows *Backstage11*, is quite loud and has a pronounced music track.

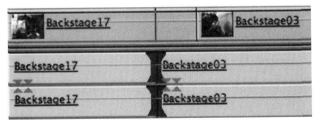

10.16 Roll or Extend Audio Edit

4. As you did with *Backstage05* earlier in the sequence, suppress its sound completely by dragging the level line down to the bottom.

For the next shot, *Backstage03*, I want to fade up the sound, but as so often happens when working with video, I want the fade to come up before the shot begins.

Use a Roll edit or Extend edit to move the audio portion of the shot earlier in the sequence.

1. To do this, again hold down the **Option** key and click on the edit point in the audio tracks between *Backstage17* and *Backstage03* on A1/A2.

2. Now either use the Roll tool to move that audio edit about a second earlier, or do an Extend edit, moving the playhead about one second earlier and pressing the **E** key to create a split edit that looks like Figure 10.16.

3. To complete the fade, with the edit still selected, press **Command-Option-T** to add the crossfade.

I would like to fade in the overlapping *Backstage11* a little earlier. To do this I need to ripple the sequence to move the overlapping on A3/A4 so that they butt up against each other. We'll do this with the Ripple tool.

10.17 Multitrack Ripple Edit

4. With the Ripple tool, select the left side of the edit between *Backstage04* and *Backstage11*.

5. Hold down the **Command** key and click just to the left of the audio portion of *Backstage11*, in the empty space between it and the previous shot (see Figure 10.17). You can now ripple the empty space together with *Backstage04*.

6. Pull the edit until the audio tracks collide on A3/A4.

In the Viewer

Let's add the fade at the beginning of *Background11* in the Viewer.

1. Switch back to the Selection tool with the **A** key, and double-click on the audio portion of the clip.

This opens the clip to the Viewer but with the Stereo (a1a2) tab in front (see Figure 10.18). Here you can see the clip's audio waveform. Notice the pink line in the center of the audio track. As you move the cursor over the line, it changes to the Resizing tool we saw earlier, which allows you to raise and lower the audio level.

10.18 Stereo (a1a2) Viewer

At the top of Figure 10.18, you'll notice the **Level** slider and the **Decibel Indicator** box. It's currently at 0, which is the level at which the audio was captured. You can raise and lower the audio levels with the slider if you wish.

As you move the pink line up or down with the Resizing cursor, both the Level slider and the Decibel Indicator box at the top move. A small window appears in the waveform as well that shows the amount in decibels that you're changing the audio level (see Figure 10.19). Notice also that, because this is a stereo pair, you are seeing two waveforms in this window, and that they move together when you raise and lower the level of one track.

To add a keyframe, either use the Pen tool or hold down the **Option** key as the cursor approaches the level line. The cursor changes into the Pen tool.

10.19 Decibel Level Change Indicators

2. Go about one second into the shot in the Viewer and add a keyframe.

3. Go back to the beginning of the clip and add another keyframe there.

4. Pull down the keyframe at the beginning of the shot so that the audio fades up from the beginning of the shot (see Figure 10.20).

There are several ways to delete an audio keyframe:

- Grab it and pull it down out of the audio timeline.

- If the Pen tool is active, hold down the **Option** key when you're over the keyframe. The cursor will change into the Pen Delete tool (see Figure 10.21).

Tip

Zoom a Marquee: You can also use the Zoom tool to drag a marquee along a section of the waveform to zoom into just that portion of the display. This technique will work in the Viewer, the Canvas, and the Timeline.

10.20 Audio Fade-In

- Use the shortcut menu by right-clicking on the keyframe and selecting **Clear**. To move the keyframe, grab it and slide it left and right along the line.

10.21 Zoom Tool in the Waveform with Audio Slice

One of the great features for editing sound in the Viewer is that you can do it with great precision, down to 1/100th of a frame. To do this you have to zoom into the waveform, either with the scaling tab at the bottom of the Viewer window or with the Zoom tool (see Figure 10.22), which you can call up with the **Z** key. To zoom out, hold down the **Option** key while you click in the waveform. You can also use **Command-+** to zoom in and **Command--** to zoom out. The black band in Figure 10.22 represents one frame of video, and you can zoom in farther still. Notice the tiny slice of audio that has been cut out of the track, less than one video frame in length.

FCE has the ability to automatically record slider movements while playing back a clip in the Viewer. This is switched at the bottom of the **Editing** panel in the **User Preferences** by checking the box for **Record Audio Keyframes**.

Because the Viewer is a pretty cramped space, a nice trick is to pull your Stereo (a1a2) tab out of the Viewer and dock it into your Timeline as in Figure 10.23. Then as you play back your audio, you can monitor it on the meters and ride the levels up and down as you like. When you stop playback, the keyframes necessary to reproduce your level control will be added to the clip.

Fixing Soft Audio: Sometimes audio is too low to be as forceful as you'd like, even after you crank it up with FCE's level controls. A neat little trick is to double up the audio tracks. Put another copy of the same sound on the track below. A simple way to do that is to hold down the Option-Shift keys, grab the upper of the two audio tracks, and drag them down onto the tracks below until you see the downward-pointing Overwrite arrow. Drop the audio on the tracks below. You will have created a duplicate. Now push that audio level up as well.

You can merge the new audio tracks into the sync clip. FCE has the ability to merge up to 24 tracks of audio with a single track of video. This is normally done in the Browser, but you can still do it in the Timeline to your audio-doubled clip. Select the clip, then Command-click the duplicate audio tracks to select them as well, and use Modify>Link or Command-L to link them all together as a single clip with four or more audio tracks. You'll get an out-of-sync error as in Figure 10.24, but you can ignore it.

10.23 Stereo (a1a2) Tab in the Docked Timeline

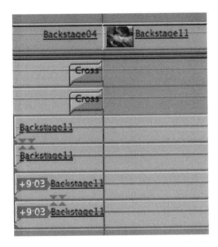

10.24 Doubled Audio Tracks in the Timeline

Sometimes when you move an unlinked audio track, it may accidentally slip out of sync with the video material. If that happens, you'll see time indicators in the Timeline tracks (see Figure 10.25) showing you how far out of sync the clips have slipped. The time slippage shows in a red box. The minus number means that the audio is three frames ahead of the picture. A plus number would indicate that the audio is behind the video.

10.22 Zoom Tool in the Waveform with Audio Slice

10.25 Out-of-Sync Audio

10.26 Out-of-Sync Shortcut Menu

If the audio does slip out of sync, the easiest way to get it back in sync is to right-click on the red box and choose from the options available in the shortcut menu (see Figure 10.26).

You could also nudge the clip back into sync. Option-click on the audio to select the audio portion of the clip. With only the audio selected, use the [or] keys to slide the clip forward or backward. As it moves, the time displays will update and finally disappear when the clip is back in sync.

10.27 Typing in a Numeric Value to Move Audio

You can also select the audio portion of the clip (or whichever portion has free track space around it) and type plus or minus the value to bring up the Move box as in Figure 10.27.

Middle of the Sequence

Let's finish off the *Rough Cut Copy* sequence. There are only a few more levels to tweak. Farther along in the **Timeline** is another portion of *Backstage05*. This time we do want to use the sound.

1.   Again with the **Option** key, select the audio portion of *Backstage05* and move the stereo pair down to A3/A4.

2.   Extend the front of the sound until it butts up against *Backstage11*, also on A3/A4.

3.   Extend the end of the sound as far as it will go, which isn't that far.

Between *Backstage03* and *05* are two shots, *Backstage09* and *10*. Both of these shots are quite loud.

4. Marquee-drag or **Command**-click to select the pair of them, and use **Modify>Levels** or **Command-Option-L** to reduce their levels to –9dB.

5. To smooth the transition between *Backstage09* and *Backstage10*, add a crossfade transition between the pair (**Command-Option-T**).

6. Extend the end of the audio on *Backstage10* so that it's underneath the following shot *Backstage05*.

7. With the Pen tool, make a slow fade-down on the audio of *Backstage10* that you extended under *Backstage05*. Or you could add a crossfade transition on the end and lengthen it.

8. Add a crossfade transition to the beginning of *Backstage13* that follows *Backstage05*.

9. With the Pen tool, add a slow fade-out to the end of *Backstage13*.

The middle portion of the sequence should now look like Figure 10.28.

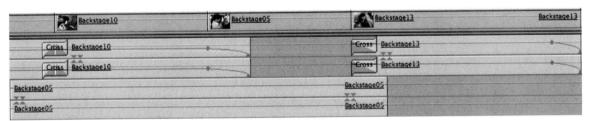

10.28 Middle Portion of the Completed Sequence

10.29 Changing Spread Value

🐭 *Note*_____

Pan Values: In addition to the pink levels line in the Viewer, there is a purple pan line. In a stereo pair such as this material, the pan lines are defaulted to −1. This indicates that the left channel is going to the left speaker and the right channel to the right speaker. By moving the lines up toward zero as in Figure 10.29, the two tracks are centered between the speakers. Going to 1 will make the channels cross over and swap sides. You can also type in a value in the Pan slider box.

When you have a multitrack recording with separate Mono (a1) and Mono (a2) sound, the Viewer appears with separate tabs, one for each channel. Level and Pan values can then be set separately for each channel, one set to −1 and the other to 1. This allows you to move the audio from one side of the stereo speakers to the other.

When you're working with separate channels using the pan line, you can shift the sound to come from either the left side or the right side. Moving the Pan slider to the left to −1 will move all of the sound to the left speaker, and moving the Pan slider all the way to the right to 1 will move the sound to the right speaker. As with Level, Pan values can be keyframed. The classic example is the racing car that approaches from the left with all sound coming from the left speaker, roars by, and disappears to the right while the sound sweeps past to the right speaker.

A little trick to quickly get the channels centered between the speakers is to select the clips in the Timeline and use the keyboard shortcut Control-period to center the tracks to the zero value.

End of the Sequence

There is an interesting little problem in the ending portion of the sequence that will again require a Ripple edit of empty space.

1. Pull the audio tracks for Backstage02 down onto A3/A4 and extend them front and end as far as you can.

2. There is one more stereo pair to pull down onto A3/A4, the last shot, *Background14*. Bring the audio down to A3/A4 and extend the front until it meets *Backstage02* on A3/A4.

I want to put a crossfade transition between the two shots on A3/A4, but I can't because there isn't enough media available on the end of *Backstage02*. I need to ripple that shot back by 15 frames to create enough space for the overlap.

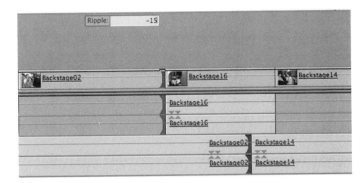

10.30 Selecting the Ripple Edits and Numerically Editing

3. With the Ripple tool, select the left side of the edit at the end of *Backstage02*.

4. Holding down the **Command** key, click just to the left of the beginning of *Backstage16* tracks on A1/A2, as shown in Figure 10.30.

5. Pull the edit point to the left so that it moves 15 frames, or edit it numerically (Type *–15* and press the **Return** key). As you type, a little box will appear at the top of the Timeline window telling you that you're rippling the edit as in Figure 10.30.

6. With the edits still selected, both the A3/A4 tracks and the empty space on A1/A2, apply the crossfade with **Command-Option-T**. This will add the crossfade to all four tracks, between *Backstage02* and *Backstage14* on A3/A4, as well as to the beginning of *Backstage16* on A1/A2.

For normal speech it's probably best to keep the recording around –12dB, perhaps a little higher for louder passages, a bit lower for softer ones. Many audio CDs are very heavily compressed, right up to the limits of digital audio. If you see your audio meters hitting the top of the scale, lighting up the two little orange indicators at the top, bring down your audio levels a few dB. You'll probably find you have to do this for most audio CD material. Monitor not only single tracks but also your mixed track. Often a single track will not exceed peak level, but a mix of all your tracks may send your meters well into the red.

10.31 Audio Meters

✈*Tip* _____
Metering: Key tools for working with sound in Final Cut are its audio meters (see Figure 10.31). The standard audio level for digital audio is –12dB. Unlike analog audio, which has quite a bit of headroom and allows you to record sound above 0dB, in digital recording 0dB is an absolute. Sound cannot be recorded at a higher level. It gets clipped off. Very often on playback of very loud levels, the recording will seem to drop out completely and become inaudible as the levels are crushed beyond the range of digital audio's capabilities.

✈*Tip* _____
iMovie Sound Effects. It is possible to bring iMovie sound effects into Final Cut Express, such as those great Skywalker sound effects. The trick is to know where they are and to copy them to somewhere else. Do this very carefully.

1. Right-click on the iMovie application inside your *Applications* folder.
2. From the shortcut menu, select Show Package Contents.
3. Go inside the *Contents* folder to the *Resources* folder and find inside that the *Sound Effects* folder.

Most of the iMovie sound effects are AIFF files. Copy what you need from that folder. Do not move them. The Skywalker sounds are MP3s and should be converted to AIFF using iTunes or the QuickTime Pro Player, if you have that.

Voice Over

Final Cut Express has a feature called **Voice Over**, which allows you to record narration or other audio tracks directly to your hard drive while playing back your Timeline. Voice Over is most valuable for making *scratch tracks,* test narrations used to try out pacing and content with picture. It could be used for final recording, although you'd probably want to isolate the computer and other extraneous sounds from the recording artist. Many people prefer to record narrations before beginning final editing so that the picture and sound can be controlled more tightly. Others feel that recording to the picture allows for a more spontaneous delivery from the narrator. However you use it, Voice Over is an important tool in the application.

10.32 Voice Over Tool

Voice Over is found under the **Tools** menu. This brings up the window in Figure 10.32. Or better still, call it up from the menus under **Window>Arrange>Voice Over Recording**, which brings a three-up display, Viewer on the left, Voice Over in the center, Canvas on the right, Browser and Timeline below.

The first steps you'll have to take are to configure your recording setup for your **Source**, **Input**, and **Sample Rate**. Source defines where the sound is coming from: the computer mic input, a USB device, a camcorder, or an installed digitizing card. Input controls the type of signal being received, whether it's line level, balanced audio in, digital audio, or whatever your source device is capable of handling.

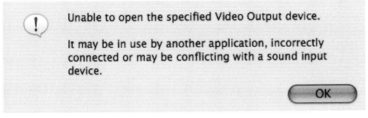

10.33 DV Device Error Message

> ▶ *Tip*
> **More RAM for VO:** Because Voice Over works in RAM, storing the sound before recording it to disk, you may need to put more RAM into your computer than the minimum requirements asked for by FCE because the audio is buffered in RAM as it's recorded. For example, 48kHz audio consumes 6MB per minute. So a half-hour track would take 180MB. Once they are recorded, all of these recordings are stored in your *Capture Scratch* folder with the project name.

10.34 Discard Warning Dialog

> ▶ *Tip*
> **DV Input:** If you're recording through a DV camcorder or other DV device, make sure that Video (at the bottom of the View menu) is switched to Canvas Playback. If it's set to Apple FireWire, the playback signal will be going out through the cable, which prevents you from recording from it. Two sets of signals going in opposite directions just won't work. If you have Apple FireWire selected in the View menu, you'll get the error message in Figure 10.33. Also make sure your camera is in camera mode and not in VCR mode. It has to be in camera mode to get the input from the microphone.

Offset adjusts for the delay taken by the analog-to-digital conversion. USB devices typically take one frame. DV cameras can be three frames or more.

Let's look at some of the controls in this panel. The large red button, the middle of the three in the top portion of the window, is the **Record** button. It will also stop the recording, as will the **Escape** key. The button to its left is the **Preview/Review** button and will play the selected area of your sequence. The button to the right is the **Discard** button. Immediately after a recording or after aborting a recording, pressing the **Discard** button will bring up the warning dialog in Figure 10.34.

The Gain slider, next to the **Input** pop-up, allows you to control the recording level based on the horizontal LCD display meter. This is fine for scratch tracks, but for finished work it is probably better to have a hardware mixer before the input for good mic level control.

Tip
Playback Levels: Don't be fooled by FCE's vertical audio meters. These display the playback levels; they do not show the recording level.

The Headphones volume does just what it says. If there is nothing jacked into the headphone output of your computer, the sound will come out of the computer speaker. To avoid recording it or the sound cues, uncheck the **Sound Cues** box.

FCE gives the recording artist elaborate sound cues, which are turned on with the little checkbox. Together with the aural sound cues in the headphones, there is visual cueing as well, which appears in the window to the right of the Record button. As the recording starts, a countdown begins, with cue tones as the display changes. It starts pale yellow and becomes darker and more orange until recording begins. Then the display changes to red. There is a cue tone at five seconds from the end of the recording as well as beeps counting down the last five seconds to the end of the recording. Recording begins during countdown and continues two seconds after the end of the recording during Finishing. Although this doesn't appear in the Timeline after the recording, you can drag out the front and end of the clip if the voice started early or overran the end.

I think the best way to work with Voice Over in the Timeline is to define In and Out points. If no points are defined, recording will begin at the point at which the playhead is parked and go until the end of the sequence or until you run out of available memory, whichever comes first. You can also simply define an In point and go from there, or define an Out and go from the playhead until the Out is reached. Because the Timeline doesn't scroll as the sequence plays, it might be helpful to reduce the sequence to fit the Timeline window. **Shift-Z** will do this with a keystroke.

Sometimes during recording you don't want to hear certain tracks, or you just want to hear a single pair of tracks. FCE makes it simple to do this with the **Mute/Solo** buttons. You open them by clicking on the tiny speaker button in the far lower-left corner of the Timeline window, which pops open the array of **Mute/Solo** buttons (see Figure 10.35). Clicking on the headphones will turn them red and solo that track, muting the others. You can turn on or off any combination of **Mute** and **Solo** buttons that you need. Notice the green **Visibility** (**Audibility**) buttons at the head of the Timeline. The difference between these and the

Mute/Solo buttons is that when audibility is switched off, that track will not play out to tape. If a track is muted, it will still output, even though it can't be heard during playback in the Timeline.

10.35 Mute/Solo Buttons

10.36 Audio File Window

Recording is always done to a destination track that has free space. Voice Over always records a mono track. It does not make a stereo recording and take up two tracks. If there is no free space within the defined area of the recording, Voice Over will create a new track. So if you record multiple takes, they will record onto the next lower track or onto a new track. The Audio File window will give you the track information (see Figure 10.36). You can name the recording in the Audio File window, and each take will be numbered incrementally.

After recording, the new Voice Over clip appears selected. You can play it back for review, but if you want to record further takes, use **Control-B** to switch off the clip audio so you don't hear it during playback of the next take.

✎ *Tip*
No Timecode in Voice Over:

There is no timecode or other identifying information other than the
assigned name with any Voice Over
recording, in case you need to
reconstruct your project at a later
date. It may be a good idea to keep
this recording preserved on tape or
on disk if you want to use it again.

After a discarded take, Voice Over will record to the previously assigned
track with the previously assigned name. After a few takes, you may want
to discard a previous take and reassign the targeted track so that Voice
Over will work with the empty tracks you vacated. Also, you should be
careful to switch off previous takes as you go so that the talent doesn't
hear the previous recording in the headphones while recording.

After a recording session with Voice Over, it would not be a bad idea to
go into your hard drive and root out old tracks that aren't needed and
may be filling up your drive. Those takes you recorded that you no longer
want can be deleted from your sequence, but they aren't automatically
deleted from your hard drive. Also remember that the recordings are only
a part of your sequence and will not appear in your Browser at all, unless
you put them there.

Summary

In this lesson we looked at working with sound in Final Cut Express. We
covered cutting with sound, overlapping and crossfading tracks, transitions, meters, and FCE's Voice Over tool. Sound is often overlooked,
seeming insignificant or of minor importance, but it is crucial to making
a sequence appear professionally edited. In the next lesson, we'll look at
some of the titling options available in Final Cut Express.

Lesson 11

Adding Titles

Every program is enhanced with graphics, whether they are a simple opening title and closing credits or elaborate motion-graphics sequences illuminating some obscure point that can best be expressed in animation. This could be simply a map with a path snaking across it or a full-scale 3D animation explaining the details of how an airplane is built. Obviously, the latter is beyond the scope of both this book and of Final Cut Express alone, but many simpler graphics can be easily created within FCE. More advanced motion graphics can be done in FCE's companion application LiveType, but that would be the subject for another book.

In this lesson, we will look at typical titling problems and how to deal with them. As always, we begin by loading the project.

Setting Up the Project

Let's begin by opening the FCE project we'll be working on from your hard drive:

1. Double-click on the project file *Lesson 11* to launch the application.

2. If necessary, reconnect the media file as we have done before.

Inside the project in the Browser you'll find a *Basic Animation* sequence that we'll look at later. There is also an empty *Sequence 1* ready for you to use, the master clip, *Kabuki*, and the *Clips* bin.

3. Begin by opening *Sequence 1*.

177

4. We'll be working only with the picture here, so deselect the a1/a2 destination tracks in the patch panel by clicking on them.

5. Drag a clip—let's say *Kabuki1*—from the *Clips* bin and drop it onto Overwrite in the Edit Overlay.

Text Generator

Now let's look at FCE's **Text Generator**.

1. To get to it, click the small **A** in the lower right corner of the Viewer.

2. Go into the pop-up menu, drop down to **Text**, slide across, and pick **Text** again, as in Figure 11.1. Or use the keyboard shortcut **Control-X**.

In addition to Text, there is also Lower Third, Outline Text, and the basic animations Scrolling Text, Crawl, and Typewriter. In version 3.5 of FCE, the important Boris title tools, Title 3D and Title Crawl, have been moved to their own submenu in the Generators. We'll look at the Boris tools in the next lesson, but let's start by looking at the way FCE's basic Text tool works.

11.1 Text Generator

Tip

Scrolling Text, Crawl, and Outline Text: Neither FCE's Scrolling Text nor Crawl should be used as a first choice. To create text animations for scrolling or rolling titles (vertical movement) or crawling titles (horizontal movement), you should use Title Crawl, which can be set to do either movement. This should always be the preferred tool. Nor should Outline Text be used. The primary text tools should always be Title 3D and Title Crawl.

Text

This is for very basic text graphics, simple on-screen words. The Text generator should be used only for very simple, quick text blocks. Let's look at the Text generator because it has many of the typical text controls you can work with in FCE. When you select FCE's basic Text tool, it immediately loads a generic text generator into the Viewer (see Figure 11.2).

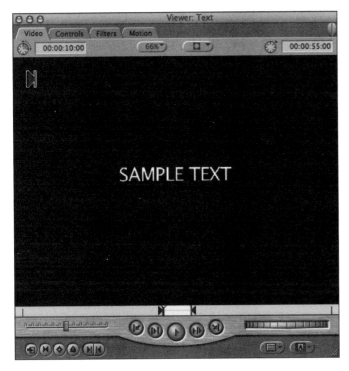

11.2   Generic Sample Text in the Viewer

Notice that this generator has:

- A default duration of 10 seconds
- A default length of two minutes

You can designate any duration for a text file up to 12 hours. However, once the text file has been placed in a sequence, its duration can no longer be extended beyond the designated duration. So if I accept the default length and I place the text file in a sequence, I can no longer make the duration go beyond two minutes. If you know you're going to need to make a very long text file, change the duration before you place it in the sequence. You can always make it shorter, but not longer. It's a good way to create a video bug, that little graphic that's always in the bottom right of your TV screen—or your warning that a tape is only a sample copy and not for distribution.

The first point to realize about this text generator is that at the moment, it exists only in the Viewer. Usually the next step I take is to put it somewhere useful, either into the Browser or the Timeline.

1. Put the playhead anywhere over the shot that's in the Timeline.

2. Drag the generic text generator from the Viewer to the Edit Overlay to Superimpose, or use the keyboard shortcut **F12**.

The text will appear above the shot, with the same duration as the shot (see Figure 11.3). Notice that the application ignores the marked Out point and takes its duration from the length of the shot underneath the playhead on V1, which is the designated destination track.

11.3 Supered Text in the Timeline

⤷Tip _____

Background: I always leave the playhead in the Timeline parked over the middle of the clip with the text supered on it. That way whatever I do in the Text controls appears a moment later supered on the clip in the Canvas. If you place a clip in the Timeline over nothing, the blackness you see in the Canvas behind the clip is the emptiness of space. You can make it a variety of colors, including checkerboard under the View>Background menu, but this is only for viewing purposes. If you want an actual color layer, use the Generators to make a color matte. Make it any color you want and place it on the layer below all other material.

You can also drag and drop the generator into the Timeline onto an empty track or the space above the tracks. Whether you drag the generic text generator to the Timeline or the Browser, you are creating a copy of that generator. Be careful not to do anything to the generator in the Viewer. I've seen countless people do this. They lay the generator in the Timeline, work in the Viewer, and then wonder why the text in the Canvas still says "Sample Text."

First, you should open the new generator you created in the Timeline.

3. Open it by double-clicking on the Text Generator in the Timeline window.

The Viewer screen will look the same, except now you'll be working on the generator in the Timeline, which is what you want. The label area at the top of the Viewer will tell you where the text came from. Figure 11.4 shows the label for text generated in the Viewer. Figure 11.5 shows the label for text that's been opened from a sequence.

11.4 Viewer:Text

11.5 Viewer:Text from Sequence 1

11.6 Plain Scrubber Bar on Clip Opened from the Browser

11.7   Dotted Scrubber Bar on Clip Opened from the Timeline

The other telltale sign that indicates whether a title or a clip has been opened from the Browser (or generated in the Viewer), or has been opened from a sequence, is in the scrubber bar at the bottom of the Viewer. In Figure 11.6 the clip has been opened from the Browser. The scrubber bar is plain. In Figure 11.7 the clip has been opened from the Timeline. The scrubber bar shows a double row of dots, like film sprocket holes.

Now we're ready to start making that graphic:

4. After you've opened the generator from the Timeline into the Viewer, click on the Controls tab at the top. You might also want to stretch down the Viewer to see all the controls (see Figure 11.8).

These are the default settings. At the top is the text input window in which you type whatever you want to appear on the screen.

5. Click on **SAMPLE TEXT** and type in *Kabuki*, press **Return**, and type *Performance*.

6. Click out of the window or tab to the **Size** box. The default is 36 point, which is quite small for video display.

7. Type in a size of *72* and press **Return**, which loads the size setting.

Above the Size slider is the **Font** pop-up menu, in which you can pick whatever TrueType fonts you have loaded in your system. It defaults to Lucida Grande, which is a pretty good font to use with video. If you have fonts on your computer that are not showing up here, then they are probably PostScript fonts. Unfortunately, FCE's titling tools do not work with PostScript, only with TrueType fonts.

An important point to note: The **Font** pop-up menu and all the settings in the text block will change all the letters for everything in the text block. You cannot control individual letters, or words, or lines of text. This applies to all of FCE's text generators except for Boris. Both **Title 3D** and **Title Crawl** have full text control, as we shall see.

> **Tip**
>
> **Computer Display:** Because much of FCE is real time, text will not require rendering on many computers. This means that as soon as the text is put into the Timeline it is at render quality. The title is rendered into interlaced DV material ready for display on a television set. That's what it is designed to do. It is not designed for display on a computer screen, which is why the text on your computer screen, and in these graphics, looks somewhat jagged and poorly rendered. You must judge your graphics output on a television set or video monitor. You cannot assess them properly on your computer monitor.

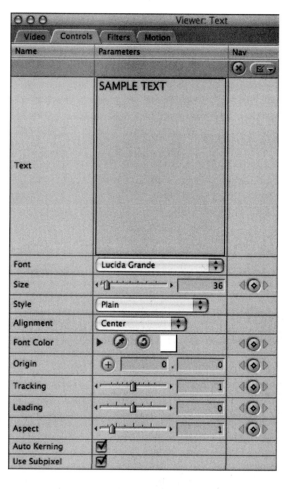

11.8   Text Control Window

▶ *Tip* _____
Sliders: *If you* have a three-button mouse with a scroll wheel, you can move any of the sliders, like the Size slider, with the scroll. Just position the cursor over it and move the wheel.

▶ *Tip* _____
No Word Wrapping: FCE's titler is limited in many ways, and word wrapping is one of them. You have to put in the line breaks where appropriate, or your text is liable to run off the screen.

The **Style** pop-up menu lets you set text styles such as bold and italic. Below Style is the **Alignment** pop-up menu.

A word of caution: Although the default setting is **Center**, the words in the text window are left-justified. Ignore that. The choice in the pop-up menu rules; the text window display isn't WYSIWYG.

The left and right alignments are not to the screen but to the Origin point, the way it works in Illustrator and Photoshop. So if you want left-justified text on the left side of the screen, you have to move the origin point about −300 or a little less to keep it in the Safe Title Area (STA), if you also set the Alignment to Left. This applies only in the Text tool. Other tools such as Scrolling Text align to the screen as you might expect, with left as the left edge of the STA, and right as the right edge of the STA (see sidebar on "Safe Areas").

✎ Note_____

Safe Areas. Televisions have a mask on the edge that cuts off some of the displayed picture area. What you see in the Viewer and the Canvas is not what you get—far from WYSIWYG—and can vary substantially from television to television. That is why the Canvas and Viewer are thoughtfully marked with a Safe Action Area (SAA) and a smaller area that is defined as the Safe Title Area (STA), the marked boxes seen in Figure 11.9. These are turned on with the View pop-up menu at the top of the Viewer and Canvas. Make sure that both Overlay and Title Safe are checked to see the SAA and STA. What's within the SAA will appear on every television set. Because television tubes used to be curved, and some still are, a smaller area was defined as the STA in which text could appear without distortion if viewed at an angle. Titles should remain, if possible, within the STA. This is not important for graphics destined only for web or computer display, but for anything that might be shown on a television within the course of its life, it would be best to maintain them. That said, more often you're seeing titles that are well outside the STA and lying partially outside even the SAA.

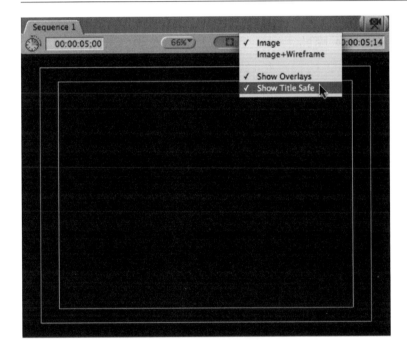

11.9   Safe Action and
        Safe Title Areas with
        View Pop-Up Menu

Font Color includes a color picker and a color swatch as well as a disclosure triangle that twirls opens to show the **HSB** sliders and **Value** boxes. The small icon between the eyedropper and the color swatch allows you to change the direction in which the color moves if you animate it. The ability to animate the controls in FCE's text tools, as well as filters and generators, is a new feature in version 3.5. We'll do a basic text animation later in this lesson.

Because of the limitations of television's color and brightness capabilities, it's important that you try to keep your luminance and chrominance val-

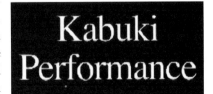

11.10 Serif Fonts

ues within the correct range. Oversaturated colors or video levels that are too high will bloom and smear on a television set. Set the HSB value so that brightness is no more than 92 percent. This may look pale gray on the computer screen, but as far as NTSC video is concerned, this is white, and it will look white on a television screen.

Fonts and Size. Not all fonts are equally good for video. You can't just pick something you fancy and hope it will work for you. One of the main problems with video is its interlacing. Video is made up of thin lines of information. Each line is switching on and off 60 times per second. If you happen to place a thin horizontal line on your video that falls on one of those lines but not the adjacent line, that thin horizontal line will be switching on and off at a very rapid rate, appearing to flicker. The problem with text is that a lot of fonts have thin horizontal lines called serifs, the little footer that some letters sit on (see Figure 11.10).

Unless you're going to make text fairly large, it's best to avoid serif fonts. You should probably avoid small fonts as well. Video resolution is not very high, the print equivalent of 72dpi. You can read this book in 10-point type comfortably, but a 10-point line of text on television would be an illegible smear. I generally don't use font sizes below 24 point and prefer to use something larger if possible.

This is often a problem with using artwork that hasn't been designed specifically for video. All sorts of issues affect images used in video: interlacing, limitation in how saturated a color can be and how bright it can be, the chrominance and luminance range limitations of NTSC, moiré patterns, and compression. Unless the artist makes the necessary adjustments while creating the work, it often looks unsatisfactory when incorporated into a video production.

You can set the **Origin** with a **Crosshair** button or with *x,y* values. You can use the crosshairs by clicking on the button and clicking wherever in the Canvas you want the center point of the text to be. The value windows are more precise. The first window is the horizontal, or *x* value; the second window is the vertical, or *y* value. The default is the center of the screen. This is centered on the baseline of the first line of text, in this case somewhere under the **b** in **Kabuki**.

You can also position the text by moving it about the screen in the Canvas. If you change the View pop-up menu at the top of the **Canvas** to **Image+Wireframe** (or use the **W** key to toggle it on or off), you can grab the text block, or any other image for that matter, and move it about the screen and position it wherever you like. Make sure the text block in the **Timeline** is selected, and a large X will appear through the image with a blue border (see Figure 11.11). This is the image with its wireframe outline. You can move the text block about the screen. If you hold down the **Shift** key, you can constrain it to moving vertically or horizontally.

Tracking is the spacing distance between the letters in a word, not to be confused with kerning, which is the spacing between individual letter pairs. The higher the tracking value, the farther apart the letters will get. Small increases in tracking will have a large impact on letter separation. As you move tracking below zero, the letters will scrunch together, and if you go low enough into negative values, the letters will flip over.

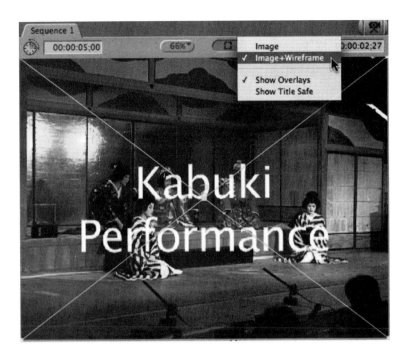

11.11 Image+Wireframe
in the Canvas

Leading (pronounced *ledding*, as in little bits of lead spacing used in hot-metal typesetting) is the spacing between lines. The default is zero. A setting of –100 moves the text up so that it's all on one line. A value of 100 moves the text down a whole line.

Aspect adjusts the vertical shape of the text. Low numbers such as 0.3 and 0.4 stretch text vertically, and higher numbers such as 2 and 3 will squeeze down the text significantly. Be careful with the Aspect control. Very little movement from the default of 1 will cause ugly antialiasing (stair-stepped edges) to appear around the text. **Auto Kerning** adjusts the letter spacing based on the letters' shapes rather than absolute values.

Lower Thirds

A lower third is the graphic you often see near the bottom of the screen, such as those identifying a speaker or location that you always see in news broadcasts. They are simple to create in Final Cut, although they are fairly limited. If you want to create something more exciting or stylish, you'll probably find it easier to do in Photoshop, Title 3D, or LiveType, which has animated lower thirds templates. Because Lower Third is so limited, it's quick and easy to use.

> ✎ *Tip*
> **Tracking:** If the Auto Kerning checkbox near the bottom of the controls is not checked, Tracking will not function.

11.12 Lower
Third

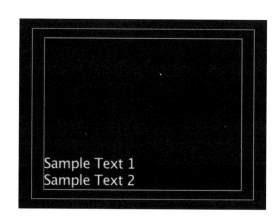

Flickering Text: Interlace flickering caused by serifs and other fine lines can be alleviated somewhat by smearing the image across the interlace lines. It is easiest to do this with text created in Photoshop, where you can apply a one-pixel vertical motion blur. You don't have to soften the whole image like this. If there are particular portions that appear to flicker, you can select them with a marquee or lasso, slightly feathered, and apply the vertical motion blur to just that portion of the image. Or you can duplicate the Text Generator in the sequence and stack one on top of the other. Apply a slight Blur or Antialias filter to the bottom copy. Only the slightly blurred edge that sticks out from underneath the unblurred copy will be visible, smearing the edge. You can also darken the lower copy to give the text a slightly harder edge.

Figure 11.12 shows the simple **Lower Third** that FCE generates. It's set down in the lower left corner of the Safe Title Area.

You can create the graphic in the Viewer before you move it to the Timeline, but remember that once you've moved it to the Timeline, what's there is now a copy. I like to move the graphic to the Timeline, and as before you can put the playhead over it and quickly see what you're doing in the Canvas.

Let's start by putting a new clip into the Timeline and adding the Lower Third to it.

1. Move the Timeline playhead to the end of the sequence by pressing the **End** key.

2. Double-click on *Kabuki2* from the *Clips* bin and Overwrite it into the Timeline.

3. Put the playhead over *Kabuki2* in the Timeline.

4. Click on the **Generators** button in the Viewer, and in the menu drop down to **Text>Lower Third**.

5. Use the Superimpose function to put the Lower Third over the clip in the Timeline.

6. Double-click on the Lower Third in the Timeline and go to the Controls tab in the Viewer (see Figure 11.13).

You'll see that the Controls are quite different for lower thirds. You have some new parameters, and you are missing a property as well. There is no Alignment pop-up menu.

11.13 Lower Third Controls

11.14 Lower Third with Bar and
Background

You have two lines of text. Unlike the regular text window, each of the two text boxes here can only hold one line of text. Each text box can be set to any font, size, or color. You can make a line as long as you want, but if you make it too long, it will run off the screen. At the bottom of the controls, you have the ability to create a background for the text and to adjust the opacity of the background.

Bar appears as a line between the text blocks. Although it has an opacity of 100 percent, it will show some of the underlying video through it. **Solid** is a block of color that appears behind the two text blocks. You can apply one or the other but not both. You could, however, add another Lower Third beneath it, with no text, just the background, as shown in Figure 11.14. The size of the background area is fixed and controlled by the size of the text it's underneath

11.15 Drop Shadowed Text

Drop Shadow

Drop shadows are important to give the image some depth and separation. It would be quite useful for our text where the white of the letters is over the bright highlights on the image below (Figure 11.15). You can add a drop shadow to your text in the Motion tab of the Viewer.

You have to activate the Drop Shadow with the checkbox in the upper left corner. The control panel, once twirled open, shows all the expected features: **Offset**, **Angle** of offset, **Shadow Color**, **Softness**, and **Opacity** (Figure 11.16).

Offset controls how far from the image the shadow appears. The default Offset works well for stills, video clips, or other large images, but not so well for text. When using Drop Shadow with the basic Text tool, you'll want to bring the value down, probably into the 2 to 5 range.

The **Angle** dial will point your shadow in whatever direction you want. The default direction, falling off to the lower right, is the most commonly used drop shadow angle. **Softness** lets you control the amount of blurring on the edges of the shadow. The **Opacity** slider defaults to 50 percent, which is probably too low for use with text. You might want to push up Drop Shadow's Opacity to 90 to 100 percent and use the Softness slider to take the edge off it.

Basic Animation

The current version of Final Cut Express HD allows you to create many more types of animation than was possible in earlier versions. Many of the text parameters in the Text Controls tab can be animated. To make an animation, you have to understand the concept of keyframes. When you change the properties of an image—in text, for instance—you define how it looks. When you apply a keyframe, you define how it looks at a

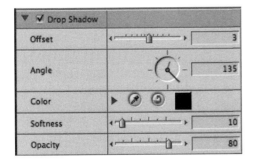

11.16 Drop Shadow Controls

particular moment in time, at a specific frame of your video. If you then go to another point in time, some other frame of video, say five seconds farther into your video and change the values for the image, you will automatically create another keyframe, which defines how it looks at that point in time. The computer will then figure out—it will *tween*—what each of the intervening frames of video has to look like over that five seconds. We've already done some animations, when we animated audio levels. Let's do a simple motion animation. We'll animate the leading and the color for the text.

1. Start by making sure the playhead is at the beginning of the Timeline, over the first stack, *Kabuki1*, and the basic text is on top of it.

2. Open the *Text* clip in Viewer and go to the Controls tab. Either grab the Leading slider and pull it down to –40 or dial in –40 in the value box. The lines of text should look scrunched together as in Figure 11.17.

3. Click on the color swatch and set the color to a very pale yellow.

4. Now click on the empty diamond keyframe buttons next to the Leading value and the color swatch (Figure 11.18). The little buttons will go green to indicate that you've added a keyframe and are on the keyframe.

5. Press **Shift-O** to move the playhead to the last frame of the clip.

6. Change the Leading value to 25. You do not have to add another keyframe; one will be added for you automatically because the value has changed.

7. Click on the color swatch and change the color value to a darker yellow. The Canvas will show the text spread out as in Figure 11.19.

8. Scrub the Timeline Ruler to see the animation in the Canvas. You may have to render it for real-time playback.

11.17 Text Leading at –40

11.18 Leading and Color
Keyframes Set

Font Color	▶	⊘	©		◁ ⊙ ▷
Origin	⊕		Ins/Del Keyframe		⊙ ▷
Tracking	◁———▯——▶		1		◁ ⊙ ▷
Leading	◁——▯————▶		-40		◁ ⊙ ▷

11.19 Text with Leading at 25
and Color Change

That's it! You've done your first basic animation. We'll do a lot more in the lessons ahead. To see the finished version of our little animation, open the *Basic Animation* sequence.

Summary

In this lesson we've looked at FCE's basic text tools and done a simple animation. In the next lesson, we will look at the considerably more powerful Boris Calligraphy and explore some of the animation capabilities it opens up.

Lesson 12

Boris Calligraphy and Advanced Titling

In the previous chapter we looked at FCE's text tools. Now we're going to look at Boris Calligraphy, which is made up of two elements: Title 3D and Title Crawl. This is actually a plug-in to FCE's Generators created for Apple by Boris FX. These supersede the FCE text tools and should be the title tool of choice for most of the work you do. These generators give the user great control and flexibility with text.

Setting Up the Project

Let's begin by opening up the *Lesson 12* project from your hard drive, and if necessary going through the reconnect process.

Inside the project in the Browser you'll find some sequences, which we shall look at in the course of this lesson. One of the sequences, *Sequence 1*, is empty, ready for you to use. There is also the master clip, *Kabuki*, and the *Clips* bin.

1. Begin by opening *Sequence 1* if it's not already open.

2. We'll be working only with the picture here, so as in the previous lesson, deselect the a1/a2 destination tracks in the patch panel by clicking on them.

191

3. Drag a clip—let's say *Kabuki3*—from the *Clips* bin and drop it onto Overwrite in the Edit Overlay.

Title 3D

Title 3D is a feature-packed tool, an application in itself, with complex animation capabilities that are beyond the scope of this book. I'm going to show you some of its principal tools, but for a thorough look at its capabilities, consult the excellent PDF in the *Boris Calligraphy Docs* folder inside the *Extras* folder on the Final Cut installation disc.

1. Call up Title 3D from the Generators pop-up menu in the Viewer.

2. Go to the submenu **Boris** and select **Title 3D**. Nothing will appear to have happened, but the Viewer will have changed.

3. Go to the Controls tab in the Viewer and click on the **Title 3D click for options button** (Figure 12.1). This will launch a separate titling window that is part of the Boris interface (see Figure 12.2).

This is the first of five tabbed windows that allows you access to Title 3D's powerful and complex tools. In fact, Title 3D has so many controls that there seem to be controls for the controls.

12.1   Title 3D Click for Options Button

12.2   Title 3D
        Interface

The window for the first tab on the left side is obviously the text window where you set up your text, font, style, size, alignment, and even justification. Unlike the FCE text box, it is truly WYSIWYG. Most important, each control can be applied to each letter or group of letters separately. So now, with little trouble, you can make a garish combination of colors and fonts, such as I have done in the sequence *Calligraphy*.

Before you do anything in this window, you may want to click on the second tab and change the default **No Wrap** to **Wrap** (see Figure 12.3). You can leave the wrap default at 512. At 512 you get a word wrapping that will fit inside a standard 720 video image's Safe Title Area. You can set whatever margins you want in this window, just as in a word processor (see Figure 12.4). In fact, many of Title 3D's controls are similar to word processors and other graphics applications, such as Adobe Illustrator.

12.3   Word Wrapping

The **Top-down Text** and **Right-to-left Reading** checkboxes at the bottom of the same window are great if you want vertical text or if you're doing Hebrew or Arabic text.

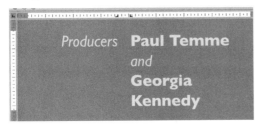

12.4   Text Window Ruler

After you've set word wrapping and any margins you want, go back to the text window to enter your text and set your font and alignment specifications. The main window allows you to enter and select text, which you can adjust with the controls at the bottom part of the window.

At the top of the text window is a ruler that allows you to set tabs for precise positioning of text elements (see Figure 12.4). The white area seen in the ruler is the active text part of the screen, and the gray area is beyond the word wrapping. Use the Tab key to navigate from one tab indent to the next. After you've set a tab, you can double-click on it to toggle between left-justified, right-justified, and center-justified. This

> **Tip**
>
> Text Control Shortcuts: If the Kerning, Tracking, or Leading value box is active, you can make the values go up or down by holding down the Option key and tapping the Up and Down arrow keys to raise and lower the values. With the text selected and holding down the Option key, you can tap the Left and Right arrow keys to increase the tracking. Or with the cursor positioned between letters, you can adjust the kerning of individual letter pairs.

tool is especially useful when making long scrolls such as movie credits, which often use columns and indents for different sections.

Let's look at some of the phenomenal text control in Calligraphy. In the bottom portion of the screen (see Figure 12.5), the first pop-up menu obviously sets the font. The two buttons to the right will move you up and down through your font list. Below the **Font** pop-up is a **Point Size Value** box. The two buttons to the right will incrementally raise and lower your point size. To the right of the font controls are six buttons that let you set the following attributes:

- Normal
- Bold
- Italic
- Underline
- Superscript
- Subscript

12.5 Text Controls

Below that, three Paragraph buttons let you set justification:

- Left
- Center
- Right

The **Tracking** slider adjusts the letter spacing globally, across all of the letters.

Kerning adjusts the spacing between individual pairs or groups of letters, as opposed to tracking, which controls the whole block of words. Kerning is important for many fonts, especially when you are writing words such as AVE, where you need to slide the A and V closer together than fonts normally place them.

The **Style** controls allow you to skew the text on the *x* and *y* axis. These were primarily designed to be used as animation controls. We'll look at these a bit later in the lesson.

Style Baseline will allow you to raise and lower letters separately, but **Style Scale X** and **Style Scale Y** will let you scale individual characters on the *x* and/or *y* axis independently from each other, allowing you to create interesting and unusual letter arrangements, as in Figure 12.6.

The buttons and pop-up menus along the bottom of the window (see Figure 12.7) have a variety of functions. The **All Styles** pop-up menu at the far left lets you change to **Basic Style**. You see basic limits in the text window. It does speed up preview, which can get quite slow with long and complex text windows.

12.6   Skewed, Scaled, and Baseline-Shifted Letters

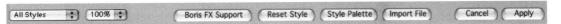

The **Percentage** pop-up menu lets you change the display size of the text window, a useful feature if you have a lot of text and want to quickly move around in it.

12.7   Pop-Up Menus and Buttons in the Title 3D Window

Boris FX Support will connect you to Boris's online web support system.

The **Reset Style** button will reset all of the parameters for the words in the text window. It will not, however, reset wrapping, tabs, justification, or margins.

The **Style Palette** is a great tool (see Figure 12.8). It allows you to create your own text style and to name and save it. This way you can replicate styles from file to file and even project to project simply and efficiently. The Style Palette is much improved in FCE 3.5, comes with prebuilt text styles, which are all customizable, a tab to save favorite fonts, useful complementary color groups, and even prebuilt color gradients.

The Import File button allows you to bring into the Text window a previously created plain text file or RTF (Rich Text Format) file. All of the justification and styles applied there will be honored in Title 3D. **Cancel** and **Apply** are self-explanatory.

> **Bitmap or Vector.** When you scale text created with the FCE text tool, the image quickly becomes jagged around the edges, yet in Title 3D you can scale the text, twisting and skewing the letters, and you'll see no apparent antialiasing or stair-stepping on the edges of the letters. This is possible because Calligraphy works with vector graphics, but FCE text creates bitmapped graphics.
>
> When a bitmapped graphic is created, the color and position of each pixel in the image are defined. If you scale that image, you have to scale the pixels, trying to create pixels where none previously existed. When a vector graphic is created, no pixels are defined. Only the shape, based on lines and curves, is defined. So if you scale a vector graphic, you're just redefining the shape; no pixels need to be created until the image is displayed on the screen.

Figure 12.9 shows what happens when a bitmapped text file (Helvetica 72 point) is scaled 300 percent and when a vector-based text file is scaled the same amount. The scaling for the vector graphic has to be done within Title 3D and not by using the Scale slider in the Motion tab.

12.8   Style Palette

12.9   Left: Bitmapped Text; Right: Vector-Based Text

This is only the first couple of tabs in Title 3D. Before we go further, let's add some text to the text window:

1. You should already have wrapping turned on, so start by making sure the alignment is set to Center.

2. Type in **Kabuki Performance**.

3. Select the text. This is important, because each character can be different, so like a word processor, the text has to be selected before making changes.

4. Set the font to Arial Black, which is perhaps the most commonly used font in video.

5. Set the point size to **72** and the text will automatically wrap to find the screen.

The third tabbed panel, **Text Color**, lets you set the text fill and opacity (see Figure 12.10). Notice the little checkbox in the upper-left corner that lets you turn off the fill, so that you only have the text outline if you want. The **Text Fill** pop-up menu lets you choose to fill the text with a color or with a gradient. If you choose **Color**, the Style Color swatch allows access to the system color picker that we saw earlier. If you choose **Gradient**, you will get access to an incredibly powerful gradient editor (see Figure 12.11), which has been even further enhanced in this version of FCE with even more radial types. The gradient style editor allows multiple color points as well as transparency. To add color stops, click below the gradient-bar display. Notice the useful little checkbox for **Live Update**, which will show your gradient on your text in the text window as you make changes.

12.10 Text Color

12.11 Gradient Style Editor

The fourth tabbed window lets you set the width and opacity for the **Text Edge**, and not just a single edge, but up to five separate edges for each letter (see Figure 12.12). Each edge can be Plain, Bevel, or Glow, and can be Center, Inside, or Outside. The slider on the right controls the softening blur for each edge. The variations possible with five edges are nearing infinite—more than anyone could need. To turn on an edge you have to make sure that the checkbox for the panel you're working in is switched on.

12.12 Text Edge

12.13 Drop Shadow

The fifth panel sets up to five separate **Drop Shadows** (see Figure 12.13). These can be a standard **Drop**; a **Cast** shadow, which slopes away from the text; or a **Solid** shadow with sides, which creates a kind of extruded text look. Drop and Cast shadows don't have Highlight or Shade color, but they have a Softness control that appears when the shadow pop-up menu is changed. Each shadow also has controls for color, distance, opacity, and angle. As with edges, be careful to turn on the checkbox for each of the shadows you want to include.

One major drawback of working with Boris Calligraphy is that while you're working in Title 3D, you cannot see the text composited on top of the image.

1. So before we start working further on the title, press the **Apply** button to create your title in the Viewer.

2. Once you've created your text, drag it to the Timeline or Superimpose it over the clip that's already there.

3. We're going to enhance it further, so double-click the Title 3D file in the Timeline to open it into the Viewer.

4. Then click on the Controls tab to open all of the controls for Title 3D. Figure 12.14 shows some of the controls for animating this tool.

5. We'll create a couple of easy animations, but first click on the Title 3D logo at the top of the controls panel to access the text again.

6. Select the text and remove any fancy edges, gradients, and drop shadows. Keep it just a simple text with a pale color.

Look at the controls panel and the sliders and dials that let you change the geometry and position of the text.

Although **Position** places the text in the screen, **Distance** makes the text appear nearer or farther away. The **Scale** value in this panel will allow you to get clean, large fonts. When working with Title 3D, scale your text here in this panel, not with Scale in the Motion tab.

Tumble, **Spin**, and **Rotate** will turn the entire text block around on the *x*, *y*, and *z* axis, respectively. A nice thing about Calligraphy is that if you have a real-time capable system, most of these motion settings, including drop shadow, will preview in real time.

The **Pivot** section controls the point around which the text tumbles, spins, and rotates. If the **Lock to Position** box is checked, the controls have no effect. With the box unchecked, the text will rotate around the selected pivot point, which can be set with numeric values or with the crosshairs button. Neither the **Tumble** nor **Spin** controls function with the X/Y controls, but their movement is affected when the Z slider is activated.

The **Transformation** sections affect all of the letters in the text block, but it affects each character individually.

Animating Title 3D

Let's make a simple motion animation:

1. In the Controls tab of the Viewer, type *300* and press **Return** to move the playhead to the three-second mark in the title.

2. Click on the diamond keyframe buttons for Distance, Scale X, and Scale Y, as in Figure 12.15.

3. Type **+1.** and press the **Return** key to go forward by one second.

4. Set the Scale X value to 270 and the Distance value to −16.

5. Render out the animation so you can play through it.

The title is static at the beginning of the scene and then zooms up and flies past the camera. The finished sequence is in the Browser and called *FlyThrough*.

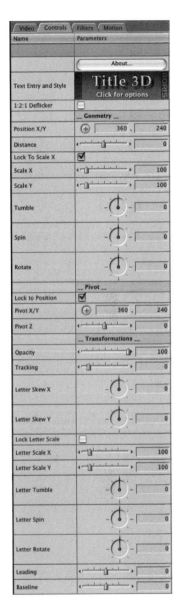

12.14 Title 3D Controls

12.15 Keyframing Distance, Scale X, and Scale Y

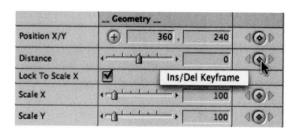

Type On

Type On is new to this version of Title 3D and allows you to create a typed-on effect with Title 3D's full text controls, making FCP's Typewriter finally obsolete. The Type On controls are at the bottom of the Title 3D controls tab. Figure 12.16 shows you the amazing amount of text control you have for your animations. To type text on the screen, first you need to animate the **Text Type On** value.

12.16 Type On Controls

... Type On ...	
Text Type On	100
Type On Order	Forward
Apply To	Letter
Always Visible	
Reveal Time	100
Acceleration	0
Overshoot	0
Decay	0
Fade	100
Shift X	0
Shift Y	0
Scale X	100
Scale Y	100
Skew X	0
Skew Y	0
Tumble	0
Spin	0
Rotate	0

1. To start, open the sequence in the Browser called *Type On*. It contains a piece of prepared text made in Title 3D.

2. Put the playhead at the beginning of the sequence (**Home**) and double-click on the text in the sequence to open it into the Viewer.

3. Go to the Controls tab and scroll down to the Type On area of the text.

4. The first value, Text Type On, is the one we'll animate. With the playhead at the beginning of the clip, click on the little diamond button, turning it green.

5. Drag the Text Type On slider all the way down to zero, or dial 0 into the value box. The text will disappear from the Canvas.

6. Go to the end of the clip. **Shift-O** right in the Controls window is the easiest way to do it.

7. Now drag the slider all the way up to 100, or type in the value.

You'll probably have to render this out. With the text clip selected, press **Command-R** to render it. Play it from the beginning, and you'll see your text type onto the screen. The rest of the controls in the section are for complex animation features for making the text bounce, curve, and scale.

Title Crawl

Title Crawl is accessed from the **Generators** pop-up menu inside the Boris submenu and shares many of the same controls as Title 3D. The text window that's evoked when Title Crawl is called up functions identically in both Calligraphy title tools. The difference is seen in the Controls tab of the Viewer (see Figure 12.17). Here there are far fewer options: no Geometry, no Transformation.

12.17 Title Crawl Controls

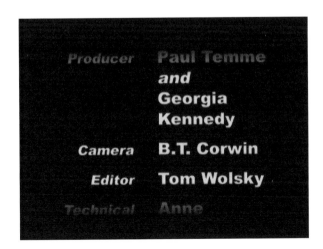

12.18 Masking and Blending in Scrolling Title

The Animation pop-up menu lets you set:

- None (the default, and rather pointless)
- Roll (Scroll)
- Crawl

★ *Tip*

Interlace Flickering: If you're doing text animation on interlaced video, check the 1:2:1 Deflicker box to reduce interlace flickering.

Mask Start, Mask End, Blend Start, and **Blend End** are interesting controls. These allow the scroll to fade in as it comes in off the bottom of the screen and fade out as it disappears off the top (see Figure 12.18). Mask Start and End control where on the screen the fades start and end. The Blend Start and End allow you to separately control the amount of fade at the top and bottom of the screen.

The **Reverse Direction** checkbox does just that: makes a roll reverse from the default bottom-to-top direction to top-to-bottom, and reverses direction of the standard right-to-left crawl to left-to-right.

To do a Crawl—a horizontal stream of text across the screen—first make sure **Word Wrap** is switched off in the second tab of the text window.

The speed of the Roll or Crawl is determined by the amount of text in the text window and the duration of the text block in the Timeline: the longer the block, the slower the motion. You should be aware that although Title 3D is vector based, Title Crawl is not; it produces bit-mapped graphics.

Once you've made your Title Crawl, place it in the Timeline and try it out for speed. To test the speed without rendering the whole item, mark In and Out points in the Timeline, make sure nothing is selected in the Timeline, and press **Command-R** to render that section. Pick a piece in the middle of the title so you get a representative section. If it seems too fast, stretch out the title; if it's too slow, shorten it and test again.

Nesting

The power of FCE's titling tools is in their great flexibility and the great amount of control you have over your graphic elements. In the project Browser is a sequence called *Title and Background*, which consists of several FCE titling tools. The output appears in Figure 12.19, but if you open it in FCE, you'll see it in color. I'll show you how it was built up.

If you open the sequence *Title and Background*, you'll see that it is made up of two layers. On V1 is a video clip twice, and on V2 is a text block called *Title Composite* and another called *Title Composite Japan*. These are nests. Nesting is an important concept to understand in FCE. Because you can have sequences within sequences in FCE, you can also group lay-

12.19 Title and Background

ers together into nests to form a sequence of their own. You'll notice in the Browser there are sequences called *Title Composite* and *Title Composite Japan*. These elements appear on V2 in *Title and Background*. Let's build these nests together.

Text

1. Start by duplicating *Sequence 1* in the Browser. Select the sequence and use **Edit>Duplicate** (**Option-D**).

2. Rename the sequence *Title Composite 2*, to distinguish it from the one that's already in the Browser.

3. Open *Title Composite 2* by double-clicking on it or by selecting it and pressing **Return**. Delete anything that may be in the sequence.

4. In the Viewer, from the Generator pop-up menu, select **Boris>Title 3D**.

5. Go to the Controls tab and click on the Title 3D button to bring up the text window.

6. Go to the second tab in the Title 3D window and change the pop-up menu to Wrapping.

7. Return to the first tab and type in **KABUKI**.

8. You can use whatever text, color, or settings you want, but this is how I built the text:

Font	Arial
Style	Bold
Point Size	96
Color Fill	muted red: R 200, G 68, B 88
Edge Style	Plain, Inside, Black

Edge Width	3
Edge Softness	2
Drop Shadow	Default: Drop Shadow, Angle 45
Shadow Color	Green: R 20, G 96, B 19
Shadow Distance	6
Shadow Opacity	100
Shadow Softness	3

9. When you've finished making the text, click the **Apply** button.

10. Switch back to the Video tab in the Viewer and edit the text onto V1 in the sequence.

Background

1. In the Timeline, move the playhead over the middle of the text block you just edited into the sequence.

2. From the Viewer, drag another copy to the Canvas Edit Overlay and drop it on Superimpose.

You now have two exact copies one on top of the other. The top one will be our text, while the bottom one will be converted into the soft, white background layer.

3. Double-click on the Title 3D text block on V1 in the Timeline to bring it back into the Viewer.

4. Go to the Controls tab and click on the Title 3D button to bring up the text window.

5. Select the text, go down to the Drop Shadow tab, and switch off the drop shadow.

6. Next go to the third tab, the color tab, and in the upper left corner switch off **Fill On**.

7. Finally go to the fourth tab, the edges tab, and set the edge as follows:

Edge Style	Plain, Center, White
Edge Width	Type in 80
Edge Opacity	80
Edge Softness	2.5

Why do I put the second edge on a separate layer? There are a couple of reasons. The main one is that it allows me to put the drop shadow on top of the soft background; otherwise, the drop shadow would be behind it and hardly visible. It also allows me to place elements between the text and the background.

Your Canvas should now look something like Figure 12.20.

12.20 Text and Background Layer

Color Mattes

1. Placing the cursor at the head of the V1 track, anywhere near the locks or auto select buttons, right-click, and from the shortcut menu, select **Add Track** (see Figure 12.21).

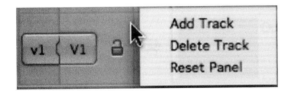

12.21 Add Tracks

2. Do this three times so that you have a total of three empty tracks between the two layers with the text blocks.

3. In the Viewer from the Generators button, select **Matte>Color**, as we did to make the color backing for the Page Peel transition in Lesson 8 on page 139. Again this will fill the screen with midtone gray.

4. Drag it to the Timeline and place it on the empty V2 you created.

5. Double-click the Color Matte in the sequence to open it back into the Viewer.

6. Go to the Controls tab and set the color to the same dark rose as the KABUKI title. Use the color picker if the title is visible in the Canvas. It should be if the playhead is sitting over the clips.

12.22 Crop and Opacity Settings in Motion Tab

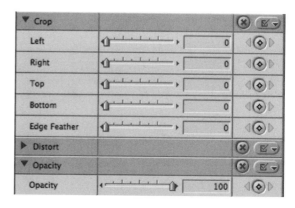

7. After setting the color, go to the Motion tab and twirl open the Crop and Opacity controls (see Figure 12.22). I used these settings:

Top	62
Bottom	31
Opacity	75

We'll look at the other controls in the Motion tab in detail in the next lesson.

8. Open another Color Matte, and place it on the track above the red bar you just created.

9. Make the color of this matte green as before (R 20, G 96, B 19). You can access the system color picker by clicking on the swatch and choosing the RGB sliders to set your color values.

10. In the Motion tab, set these Crop values:

Top	60
Bottom	38

11. We have one more color matte to make. Generate the matte and bring it to the sequence below the uppermost Title 3D block.

12. Set the same green color and these Crop values:

Top	70
Bottom	32

Your sequence should have five layers in it (see Figure 12.23):

- Background blur made from the KABUKI Title 3D block on V1
- Three color mattes on the layers above
- At the top, the Title 3D block that holds the text KABUKI

12.23 Timeline after Making Text and Matte Layers

Putting It All Together

1. Duplicate *Sequence 1* again.

2. Open the duplicate and delete anything that may be in it.

3. Set V1 as the destination track in the patch panel, and deselect the patching so there are no audio tracks.

4. From the *Clips* bin, select the clip called *Kabuki3*. Use Overwrite in the Canvas or drag it directly onto V1 of the empty sequence.

5. Move the playhead so that it is over the clip on V1.

6. Drag *Title Composite 2* from the Browser to Superimpose in the Canvas to place it above the video clip.

Reusing the Title Block

Here's what else makes this beautiful: suppose I've built this complex text block, and I want to change the actual text but nothing else.

1. Duplicate *Title Composite 2* in your Browser.

2. Change the name of the duplicate to *Title Composite Japan 2* and open it by double-clicking on it.

3. Double-click on the top Title 3D block to open it into the Viewer, and in the text window select the text and replace the word **KABUKI** with the word **JAPAN**.

4. Repeat for the Title 3D block on V1.

Nothing else changes, just the text block and the background layer. Easy, isn't it?

A nested sequence is like a clip in a sequence. If you want to apply an effect to a nest or reposition the block—lower in the frame, for instance—you can do this without adjusting each layer individually. We'll look at applying effects in a later lesson, as well as animating images about the screen.

Still Images

Often you want and need to work with still images, photographs, or graphics generated in a graphics application such as Photoshop or Photoshop Elements. What you should first know about working in Photoshop is that you should use only the RGB color space—no CMYK, no grayscale, and no indexed color. They don't translate to video.

One problem with using Photoshop is the issue of square versus rectangular pixels. Because Photoshop is a computer program, it works in square pixels exclusively, but the DV format uses rectangular pixels—tall, narrow pixels that allow for greater horizontal resolution. This presents a minor problem in the earlier versions of Photoshop, but it has been corrected since the release of Photoshop CS and CS2, which allow you to preview images with rectangular pixels and has guides for both Title and Action Safe areas.

The important point is to understand how FCE handles still image files. It handles different types of images in different ways. Single-layer files are treated one way; Photoshop files with multiple layers or transparency are treated another way. Single-layer files are treated as graphics files, and FCE understands that they come from a square-pixel world. Multilayer files are treated as sequences, and FCE would not presume to alter the dimensions of a sequence you created. It assumes that you did it correctly.

The recent versions of Photoshop and Photoshop Elements have presets for working in DV, NTSC, and PAL, 4:3 as well as widescreen. These should be used whenever you're making a multilayer or transparent image for use with FCE 3.5. For HDV material, use either the HDV 1,440×1,080 Anamorphic preset if you're working in 1080i or the HDV 720 preset if you're working in 720p.

You're not always making a graphic that needs to fit in the video format. Sometimes you're making a graphic that is much larger, one you want to move around on to make it seem as if you're panning across the image or zooming in or out of the image. To do this, you need to make the image much greater than your video format, perhaps 2,000 by 2,000 pixels or more.

If you are working with a Photoshop layered image, you still should squeeze the image down to rectangular pixels before you bring it into FCE. Here's how you should make them:

1. Create your multilayer image or image with transparency, and before you save it, go to **Image>Image Size**.

2. Uncheck to switch off **Constrain Proportions**.

3. Switch the pixel value for the vertical height of the image to percentage, and then reduce the height of the image to 90 percent or, if you want to be precise about it, 89.886 percent.

You should only do this for Photoshop files that are multilayer or with transparency—files that import as a sequence. This is not necessary for single-layer images without Photoshop transparency. FCE understands that these are square-pixel images brought into the video world and will handle them appropriately. If they are layered files with transparency, FCE treats these as separate sequences and does not adjust for square pixels.

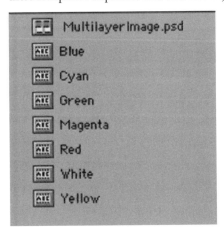

12.24 Layers Pulled from Inside a Multilayer Photoshop File

➤ *Tip*
Bringing in the Layers: If you do bring your Photoshop sequence into FCE as layers and you decide you would rather work with it as a single-layer file, use this easy trick: open the Photoshop sequence, and with the playhead over the layers, go to Modify>Make Freeze Frame (Shift-N). That will make a still image of all the layers. You can drag that still image into the Browser, rename it, move it wherever you want, and use it again and again. What's nice about this technique is that it preserves the transparency of the Photoshop file; all of the layers will be merged, but the transparency will remain intact. If you want to preserve the layers as individual images, select all of the layers and drag them to the Browser. They will appear as individual images with their Photoshop layer names as in Figure 12.24. All of the colored layers have been pulled out of the sequence Multilayer.psd.

When you import an oversized Photoshop file and place it inside a sequence, FCE will scale the image. If the still is smaller than the image resolution—say, a 500×200 image in a 720×480 DV sequence—the application will place it in the center of the screen with blackness around it. If the image is 400 pixels wide by 800 pixels tall, FCE will scale it to fit inside the window, as in Figure 12.25. If you do want to use the image at its full size so that you can move across it, the first step you'll have to do is return it to its full size:

1. Double-click on the image in the Timeline to open it into the Viewer.

2. Go to the Motion tab in the Viewer and set the Scale value back to 100.

12.25 Large Image in the Canvas Showing Scale in the Viewer

Resolution

For people who come from a print background, an important point to note is that video doesn't have a changeable resolution. It's not like print where you can jam more and more pixels into an inch of space and make your print cleaner, clearer, and crisper. Pixels in video occupy a fixed space and have a fixed size, the equivalent of 72dpi in the print world, which happens to be the Macintosh screen resolution. Dots per inch are a printing concern.

Forget about resolution. Think in terms of size: the more pixels, the bigger the picture, just the way digital still cameras work. Do not think that you can make an image 720×480 at a high resolution such as 300dpi or 600dpi and be able to scale it up and move it around in FCE. Certainly you'll be able to scale it up, but it will look soft, and if you scale it far enough—to 300 percent, for instance—the image will start to show pixelization. FCE is good at hiding the defects by blurring and softening, but the results are not really as good as they should be. FCE is a video application and deals only with pixel numbers, not with dpi.

Scanners, on the other hand, are designed for the print world where dpi is an issue. Because scanners generate lots of pixels, this is very handy for the person working in video. This means that you can scan a four inch by three inch image at, let's say, 300 or 600dpi, which is a quite small image, and your scanner will produce thousands of pixels, which will translate into video as a very large image. You now have an image that's much larger than your video format of 720×480 pixels.

If your scanner can generate an image that's 2,880 pixels across, it's making an image four times greater than your DV video frame. You can now move that very large image around on the screen and make it seem as if a camera is panning across the image. Or you can scale back the image, and it will look as if the camera is zooming back from a point in the image. Or

Pulling Photoshop Effects. Another problem many users encounter with Photoshop images is with effects applied in Photoshop, such as drop shadows to text layers or any of the hundreds of image effects the application can do. None of the effects seems to appear when the file is imported into FCE. The problem is that the effects are not applied to the image but exist as code attached to the file, so they can be changed at any time without having to recreate the layer. It's like nondestructive editing in FCE. There is a way around this, however. Merge the layer with the effect into an empty layer. Make a new blank layer beneath each layer you want to rasterize; then from the Wing menu of the Layers palette, choose Merge Down (see Figure 12.26). This fixes the effect with the image onto the empty layer, but now the layer effects are no longer editable.

Another method, if you only have a few layers that you don't mind merging together, is to use Merge Visible. Create a blank layer at the bottom of the layer stack and press Command-Option-Shift-E. Unlike the normal Merge Visible from the Photoshop Layer menu, this keyboard command will not collapse the layers into a single layer but will copy the content of all the visible layers and merge them into the single blank layer. With this method you still have the editable layers in the Photoshop file. If you switch off the visibility for the upper layers in Photoshop, when the file is imported, the merge layer will be visible and the other layers will be present, but their track visibility will be switched off as it was in Photoshop.

This is something you should do at the very end: merge the layers as needed, while keeping an original PSD file copy in its original format with the original images, text layers, and effects, separated and still editable.

reverse the process and make it look as if the camera is zooming into the image. We'll look at these topics in Lesson 14, "Animation Effects," on page 236.

Working with a single-layer file within FCE has one advantage: it's simpler. One of the issues that arises with Photoshop sequences in FCE is the problem of doing transitions between them (see "Transitions between Sequences" on the next page.

Transitions with Still Images: If you want to put together a group of still images with transitions between them, you can simplify the process in a couple of ways. When you import the files, make sure you leave enough room in your Still/Freeze Duration preference to accommodate the transitions. Sequentially number the stills you want to import and place them into a separate folder on your hard drive. Next import all of your stills as a single folder using Import>Folder so they come in as a bin. Then drag the bin from the Browser straight to the Edit Overlay and drop on Overwrite (or Insert) with Transition. All of the stills will miraculously dump out of the bin and appear in the Timeline with a cross-dissolve between them. The technique works beautifully with flattened PSD files or other image formats such as JPEGs.

Fading

Very often you'll want to fade in the graphic and fade it out again. Take another look at the sequence called *Title and Background*:

1. Click on the **Clip Overlay** button (**Option-W**), the button in the far lower-left corner on the Timeline window.

12.26 Merge Down

The files now have lines in them near the top. This is the opacity value of the clips. With the lines all the way to the top, their values are 100 percent. You'll notice that the line ramps down at the beginning and end of each of the graphics clips in the lesson sequence. This will fade in and fade out the Opacity from 0 to 100 and back again. This works exactly like the control we used for audio levels.

2. Grab the level line and pull it down to change the overall level.

3. Use the Pen tool (**P**) to make opacity keyframes on the level line and to pull down the opacity as needed.

The global Levels tool, **Sequence>Levels** (**Command-Option-L**), will also affect the opacity levels of multiple video or title clips. We saw this feature in Lesson 10, "Controlling Audio Levels" on page 161. Unlike audio keyframes, you can also smooth the opacity keyframes to ease into the fade by right-clicking on the keyframe. In the sequence *Title and Background*, the first clip has had the fade smoothed, while the second has not.

Transitions between Sequences. Because FCE allows you to place sequences within sequences, such as these nested Photoshop or graphics sequences we've been working with here, it sometimes becomes necessary to create transitions between them. This presents some problems. FCE treats each sequence as a complete piece of media. So as we've seen, if you have used the media to its limits, you can't create a transition.

Though each layer in a Photoshop sequence can be any length you want, when the sequence is laid into another sequence, the final sequence assumes that the limit of the media is the limit of the nested sequence. It will not go burrowing into the nest to extend the media for each layer to make room for the transition. So if you want to create a transition between sequences, you have to ripple the outgoing sequence and the incoming sequence to allow room for the transition.

Summary

In this lesson we've gone through Boris Calligraphy's Title 3D and Title Crawl, and looked at working with still images and Photoshop files. But that isn't all there is to titling. There's also LiveType, which is a truly powerful titling and animation tool. We'll look at animation next, creating moving images on the screen inside Final Cut Express HD.

Lesson 13

Animating Images

Final Cut Express has considerable capabilities for animating images. It allows you to enhance your productions and create exciting, interesting, and artistic scenes. In this lesson we will concentrate on FCE's motion capabilities.

Setting Up the Project

One more time, let's begin by opening up the lesson from your hard drive.

1. Open *Lesson 13*, and if necessary, go through the reconnect process.

2. Open *Sequence 1*, which is empty.

3. We're going to deal only with video tracks for much of this lesson, so the first step, as we did in the previous lesson, is to switch off the destination tracks for A1 and A2. In the patch panel, click on the a1/a2 buttons at the head of each track.

4. Next drag a clip—let's say *Archers1*—from the *Clips* bin and drop it onto Overwrite or Insert in the Edit Overlay.

Because the audio tracks were untargeted, only the video portion of the clip will appear in the Timeline.

5. Use the **View** pop-up menu at the top of the Canvas to select **Image+Wireframe** (see Figure 13.1).

13.1   Canvas View Pop-up Menu

Select the clip in the Timeline, and the image in the **Canvas** will appear with a wireframe indicator. The large X through it defines the corners and boundaries (see Figure 13.2).

Let's also set the window arrangement for compositing.

6.   Go to the Window and choose **Arrange>Compositing.**

Your window layout should now look something like Figure 13.3.

7.   Double-click on the clip in the Timeline to open it in the Viewer, and then click on the Motion tab at the top to open it.

13.2   Image+Wireframe
        Clip in the Canvas

The Motion tab (Figure 13.4), which we've seen briefly before, holds all of the motion parameters that can be keyframed in FCE. Most of them, with the exception of Opacity, Drop Shadow, and Motion Blur, can be keyframed in the Canvas. Motion Blur cannot be keyframed at all. We saw how to keyframe Opacity at the end of the last lesson.

Once you start twirling open the little triangles, which the FCE manual calls *disclosure triangles*, you might need to stretch down the window. Notice that each of the sections—Basic Motion, Crop, Distort, Opacity, Drop Shadow, and Motion Blur—has a button with a red X on it. This allows you to reset the values for that parameter.

13.3 Compositing Window Arrangement

13.4 Motion Tab

Keyframing

The basic concept of keyframing is that you mark the properties for a clip at a particular frame. You mark them by setting a *keyframe.* If you go further forward or backward in time by moving the playhead and changing the parameter values for the clip, another keyframe will automatically be set. The application calculates how fast it has to change the values to go from one state to the other. If the keyframes are far apart in time, the change will be gradual. If the keyframes are closer together, then the change will be more rapid.

It's easy to set a keyframe in FCE. With the clip selected in the Timeline, click the **Keyframe** button (the little diamond at the bottom right of the **Canvas**), or press the keyboard shortcut **Control-K** (see Figure 13.5).

13.5   Keyframe Button

This sets an initial keyframe for those properties in the Motion tab that are keyframeable. It will not set keyframes for Opacity or Drop Shadow. When a keyframe is set, the wireframe for the clip turns green in the Canvas. The wireframe will also display a number that indicates the track number of the track where the clip is. To delete a keyframe that you've set, right-click on the image in the Canvas and select Delete point from the shortcut menu (see Figure 13.6).

13.6   Keyframe
Shortcut Menu

Let's look at the parameters in the Motion tab that can be keyframed and what you can do with them.

Scale

The first keyframeable property in the Motion window is **Scale**, a simple slider and value box that lets you set a size. Because FCE deals exclusively in bitmapped images, stills, video, and text files made up of pixels, it's generally not a good idea to scale upward, not much above 110 to 120 percent.

While the sliders and value boxes in the Motion tab give you precise control, the easiest way to scale or control the other motion parameters is in the Canvas. With the Canvas set to Image+Wireframe, grab one of the corners and drag. The image will, by default, scale proportionately. If you want the image to be distorted, hold down the Shift key while you drag (see Figure 13.7).

13.7 Image Scaling Distorted

If you hold down the **Command** key while you drag an image's corner to scale it, you add the Rotation tool so that you can scale and rotate at the same time.

Rotation

Rotation is controlled with the clock dial or with values. There is a limit on how far you can take rotation. No more than 24 rotations seem possible. To get there, you can either:

- Keep dialing in more turns of the screw or
- Type in a value

Each notch of the "hour" hand is one revolution. It would be nice if separate value boxes for revolutions and degrees had been included. At the moment, you either have to:

- Twist the dial around lots of times or
- Calculate, such as 22 revolutions times 360 degrees equals 7,920 degrees

As with Scale, Rotation can be created in the Canvas. As you move the cursor near one of the edges of the image, it changes into a rotation tool (see Figure 13.8). You can grab the image and swing it around the anchor point, which we'll see in a minute. For the moment, rotation is happening around the middle of the image. It's a little easier to rotate the image if you grab nearer to the corner, but don't get too close or you'll grab the Scale point.

13.8   Rotation Tool

⇒Tip
Rotation Tip: Holding down the Shift key will constrain the dial to 45-degree increments, and holding down the Command key will give you a little finer control over the movement of the dial.

Center

Center is the position of the clip, where the image is on the screen. FCE counts the default center position, 0,0, and counts outward from there, minus x to the left, plus x to the right, minus y upward, plus y downward. The crosshairs allow you to position an image with a click in the Canvas.

Straight Motion

Let's set up a simple motion for a clip. You should have the clip *Archers1* at the beginning of an empty sequence and have it loaded in the Viewer open to the Motion tab.

1. If you have done any movement to the clip, reset the parameters by clicking on the red **X** buttons in the Motion tab.

2. Make sure that the Canvas is in Image+Wireframe and that the playhead is back at the start of the sequence.

We're now going to move the clip off the screen.

If you need to position an image outside of the Canvas, first reduce the size of the display in the Canvas.

3. Go to the **Zoom** pop-up menu (see Figure 13.9). To do this, it's simplest to set the pop-up menu to **Fit All**, which should reduce the size of the image, revealing some of the grayboard around it. You might

want to stretch out the Canvas area a little to give you even more room, or reduce it further, maybe down to 25 percent to see lots of the outside area.

4. Grab the image and move it off the screen (see Figure 13.10). Or click on the Center crosshairs in the Motion tab and then mouse down out in the grayboard and drag to reposition.

5. Make sure the playhead is at the beginning of the Timeline. Press the **Home** key if it isn't.

6. Once the clip is positioned off the screen, use **Control-K** to set a keyframe or click the Keyframe button in the bottom right of the **Canvas**.

Notice in the Motion tab that all of the motion properties have keyframes that have become green, and if you look closely in the area to the left of the motion properties called the *keyframe graph*, you can see a keyframe has been added to the graph (Figure 13.11). This is a new and powerful feature in version 3.5.

7. To make our animation, go forward five seconds in time and move the playhead exactly, make sure the clip in the Timeline is deselected (**Command-Shift-A**) and type **5.** and press **Return**. You'll see both the playheads in the keyframe graph and in the Timeline move. You can also hold down the **Shift** key and tap on the **Right** arrow key five times to move forward five seconds.

8. Drag the clip across the screen to the other side, creating a line with a string of dots on it.

13.9   Zoom Pop-up Menu

13.10 Moving an Image off the Screen

13.11 Keyframes in the Motion Tab

Tip

Straight Lines: If you hold down the Shift key while you drag the image, its movement will be constrained to right angles, either straight horizontally or straight vertically, depending on which direction you drag the clip.

You have created a straight linear motion of the image across the screen (see Figure 13.12). Notice that while at the first keyframe the wireframe was green, at the second keyframe only the dot in the center of the wireframe is green, because only the Center position value has changed. Also notice in the keyframe graph and the Center parameter a new keyframe has been added (Figure 13.13), but only for that parameter, because the Center position parameter is the only one that has changed. In the Canvas, the center point turns green when the playhead is on the keyframe. It's visible only when the clip is selected. When the clip isn't selected, there is no indicator.

13.12 Linear Motion Path

13.13 Center Keyframes and Keyframe Graph

13.14 Curved Motion Path

Curved Motion

There are two ways to create a curved path:

- Pull out the path from the linear motion.
- Create a curved path by using Bezier handles.

In the first method, when you place the cursor on the line, it changes from the regular Selection tool into the Pen tool. You can drag out the line so that it's a curve (see Figure 13.14). This creates a new keyframe.

Notice also the two bars sticking out from the dot on the curve. The bars have two handles each, represented by little dots, one slightly darker than the other. These bars are called Bezier handles.

The second method doesn't create an intermediate keyframe. There are normally no handles to adjust the arc on either the start point or the end point of the motion, but you can quickly add these by right-clicking on the point and selecting Ease In/Ease Out from the shortcut menu (see Figure 13.15).

When you select either Ease In/Ease Out or Linear, the Bezier handles will appear. These can be used to pull the line into an arc (see Figure 13.16). Pulling the knob on the end of the handle allows you to adjust the arc of the curve. Each side of the arc, at the start, end, and any intermediate points, can be adjusted separately to make complex movements.

➤ Tip

Speed of Motion: The spacing of the little dots along the motion path indicates the speed of the motion. If the dots are bunched together, the motion is slow, whereas if they're more separated from each other, the motion is fast.

13.15 Ease In/Ease Out Menu

13.16 Curved Motion with Bezier Handles

Changing Speed

✒️*Tip*
Starting Off-Screen: If your animation starts off the screen, generally you use the Linear for Bezier handle. This adds the handle but no easing. The assumption is that the object arriving from off-screen is already in motion at full speed and does accelerate as it enters the frame.

Normally objects don't arrive at speed instantly, nor do they stop instantly; so if your image is starting or stopping on the screen, you probably want it to accelerate or decelerate rather than jerking into motion. In graphics animation this is called *easing*: you ease into a motion, and you ease out of a motion. This easing is controlled by the darker set of points, halfway along the Bezier handles (see Figure 13.16). These are the *acceleration handles*. They control the speed at which the image moves through the keyframe, the rate of deceleration as it approaches the keyframe, and the acceleration as it leaves the keyframe. If you pull the handles apart, the motion will be faster. If you push the handles inward toward the keyframe point, the motion will slow down. The image will decelerate as it comes to the keyframe and then accelerate away.

If you want the motion to smoothly pass through the point without changing speed, make sure those handles are not moved, or right-click on the keyframe and choose Linear. In the sequence in your Browser called *Curved Motion Path*, I have created a simple motion path that shows this feature. On a slower computer you might have to render this out, depending on your RT settings.

✒️*Tip*
Adjusting Bezier Handles: If you want to make the curves or the motion even more complex, you can adjust each end of the Bezier handles independently. If you hold down the Command key and grab a handle, it will move separately from the other handle (see Figure 13.17).

You'll clearly see the deceleration and acceleration as the image passes through the intermediate keyframe. Notice that the image moves much quicker in the first part of the movement and slower in the second portion. This happens because the first portion of the movement is shorter both in time and distance.

13.17 Separate Bezier Control Handles

One great feature of FCE is the ability to move the entire motion path you've created. You can move the whole path as a single entity to whatever position on the screen you want. This can be very useful if you've made a horizontal movement—say, left to right across the screen—that slides a clip through the upper portion of the screen. Later you decide it would be better for it to slide across the lower portion of the screen. Rather than resetting all the motion path keyframes, simply move the entire path. To do this, make sure the Canvas is in Image+Wireframe mode. Hold down **Command-Shift**, and when the cursor is over the clip, it will change to the Hand tool (see Figure 13.18). Grab the clip and move it. The whole motion path will move as a single group.

13.18 Using the Hand Tool to Move a
Motion Path

Other Motion Controls

Anchor Point

The anchor point is the pivot point around which the image swings. It's also the point around which scaling takes place. For some reason that escapes me, Anchor Point, unlike Center, does not have crosshairs for positioning it. Fortunately, there is a way to move it in the Canvas (see Figure 13.19).

13.19 Anchor Point Moved with the
Distort Tool

1. Select the Distort tool (keyboard **D** for distort), and grab the center point of the clip. Drag it to where you want to position the anchor point. The point you're moving with this tool is actually the anchor point.

We'll look at the Distort tool on the next page.

2. Apply a rotation to the image.

Notice that it doesn't swing around the center of the image but rather around this new point. If you pull it out to the upper-right corner, that's where the image will pivot. Take a look at *Anchor Point Sequence*. Two images swing through the frame with opposing anchor points.

Notice also that on the second clip, I have animated the center as well as repositioning the anchor point. It moves slightly differently, more tumbling than simply rotating. Be careful with animating multiple parameters: once the anchor point has been moved, it can lead to unexpected results.

> ✒️*Tip*
> **Anchor Point Keyframe:** If the clip is deselected, the anchor point keyframe is not indicated in the Canvas. If the clip is selected, however, the track number will turn green to show that the playhead is over an anchor point keyframe.

Crop

Crop allows you to cut the image from the sides. In addition to the Canvas, this can be done in the Motion tab with the Crop controls hidden under the twirly disclosure triangle (see Figure 13.20). Notice that each of the sides in the Crop function can be keyframed separately.

13.20 Crop Controls

Crop Tool - c

13.21 Crop Tool

If you have specific values, or if you want to reduce the image by precise amounts—such as equally from all sides—then this is the place to do it. To crop in the Canvas, you'll need to use the Crop tool. The Crop tool is in the tools and can be called up with the letter C, just as in Photoshop (see Figure 13.21). As with the other motion controls in the Canvas, it will work only while you're in Image+Wireframe.

13.22 Cropping the Image in the Canvas

The Crop tool in FCE doesn't work very much like Photoshop's. You can't simply drag a marquee across the image to define the section you want to keep.

1. Select the image, and with the Crop tool, grab one edge of the image. As the tool gets near the edge, it changes into the Crop icon, indicating that the cursor is acting in Crop mode.

2. Grab the edge and pull in the image to crop (see Figure 13.22). Or you can grab the corner and crop adjacent sides at the same time.

Notice at the bottom of the Crop control panel in the Motion tab the slider for Edge Feather. This softens the edges of the image and can be very attractive, particularly when there are multiple images on the screen (see Figure 13.23).

Distort

The **Distort** tool allows you to squeeze or expand the image, either maintaining its shape or pulling it apart. Be careful, though. Remember that these are pixels you're dealing with, and making pixels bigger can make them blocky and ugly. What's remarkable is how much you can distort the image and still get away with it. As with other tools, there are two or more places to do everything. We already saw one way to distort the image by grabbing a corner with the Selection tool and dragging the image around while holding down the **Shift** key. This distortion alters the aspect ratio of the image but maintains its rectangular shape. This can also be done with the slider at the bottom of the Distort control panel (see Figure 13.24).

> ✦ *Tip*
> **Crop Line:** If the clip is selected in the timeline, when the playhead reaches a Crop keyframe, the crop line shows as mauve. If the clip is not selected, no indicator appears in the Canvas.

13.23 Two Clips in the Canvas
Cropped and Feathered

➤ *Tip*
Double Crop: If you hold down the
Command key while you drag one
edge of the image with the Crop tool,
the opposite side will be cropped
equally. And if you use the Command key and drag from one of the
corners, you can crop all four sides
proportionately and simultaneously.

▼ Distort			
Upper Left	−360 ,	−240	◀◉▷
Upper Right	360 ,	−240	◀◉▷
Lower Right	360 ,	240	◀◉▷
Lower Left	−360 ,	240	◀◉▷
Aspect Ratio		0	◀◉▷

13.24 Distort Control Panel

Moving the **Aspect Ratio** slider to the left, into negative numbers, will
squeeze the image vertically so it mashes down into a narrow slit. Pulling
the slider to the right into large positive numbers will squeeze it horizontally, so that it's a tall, thin image. The slider ranges from −1,000 to
1,000. The image can't be squeezed until it's gone, but it does come close.

You could dial in values into the corner-point boxes, which will move the
corner points to any position you want, but the easiest way to use Distort
is with the Distort tool, which is underneath Crop in the tools. Select it
with the **D** key. The Distort tool lets you grab a corner in the Canvas and
pull it around and really mess the image up if you want (see
Figure 13.25).

13.25 Distorted Image in the Canvas

Anything becomes possible with these kinds of tools. Now that images are digital, they can be twisted and distorted, shaped and sized, and blended any way you can imagine. I hope you see the potential for creating almost any possible transition.

I've made a simple one using Distort, Scale, and Center animation. Look at *Transition Sequence*. A few pulls on Distort tool, a little scaling, and the image shoots off. If you apply motion or any other effects to a clip, the whole clip has to be rendered out, even if all of the values remain at default for the greater part of its duration.

The simplest way to get around this problem is to cut the clip—**Control-V** or **Blade**—and separate the normal section from the twisted section. You can see what I did in *Transition Sequence*. Just be careful you don't move elements around so that the two parts get detached from each other.

There are still a few more elements to look at in the Motion panel.

Opacity

The uses for **Opacity** are pretty obvious. The transparency of the image can be decreased from 100 percent opaque to zero opacity. It's a useful way to do simple fades, as we saw in the Timeline with titles in the previous lesson on starting on page 211. Whatever is adjusted in the Timeline with the Pen tool will also appear reproduced in the keyframe graph in the Motion tab, or you can keyframe and control the Opacity in the Motion tab.

> **Tip**
> **Proportional Distortion:** If you use the Distort tool and grab one corner while holding down the Shift key, you will distort the image proportionately. Dragging the upper-left corner in, for instance, will make the upper-right corner move inward the same amount. It's an easy way to create perspective. It's also an easy way to bend the image inside out so half of it is flipped over on itself.

13.26 Drop Shadows against White Matte

Drop Shadow

Drop Shadow gives a multilayered image a three-dimensional appearance. It gives titles and moving images some depth and separation (see Figure 13.26). FCE's Drop Shadow is pretty basic, but it works fine. The control panel has all of the expected features of Offset, Angle of offset, shadow Color, Softness, and Opacity (see Figure 13.27). Note that Drop Shadow has to be activated with the little checkbox in the upper-left corner of the control panel.

13.27 Drop Shadow Controls

What might seem puzzling about the **Offset** slider is that it goes into negative numbers. Angle would seem to do the same thing as Offset, but when you animate them, they behave differently. Open *Shadow Sequence* from the Browser and play through the first two shots. In the first shot, Offset is animated and the shadow slides underneath the image. In the second shot, Angle is animated and the shadow circles the image.

The **Angle** control lets you change the direction in which the shadow drops onto the underlying layers.

Softness lets you control the amount of blurring on the edges of the shadow. Though the slider goes up to 100, I'm quite disappointed in how little effect it has. Shadow softness in FCE reaches no more than about 10 percent into the shadow area, so you're forced to rely on Opacity to soften the shadow area, which is not the same look. It lacks the subtlety of other compositing applications.

Look at the third clip in the *Shadow Sequence*. It uses the shadow to help create the illusion of three-dimensionality in two-dimensional space. By hardening the shadow and reducing the offset, while increasing the opacity of shadow as the clip becomes smaller, you can create the impression that the clip is getting closer to the gray background.

The default drop shadow settings work well for stills and other large images, but not so well for text. If you're using this drop shadow with the basic **Text** tool, you should bring down the **Offset** value and push up the **Opacity** value. For thin objects such as text, the first is too high and the second too low.

Motion Blur

Motion Blur is also activated with a checkbox in the upper left of its control panel. This is not a keyframeable property. Figure 13.28 shows FCE's Motion Blur at a setting of 1,000 with four samples and with 32 samples. This was created by applying Motion Blur to a panning shot. It gives the clip the appearance of great speed because of the added blur. Sampling goes down to 1, which produces no Motion Blur at all. The stepping that occurs in the lower sampling rates is ugly and best avoided. The low sample settings can be used, though, to produce interesting effects in images that contain fast-moving objects. You will see a ghosting effect as the object moves through the screen.

13.28 Motion Blur Set to 1,000 with Four

⭐ *Tip*
_____
Moving between Keyframes:
In addition to the little triangles next to the keyframe buttons in the Motion tab, you can also use keyboard shortcuts to move between keyframes. Shift-K will take you to the next keyframe, and Option-K will take you to the previous keyframe.

Use Motion Blur if you're trying to make it look as though your animations are moving very quickly, but be warned that Motion Blur adds considerable time to all renders. It's a very long and slow calculation for each frame. If you are going to apply it, always add it last, just before you're finally going to render out your sequence.

Summary

This lesson gives you an overview of the motion parameters in FCE:

- Scale
- Rotation
- Center
- Anchor Point
- Crop
- Distort
- Opacity
- Drop Shadow
- Motion Blur

In the next lesson, we'll look at some ways to use these animation parameters to create motion effects.

Lesson 14

Animation Effects

Now that you know how FCE's motion parameters work, let's see what you can do with them. We'll go through several exercises to learn different techniques beginning with motion control, easing and pan and scan issues, creating split screens, picture in picture, and making the motion graphics open for a classic TV show.

Setting Up the Project

For this lesson we'll use the *Lesson 14* project, launch the project, and reconnect the media if necessary. The project contains several sequences, including *Sequence 1*, which is empty and should be open. The Browser also has two master clips, *Archers* and *BB.mov,* as well as two bins, *Clips* and *Graphics.*

Because we're going to be working in the Viewer a good deal, let's change our window arrangement. Use **Windows>Arrange>Compositing** and adjust the windows to suit you and your monitor.

Motion Control

One question that new users often ask is how to recreate what's called in iMovie the Ken Burns effect. This name was coined by Apple to describe a technique that antedates Ken Burns' outstanding work by many decades. The technique used by the documentary filmmaker is called motion control and is done using cameras mounted vertically to shoot down on images as they move across them. These days motion control is done on special rostrum cameras that are computer controlled and can be programmed to make very complex motions with great precision. Some of this can now be simulated in inexpensive desktop software. Though not as simple as in iMovie, it's relatively easy to do in Final Cut Express. We'll do a slow push into two still images. Let's begin by bringing the two files into the Timeline.

1. Start by opening the *Graphics* bin and dragging *LongShot.jpg* into *Sequence 1* onto V2.

2. Next Overwrite *Leaves.jpg* from the *Clips* bin into the Timeline after the first still.

The images are both 1,500×1,125 pixels in size, much larger than the size of the regular NTSC DV frame, which is 720×480 pixels. Whenever you bring a still image into an FCE sequence, the application will always try to fit the image to the sequence size as best it can. If the image is tall and narrow, a vertical shot, the application will scale it so it fits vertically in the frame. In this case, the images are scaled down to 48 percent to fit into the Canvas.

3. We'll work on *LongShot.jpg* first, so double-click on the image in the Timeline to open it into the Viewer and look at the Scale value in the Motion tab.

To create the motion control effect, we're going to want to animate this Scale value.

4. To do this, make sure the playhead is at the beginning of the clip. Press the **Home** key.

5. Click on the keyframe button in the Motion tab that's opposite the Scale value.

Because I know I'm going to add a Cross-Dissolve to this, I don't want the animation to stop at the end of the shot or it will stop during the transition. I have to extend the animation through the handles that the transition will create. A one-second transition will add 15 frames onto the still image. The still image is five seconds long, so I want to put my end keyframe at 5:15.

6. To go to the end point where we want the animation to end, type **515** and press **Return**, and the playhead in the keyframe graph (and the Timeline) will move to that point, 15 frames past the end of the still (see Figure 14.1).

We now want to change the Scale value of that first shot to do a slow zoom-in. Over the five-second duration of this shot, plus the transition, we'll scale the image by 20 percent.

7. Set the Scale value up to 75 percent.

You don't need to set another keyframe, because the value has changed, so FCE will automatically add the keyframe when you change the value. If you play the Timeline, you'll see the slow push-in, which does not end at the end of the shot.

Let's work on the *Leaves.jpg* shot next. We want the motion to begin before the beginning of the clip, so when the transition creates the handles it needs, the animation will have already begun.

14.1 Playhead in the Keyframe Graph

8. Double-click on *Leaves.jpg* in the Timeline to bring it into the Viewer.

9. The shot begins at 5:00 in the Timeline, and we want the motion to start half a second earlier, so type **415** and press **Return** to move the playhead before the start of the clip.

10. Click the **Scale keyframe** button to add a Scale keyframe.

11. Go to the end of the clip using **Shift-O**.

12. Set the Scale value to 75.

13. Play through the Timeline.

To complete the animation, we just need to add the Cross-Dissolve between the two shots.

14. Select the edit point in the Timeline, and press **Command-T** to add the default transition.

That's it. If you step through the transition, you'll see that the animation is continuous, which would not happen if you put the keyframes right at the end of the first shot and the beginning of the second. The motion would stop for one shot in the middle of the transition and start for the other. In the *Motion Control* sequence I've laid out the animation both ways, with these step-by-steps first, and then without the motion overlap—a subtle difference, but quite noticeable to the viewer.

↳Tip

Transition Glitch: If you're working in real time, you will probably
notice a little glitch in the transitions
start and end. This is FCE's Dynamic
RT changing resolution on-the-fly to
keep real-time playback. To see it
play smoothly, render it out using
Sequence>Render Only>Preview.

Pan and Scan

Pan and scan is another slang term for motion control on large-size still images. It does raise some issues working in Final Cut, both Express and Pro. I have set up a sequence that illustrates some of the problems. If you open *Pan Sequence*, you'll see that it contains four copies of a still image. It's a PICT file called *Pict*, but it could as easily be a Photoshop file, PNG, or TIFF.

In the previous lesson, I said you should forget about image resolution as far as video is concerned and think only in numbers of pixels. In the print world for which scanners are designed, resolution is critically important. If you're scanning images such as this one to use in FCE, you can scan it at a high resolution, like 300 or 600dpi. Ideally, you'd want to calculate the area you're going to zoom into based on an image that's a multiple of 720 pixels across at 72dpi. Often it's simpler just to scan more than you need and adjust it in Photoshop or even leave it to Final Cut. By scanning at high resolutions, the scanner will generate lots of pixels. FCE will translate this into a very large image, not a small image at high resolution as a print system would do.

In the *Pan Sequence*, I've done motion control on *Pict* four times. Look at them one at a time. On real-time systems, these movements will not need rendering to play back on the computer screen.

In the first image, the image starts out centered in the screen and zooms into a point in the upper-right corner of the image.

A couple of problems are apparent:

- The image jerks into motion; acceleration is not smooth.
- The zoom-in seems to get slower and slower as it progresses.

This latter is a difficult problem and pretty much impossible to deal with when using the motion controls in Final Cut. It is totally unnatural and the bane of trying to create motion that looks like a camera moving over an image and zooming as it goes.

But first let me show you how to add easing:

1. Copy the first *Pict* image inside the *Pan Sequence*. Select it and press **Command-C**.

2. Switch to *Sequence 1* and clear any content in the sequence by delet-ing it.

3. Paste the image into the empty sequence with **Command-V**.

4. Select the image, and in the Canvas **View** pop-up menu, switch on **Image+Wireframe**.

If you're partway through the motion, you'll see a trail of dots as well as the wireframe indicating the motion path of the center animation. If you set the Canvas in the **Zoom** pop-up to **Fit All**, you'll also see both green start and end center keyframes at the beginning and end of the motion path (Figure 14.2).

5. To add easing to the movement, right-click on each of the green dots on the ends of the motion path, and from the shortcut menu choose **Ease In/Ease Out** (Figure 14.3).

This will add the easing as well as the Bezier handles we saw in the last lesson, which would allow us to bend the motion path. If you play this back you'll immediately see a problem: the image overshoots the motion and then comes back into the screen.

14.2 Image with Motion Path

To alleviate this we'll add easing to the Scale value as well. This is a new feature in FCE 3.5, which has never been available in the application.

6. Double-click the *Pict* image in the sequence and go to the Motion tab in the Viewer.

7. To give you more room to work with, pull down the separator bar between the Scale and Rotation value controls as in Figure 14.4. You can do this for any of these areas, but it's most useful for Scale.

8. Next, right-click on each of the Scale keyframes, and from the shortcut menu select Smooth (Figure 14.5). This is equivalent in the Motion tab of easing for Center animation and will give you a curved value ramp indicating the acceleration and deceleration of the scaling.

14.3 Easing Center Point

14.4 Separating Scale and Rotation Values

14.5 Smoothing Scale Keyframes

This is better, but it's still not right. The animation doesn't shoot as far off the screen, but it still swings off a little. This is because the smoothing rate of Scale and the Ease In/Ease Out rate of center-point animation are different, so that the image still shoots off the Canvas and slowly comes back into frame. You can see this in the second animation in the *Pan Sequence*.

The third version of *Pict* in the *Pan Sequence* compromises by limiting how far into the corner the keyframes allow the motion to go. By leaving room for easing to overrun and swing back, the move is more acceptable. At least it doesn't shoot off the Canvas.

Scaling takes place around the anchor point, so if you scale to zoom and pan off to one corner at the same time, the image is moving farther and farther away from the point on which the scale is changing.

In the fourth animation, to try to correct this issue and the problem of the mismatched animations, another animation is added, the anchor point, which is not normally animated. Using the Distort tool, I dragged out the anchor point so that rather than moving farther and farther off the screen as the image moved, it remained centered in the screen. This produces a different result—not great, but acceptable, still sometimes subject to overshoot, especially on very large images.

The bottom line is you have three basic choices:

- Live with the jerky motion and lack of acceleration and deceleration.

- Apply easing to the center keyframes and leave room for the overshoot on the zoom-in.

- Or animate the anchor point as well to try and compensate for the overshoot.

Which option you use probably depends on the situation. Sometimes one might work better than another.

Split Screen

This is a common request for all sorts of purposes, for showing parallel action such as two sides of a phone conversation or to show a wide shot and a close-up in the same screen. It's easy to do if the video was specifically shot for a split screen. For a phone conversation, for instance, it should be shot so that one person in the phone conversation is on the left side of the frame and the other person is on the right side of the screen.

Look at the *Split Screen Sequence* in your Browser. Don't bother rendering it out; they're just still frames. In the first clip, Rich was shot on the left of the screen and Anita on the right. I had to crop the picture of Anita from one side, and because neither image left enough space for the other person, I had to move Rich farther to the left and Anita farther to the right.

14.6 Split Screen with Bar

Some people like to add a bar that separates the two images as in Figure 14.6. That's easy to do. Use the Generators to create a color matte and place it on the top track, as in *Split Screen Sequence*. Crop the matte left and right so that only a narrow stripe is visible over the join of the two frames.

Picture in Picture

By now you've probably figured out how to make a Picture in Picture (PIP). You just scale the image down to the desired size and position it wherever you want on the screen.

One note of caution about PIPs: many video formats, such as material converted from analog media, leave a few lines of black on the edges of the frame, as we saw when doing transitions. These are normally hidden in the overscan area of your television set and never seen. However, as soon as you start scaling down images and moving them about the screen, the black line becomes apparent. The easiest solution is to take the Crop tool and slightly crop the image before you do your PIP so as not to get the black lines, which give the video an amateur look. You might also want to add a border to the PIP to set it off, but that's for Lesson 15 when we look at "Bevel Border" on page 257.

A nice touch to add to PIPs is to give them a drop shadow from the Motion tab. This will help separate it from the underlying image and give a screen a sense of three-dimensionality.

Brady Bunch Open

This is one of the classic show opens on American television. It's relatively easy to reproduce in FCE using the techniques we've learned here. In the Browser is a clip called *BB.mov*. Play through it. This is the sequence we're going to build. It's based on the timing of the original show's open. If you know the Brady Bunch song, sing along. In building this sequence, we'll use still images rather than movie clips to conserve storage space.

1. Open the *Brady Bunch Sequence*.

2. You might have to render it out to play it at real speed, but it shouldn't take very long. Or use **Option-P** to play through the sequence as quickly as your computer can.

3. We're going to replicate this sequence. Look through it closely to get an idea of where we're going.

4. Make a copy of the *Brady Bunch Sequence* and open it. This sequence has markers set in where events will occur.

5. Use **Command-A** to select everything in the sequence and delete it.

6. To begin, you might want to lay *BB.mov* on V1 in your Timeline and lock the track. That way, it can act as a guide.

Sliding White Bar

The first step we have to take is to create the white bar that slides across the screen. That's easy enough.

1. From the Generators, make a color matte. In Controls, change the color from the default gray to full white.

2. This bar moves across the screen very quickly, so set the duration to about two seconds. You'll need even less than that, but if you make it too short, it may be difficult to work with in the Timeline.

3. Crop the top and bottom with the Crop tool in the Canvas. In the Crop controls, the Top value is 48.75 and the Bottom value is 47.92, creating a narrow bar. You could bring it into the Timeline first and then bring it back to the Viewer to crop it, but we know we're going to create a thin white line, so we may as well do it before loading it into your work sequence.

4. Drag the bar onto V3 at the head of the Timeline, leaving a video track free below it.

I'm assuming that you've placed *BB.mov* on V1 as a guide and have locked that track.

5. Slide the bar off the screen to the left so that you start in black. Open the white bar from the Timeline into the Viewer so you can set its Center coordinates to x –720, y 0.

6. Make sure the playhead is at the beginning of the clip, and set a Center point keyframe. This is the value we'll animate to make the motion.

7. Move the playhead to about 22 frames into the sequence.

8. With the Canvas in Image+Wireframe mode, using *BB.mov* as a guide, slide the bar across the screen to its end position, which is when about half the bar is off the screen on the right side. Hold down the **Shift** key as you slide it to constrain the movement to horizontal. Its Center coordinates should now be x 360, y 0.

9. In the Motion tab, add an Opacity keyframe. We are going to do a quick fade-out, so move three or four frames forward in time and then drag the Opacity slider down or type in a value of 0.

The keyframes you're adding are visible in FCE's new keyframe graph.

10. Move the playhead back to where the bar begins to fade out before you bring in the first image.

Fixing the Headshot

1. Open the bin in your Browser called *Graphics*.

It's probably best to leave it open. In the *Graphics* bin are the headshots of this sequence and the image for the pan and scan sequence we dealt with earlier. These are mostly PICT files and a few titles made with Title 3D. We'll get to those later on page 249.

2. Drag *HeadshotPink.pct* to V2 to the point where the bar begins fading out (see Figure 14.7).

14.7   Headshot and White Bar

At this point, the headshot will fill the frame with the white bar over it. We have to scale down and reposition the headshot.

3.   Open *HeadshotPink.pct* into the Viewer from the Timeline and pull down the Scale value. I scaled it down to 52.3.

4.   In the Canvas, slide the image to the right. For precision set the Motion tab values to *x* 166, *y* 0.

Next we have to crop the image.

5.   Select the Crop tool from the tools (keyboard shortcut **C** for crop). With the Crop tool, pull in the left and right edges a little bit. Crop the top and bottom until the headshot is a narrow slit hidden underneath the bar. Or hold down the **Command** key as you drag with the Crop tool to proportionately crop the image from both top and bottom. The settings used in the sequence are:

Left	6.38	**Right**	11.28
Top	50	**Bottom**	50

14.8   Scaled and Positioned Headshot

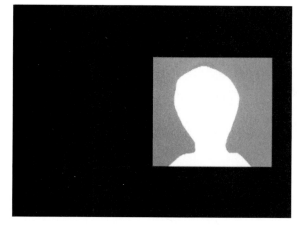

6.   In the Viewer, set keyframes for the Top and Bottom Crop values.

7.   Go forward about 14 frames into the clip. Type **+14** and press the **Return** key.

Be careful you don't do this in the Timeline, because if you don't drop any selected clips, you'll move the clip 14 frames in the Timeline rather than moving the playhead 14 frames.

8.   Open up the image by changing the Top and Bottom Crop values back to 0.

You've made the first part of the animation: the bar slides across the screen, stops, and fades out, and the headshot wipes open to reveal the picture as in Figure 14.8. Don't worry about the lengths of the clips yet. We'll fix that later.

Middle Headshots

Now we're ready to bring in the next set of headshots.

1. Go down to *Marker 1* in the timeline by using **Shift-Down Arrow** to take you to the next marker; **Shift-Up Arrow** takes you to the previous marker.

This is the point where the three headshots of the girls appear on the left.

2. From the *Graphics* bin, drag in the image *HeadshotGreen.pct* and place it on V3, the track above the pink headshot.

3. Again, first we have to scale and position it so that it's in the lower-left corner of the screen. The settings I used are:

Scale	29.59
Center	x –231, y 147
Crop Right	3.85

Next we need to fade in the image by ramping up the opacity. This again is a fairly quick fade-in, about 14 frames.

4. Set an Opacity keyframe at the beginning of the clip, and pull the value down to 0.

5. Move forward 14 frames, and bring the Opacity slider back up to 100.

We need two more copies of this image to make up the three headshots on the left of the screen. We'll do this by duplicating the one in the Timeline.

6. Hold down **Option-Shift** and drag *HeadshotGreen.pct* in the Timeline from V3 onto V4 to duplicate it.

7. Repeat the **Option-Shift**-drag from V4 to make another copy on V5.

At this stage, all three copies of *HeadshotGreen.pct* are on top of each other.

8. Select the clip on V4 and in the Canvas drag it upward, holding down the Shift key to constrain direction, and position the image about the center line of the screen.

9. Repeat for the clip on V5, dragging it up vertically to the top third of the screen. I used these Center position settings for the three layers:

V5	x –231, y –148
V4	x –231, y –1
V3	x –231, y 147

At *Marker 2*, where the fade-ups on the green headshots end, the screen should look like Figure 14.9.

14.9 Four Headshots On-Screen at *Marker 2*

Extending

So far, so good. Next you should extend the image files in the Timeline all the way down to *Marker 3*. You could drag them out to *Marker 3* with the Selector tool (A), or you could do an Extend edit.

1. Position the playhead at *Marker 3*.

2. **Command**-click on the edit points at the end of each clip in the Timeline, the green headshots as well as the pink headshot.

3. Press **E** to do an Extend edit.

Voilà. All of the clips will be extended to *Marker 3*, as shown in Figure 14.10.

At *Marker 3*, all four shots end, and we cut to black, but not for long. Next we have to bring in a new white bar from the right side.

4. Copy the white line from the beginning and paste it at the next marker on V3.

The line will appear with all of its motion and opacity just like the first time you made it. The only problem is that it's moving in the wrong direction.

Auto Select. In this version of FCE, you can simply copy and paste a clip on one track to another position on the same track. If you need to copy a clip from one track to another, you have to use the Auto Select buttons. To do this, select the clip you want and copy it. Then switch off all the Auto Select buttons except for the track you want to paste to. The easiest way to do this is to Option-click on the Auto Select button on the track you want to paste onto. This switches off auto select for all of the tracks except for the track you Option-clicked on.

The patch panel has several distinct functions. One of them, Destination Track selection, controls how material gets placed into your sequence. Auto Select is similar. It controls how edits—such as an Add edit—are executed, which items are copied, and even where items are pasted. If you copy a clip from the Browser and paste it into a sequence, this is controlled by the Destination Track selection. However, if you copy a clip from inside a sequence, either the one you're working in or another sequence, and paste the clip or clips into the Timeline, the Destination Tracks do not determine where the pasted material goes. That is set by the Auto Select function.

5. Open the copied clip at *Marker 4* into the Viewer.

6. Holding down the **Shift** key, slide the clip in the Canvas, which should still be in Image+Wireframe mode, across the screen and off the right side. This is the bar's new start position, which should be at *x* 720, *y* 0.

7. Go to the point where the fade-out begins, which should be at 16:00.

8. Slide the bar to the left to its end position, mirrored from the first time you did it. The Center position should be *x* –360, *y* 0.

9. From the *Graphics* bin, drag *HeadshotBlue.pct* onto V2 in the Timeline, placing it at the point where the bar begins its fade-out.

14.11 Paste Attributes

10. Select the clip *HeadshotPink.pct* that's on V2 and copy it.

11. With *HeadshotBlue.pct* selected in the Timeline, go to the **Edit** menu and choose **Paste Attributes** (**Option-V**). This brings up the dialog box in Figure 14.11.

12. Select **Basic Motion** and **Crop** from the dialog box. Because we've lengthened *HeadshotPink.pct*, make sure the checkbox at the top of the window for **Scale Attribute Times** is deselected. The default is for the box to be checked.

This duplicates the position and animation of the earlier shot. This ability to copy the attributes of a clip and to paste these attributes to one or more clips—pasting the copied clip's motion, filter, and audio settings—is a very powerful tool in Final Cut Express.

Now we have to reposition the blue headshot clip to the left side of the screen.

13. Holding down the **Shift** key, slide the image in the Canvas to the left so that it's underneath the white bar with a Center value of *x* −174, *y* 0.

Adding More Headshots

1. Right-click in the Timeline Ruler, and from the shortcut menu select **Marker 6** to jump down to that point.

2. Bring in the clip *HeadshotRed.pct* from the *Graphics* bin and place it on V3.

3. Copy the green headshot that's earlier on V3.

4. Select the new red headshot and again use **Paste Attributes** (**Option-V**). Apply **Basic Motion**, **Crop**, and **Opacity** with **Scale Attribute Times** deselected, as previously.

5. Now reposition its center so that it's on the opposite side of the screen with a Center value of *x* 232, *y* 147.

6. Again, Option-Shift-drag the copies of the clip from V3 to V4 and V5.

7. Holding down the **Shift** key to constrain movement, reposition the clips so that they appear one above the other on the right side of the screen. The Center values I used for these three shots are:

V5	x 232, y −148
V4	x 232, y −1
V3	x 232, y 147

8. Again, extend the green headshots and the blue headshot all the way down to *Marker 7*.

Again, the screen cuts to black.

New Headshots

1. Go down to *Marker 8* and bring in the clip called *HeadPinkSmall.pct* and place it on **V2**.

Though the image is the right size for the start of this section, the application will want to scale it for some reason. It's also in the wrong place.

2. First open the clip into the Viewer and reset the Scale value to 100.

3. In the Canvas, drag it straight up to the top of the frame so that the top edge of the image is at the top edge of the screen. My setting for the Center was *y* –129.

4. Go to *Marker 9*, and in the Viewer set a keyframe for the Crop Bottom value.

It's often easier to work backward in animation: to start with the end position on the screen and then animate the wipe-on.

5. Now go back to *Marker 8* and push the Crop Bottom value up to 100.

That's your start keyframe position to give you a quick wipe-on of the picture.

Marker 10 is where the next image comes in.

6. At *Marker 10*, place *HeadBlueSmall.pct* on **V3**.

7. Reset the Scale value for the new clip back to 100 and reposition to the bottom center of the screen. My Center value was *y* 125.

8. Go to *Marker 11* to set a Crop Top keyframe.

9. Go back to *Marker 10*, and again push the crop value up to 100.

At *Marker 11* both pictures should now be on the screen as shown in Figure 14.12. We're ready now to bring in the rest of the headshots.

14.12 Two Headshots On-Screen at *Marker 11*

Final Headshots

At *Marker 12* we'll first have to place keyframes on both the pink and blue headshots. Both images need to scale down slightly and have the left and right sides cropped so the images fit into their final position.

1. With the playhead at *Marker 12*, select both headshots and click on the **Keyframe** button in the Canvas to set a keyframe for the two

headshots. This is the simplest way to add a bunch of global motion keyframes for clips.

2. Change the scale of the Timeline window so that you can see most of the Timeline. The simple way is to use **Shift-Z** for **Fit to Window**.

3. Position the playhead at *Marker 13* to place the next headshots. **Shift**-select the three green headshots from near the beginning of the sequence and copy them.

4. **Option**-click on the **Auto Select** button for V4 to make sure it is the only one selected.

5. Paste the clips into the Timeline. It doesn't matter if the other tracks aren't selected.

The clips will stack on top of each other based on the lowest autoselected track, V4 in this case. The three duplicate green headshots should be on V4, V5, and V6, leaving V2 and V3 for the pink and blue headshots. Next do the same for the red headshots in the Timeline.

6. Select the red headshots and copy them.

7. Move the playhead back to *Marker 13*, and **Option**-click autoselect for V7.

8. Paste the clips into the Timeline.

Between *Marker 12* and *Marker 14* where the green and red headshots reach full opacity, the pink and blue headshots scale, crop, and slightly reposition to their final locations.

9. For the pink headshot, set the following values at *Marker 14*:

Scale	58.08	**Crop Left**	2.83
Center	x 0, y –148	**Crop Right**	5.23

10. For the blue headshot, my values at *Marker 14* are:

Scale	66.5	**Crop Left**	8.23
Center	x 0, y 139	**Crop Right**	11.16
		Crop Top	11.22

When you've positioned the clips about the screen, you should end up with the Canvas looking like Figure 14.13.

One more step needs to be taken before we put in the titles: extend the headshots down to the end of the sequence.

11. Right-click, and using the shortcut menu, move the playhead all the way down to *Marker 24*.

14.13 Eight Headshots On-screen at Marker 14

12. Then **Command**-click on the edits at the ends of all the headshots: pink, blue, the three greens, and the three reds.

13. Now do an Extend edit to stretch them out to the playhead.

Titles

We're finished with almost all of the headshots. Next we have to get the titles on the screen. I've prebuilt them for you using Title 3D. They are made with the Marker Felt font, which is the closest in the current Apple font collection to the original title style.

1. Lay the first title, *Main Title* in the *Graphics* bin, at *Marker 15* on track V10.

You'll see that it's at its full size and the right duration for the open, but we'll do a small scaling animation.

2. Go to *Marker 16*, open the title from the Timeline, and in the Motion tab set a Scale keyframe. This will be the end point of the main title animation.

3. Go back to *Marker 15* and set the **Scale** value down to 47.83.

4. Go down to *Marker 17*, and with the **Blade** tool (**B**), cut the title and throw away the rest of it.

At *Marker 18*, the next title, *Starring Title*, appears.

5. Drop *Starring Title* onto the same track as the main title.

6. Cut this title off at *Marker 19*.

7. At *Marker 20* bring in *Mom Title*. Because it overlaps with the final headshot we're going to bring in, it needs to be placed on a higher track, V11.

8. At *Marker 21* set an Opacity keyframe on *Mom Title*.

9. At the frame before *Marker 22*, set the Opacity down to zero. This will fade it out quickly.

10. Cut *Mom Title* with the Blade tool at *Marker 22*.

Final Polishing

We're on the home stretch now, just a few more steps to take. At *Marker 21* while *Mom Title* is fading out, one more headshot is fading in.

1. At *Marker 21* drag one more copy of the green headshot onto **V10** underneath *Mom Title*.

2. The final green headshot needs to be positioned, scaled, and cropped left, top, and bottom to fit the center square in the screen. The values I used are:

Scale	33	**Crop Left**	1.6
Center	x –5, y 0	**Crop Top**	5.12
		Crop Bottom	6.11

3. Set an Opacity keyframe for the green headshot at *Marker 21*, and set the value to 0.

4. Ramp up the Opacity to 100 at *Marker 22*.

5. At *Marker 22* the last title, *Alice Title*, just cuts in. Place it on V11.

6. Cut off both *Alice Title* and the center headshot at *Marker 24*.

Fade to Black

The last step we want to do is to fade to black. We could keyframe and ramp down the opacity on each of 10 layers now on the screen, but there's an easier way:

1. Make a short slug, three seconds will do, and place it on the topmost video track at *Marker 23*.

2. Set its Opacity down to zero, and add a keyframe to the slug in the Motion tab.

3. At *Marker 24* set the slug's Opacity up to 100 percent so that black fills the screen.

Congratulations! You've made the Brady Bunch open.

Summary

In this lesson we've looked at Final Cut's animation capabilities. You can use these tools to composite images one on top of another, using FCE's multilayer capabilities. We'll look at more compositing techniques in a later lesson, but first let's see how to use Final Cut's filters.

Lesson 15

Adding Special Effects Filters

In this lesson we're going to look at and work with Final Cut's filters to create some special effects. FCE offers a great variety of excellent effects. Unlike transitions that go between clips, filters are applied to single clips or parts of clips. In addition to the filters included with the application, other programmers are creating effects using Final Cut's scripting software FXBuilder, such as the collection of filters written by Christoph Vonrhein, Graeme Nattress, Klaus Eiperle, and others.

In the *Extras* folder of the DVD is a folder for CHV-FCE Plugins, which includes demo versions of some of Vonrhein's Keyframe-collection. These include the ability to add keyframes using a display built into the Canvas. There are 130 demo filters from Klaus Eiperle's *CGM DVE's Vol. 1+*, *CGM DVE's Vol. 2+*, and *CGM DVE's Vol. 3+*. Check out the HTML files and the demo movies that explain them. There are also demo versions of the G-Filters, an outstanding collection of image-control filters. And if you want a variety of film-look effects, including an excellent bleached color effect, the G Film Effects are outstanding. Read the PDF that accompanies them to learn how to fully use them. Also included is the demo version from John Wainwright of Lyric Media's Drawing Tools generators, which are very handy. Lyric also makes useful Motion Tracking plug-ins. To add new filters to FCE, place them in the *Plugins* folder while the application is closed. Drag the plug-ins into *Library/Application Support/Final Cut Express Support/Plugins*.

253

New to FCE 3.5 is the ability to animate filters. In previous versions, many effects could be faked by doing a dissolve between the clip without the effect and the clip with the effect, but in most of the effects this is more of a botch than a real effect animation. Radial Blur, Wind Blur, Zoom Blur, animated borders, all of the Distortion group of filters, garbage mattes, mask shapes, soft edges, widescreen edges, basic 3D, curl, mirror, blink effects, stop-motion blur, and viewfinder all have animateable properties that can't be reproduced with a simple dissolve. Third-party FXScript filters have also been created for Final Cut Pro that require keyframing to work. These will all now work in Final Cut Express.

Setting Up the Project

As before, begin by loading the material you need onto your media drive and reconnect the media if necessary. For this lesson we'll use the materials in the *Lesson 15* project.

Inside your project, you'll find in the Browser, the *Clips* bin, a master clip called *Dance*, and other sequences. One of the sequences is called *Effects Builder*, which demonstrates some of the filters we'll see in this lesson. As we go through the lesson, I'll show you how the effects in this sequence were made. There is also a sequence called *Video Filters*. In it each filter has been applied with its default settings to a two-second portion of *Dance1*, except for the two Color Smoothing filters, which we'll see in the next lesson. These have no adjustable controls anyway. For quite a few filters, such as the color correction filters, the default settings do nothing, but having them laid out like this lets you easily look at any filter and twiddle its knobs to see what it does.

You may have thought there were a lot of transitions. There are even more filters—84 of them, in fact—some of which aren't very useful, but there are still quite a few that allow you to do amazing things with video. Because there is so much redundancy in the filters, different filters that do basically the same things, as well as filters that don't function well in FCE, I'll only go through some of the important ones. In this chapter we'll look at some of the useful FCE filters, but some of the most important, Color Correction, Key, and Matte filters, we'll look at in the next lesson.

Applying a Filter

It couldn't be simpler to apply an effect in Final Cut Express:

1. Select the clip in the Timeline or in the Browser, and from the menu bar select **Effects>Video Filters**.

2. Pick a submenu and pick an effect.

If they're applied in the Browser, then every time that clip is used, the filter will go with it. If the effect is applied in the Timeline, it's applied only to that one copy of the clip. It is immediately applied with its default settings to the clip. If you prefer, you can drag the effect from the *Video Filter* bin inside the Effects panel of the Browser.

It's just as easy to remove an effect. Open the clip into the Viewer, go to the Filters tab, select the effect by clicking on its name, and press the **Delete** key (see Figure 15.1).

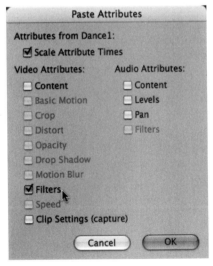

15.1 Selected Effect in Filters Tab

You can also select a clip(s) in the Timeline, and from the **Edit** menu choose **Remove Attributes** (keyboard shortcut: **Command-Option-V**). Make sure the Filters box is checked in the Remove Attributes dialog box, and the filter or multiple filters will all be removed.

Any number of filters can be added to a clip. The order in which the filters are applied can be important. The filter order can be changed by dragging the filters up and down to new positions in the order. Filters can also be turned on and off with a little checkbox. This allows you to leave a filter in place yet toggle its effect on and off to see what it's doing to the picture.

Filters can also be copied and pasted. If you select a clip that has a filter applied, you can copy the clip and use Paste Attributes (**Option-V**) to paste that filter or filters and their settings to any number of other clips simultaneously (see Figure 15.2).

15.2 Paste Filter Attributes

An important new feature in FCE 3.5 is the ability to keyframe filter values so that they can be altered over time. Look at the clip at *Marker 1* in the sequence *Effects Builder*. The middle portion of the clip *Dance2* has the effect applied to it, so that the whole clip does not need to be rendered (see the *Selective Filtering* tip). Partway through the clip, the Gaussian Blur filter comes in and ramps up from zero to 30, holds, and then ramps back down to zero. This feature makes possible effects that would have been much more complicated to do in earlier versions, or may not have been possible at all.

Favorites. Favorites are a great way to save effects, because you can not only save them as their default settings, but you can also save them as an effects pack, several effects that work together to produce a result. It's simple to do. Apply the effects and adjust them as you want them, and then with the Filters tab of the Viewer open, drag them to the Favorites bin, where you can rename them (see Figure 15.3). Notice that I created a bin within the Favorites bin, in which I put the filters, and that the stack order in which the filters were created is maintained in the bin.

The Favorites bin sounds great, but it has a serious downside, which is that Favorites are part of the application's preferences. So if you have to trash your prefs file, your favorites are gone with it. See "Favorites" on page 143 for one good solution to this problem.

15.3 Filter Pack in Favorites Bin

✎ Tip
Selective Filtering: You can add a filter to only a section of the length of a clip, which can be useful if you want to ramp up an effect while most of the length of the shot remains unchanged. To avoid having to render out the entire shot, you can apply the filter by selecting a section of the clip you want to effect with the Range Selection tool (GGG). To make the selection, stroke along the clip, the group of clips, or sections of the Timeline where you want to apply the filter. Choose the filter from the Effects menu, and you'll immediately see that only that portion of the Timeline picked with Range Selection will change the render color.

Let's begin looking at the filters by opening the empty *Sequence 1* and dragging one of the clips from the *Clips* bin into it. We'll start with *Dance1*. We'll apply some filters to this clip to see how they work.

Some Useful Filters

Gaussian Blur

Gaussian (pronounced *gousian*), named after the 19th-century German mathematician Karl Friedrich Gauss, produces a smooth blurring of the image. This blur does more, though, than just soften the picture. It allows you to blur channels separately through a pop-up menu (see Figure 15.4).

15.4 Gaussian Blur Controls

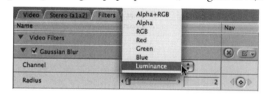

Selecting different channels can produce some interesting and unusual effects. Try applying the filter. With the clip in the Timeline selected, choose **Gaussian Blur** from the **Effects>Video Filters>Blur** menu. If you want to blur a couple of channels, apply the effect twice.

The order in which the effects are applied often makes a difference. Don't assume that because you apply Luminance blur and Blue blur you get the same effect by applying them the other way around. FCE processes the filters from the top down as they're stacked in the Filters tab. If you blur Luminance first, the color values smear, and you'll get less impact than if you blur the color value first.

The clip at *Marker 2* in the *Effects Builder* sequence shows Gaussian Blur applied twice, first with the Blue channel blurred and then with the Luminance blurred. This is followed by the same shot with the filters in reversed order: Luminance blur first and then Blue blur.

15.5   Bevel Border with a Width of 15

Bevel Border

Bevel Border is a nice touch to Picture-in-Picture effects (PIPs) and can be used to mask those nasty black edges we talked about in the previous lesson. Bevel creates a nice edge for scaled images (see Figure 15.5).

In the filter controls, the color picker is called Light Color, like the color of a gel a lighting director might put over a light that's falling across the beveled edges. You can also set the angle the light is falling from.

At *Marker 3* in the *Effects Builder* sequence, I have a short animation in which one image sucks back into a PIP, and as it does the Bevel Border appears around it. The image then pulls out to fill the screen again and the border closes down.

Channel Arithmetic

The Channel filters allow you an amazing degree of control of color and compositing. We'll look more closely at compositing in the Lesson 17 on page 290 but here the channel effects allow you to combine clips and apply color effects to them combined with compositing modes.

Arithmetic is a basic Channel effect. It composites a color to any one of the color channels R, G, or B, or all three combined, using one of the compositing modes on a pop-up menu (see Figure 15.6).

15.6 Arithmetic Channels Pop-Up Menu

Here they are called *operators,* but they are really compositing modes, which we'll look at in Lesson 17. In the *Arithmetic* sequence in your Browser, I have laid out a short clip of *Dance1* 12 times. Each clip has a different operator mode applied to its RGB value using the default color, gray. Look through these to get a basic idea of how the operators work. Most of the operators such as Add, Subtract, Darken, and Lighten are commonly known, but a couple of unusual ones, Ceiling and Floor, produce interesting results.

Channel Offset

Channel Offset is a cool filter, although you can easily take it to great extremes where strange effects will happen, especially if you use the **Repeat Edges** pop-up menu. The clip at *Marker 4* in the *Effects Builder* sequence shows you Channel Offset as applied in Figure 15.7.

Compound Arithmetic

15.7 Channel Offset Three Times with Large Offset and Repeat 8

Compound Arithmetic is based on an image placed in the Well (see Figure 15.8). Without an image there, the **Operator** pop-up menu produces little effect. It does not change by compositing with the layer below, only with itself. If an image is in the Well, the operator will apply to the image. Try it with text such as that on the clip at *Marker 5* in the *Effects Builder* sequence.

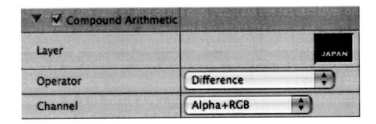

15.8 Compound Arithmetic Controls

Perspective

We'll skip the Color Correction, Keying, and Matte filter groups for the moment and devote the next lesson to them in detail. Let's move down to the Perspective group of filters and Basic 3D to start, which have become a important and powerful filters in FCE 3.5.

Basic 3D

Basic it is, but it does the job and can be used effectively for making customized effects such as bow ties, and also for animating effects. The controls for the x, y, z axes are self-explanatory (see Figure 15.9).

Notice the Center and Scale controls. Set these functions here and not in the Motion window. If you scale or reposition in Motion, the 3D will be cut off by the bounding box, as in Figure 15.10.

15.9 3D Controls

A *bow tie* is a broadcasting term for two images on the screen at the same time, often tilted toward each other to create the illusion of perspective (see Figure 15.11). Take a look at the stack at *Marker 6* in *Effects Builder*. That's a bow tie, most commonly used in two-ways (interviews from a remote site).

15.10 3D Scaled in Motion Tab and Scaled in 3D Controls

Both clips are tilted backward on the *y* axis, one by 45 degrees and the other by –45 degrees. The center points are shifted to move the images left and right, and both are scaled down to 60 to fit the screen. You can add all sorts of graphical embellishments such as borders, bars, and logos across the bottom and top.

15.11 Bow Tie

Basic 3D Animation

Let's look at creating the bow tie as an animation. In the Browser is a sequence called *Bow Tie* that already has the animation done for you.

1. Create a color matte and set the background color to whatever color you want. I used a bright blue.

2. Make the color matte five seconds in duration and edit it into the empty *Sequence 1*.

3. Switch off audio in the Timeline by clicking the **A1** and **A2** buttons in the Timeline patch panel.

4. Open the *Dance2* clip from the *Clips* bin, and with the playhead over the color matte in the Timeline, use Superimpose to edit it into the sequence.

5. Set **V2** as the destination track, open *Dance1* into the Viewer, and Superimpose that into the Timeline.

We're now ready to apply and keyframe the filter animation. As soon as the sequence starts, the two images are going to swing back into the bow tie position, which they reach at one second into the sequence. I could have just animated the top layer and already have the second layer in position, but I thought I'd rather see both images in motion. The two images hold that position until the three-second mark, and then the top image on V3 swings back and moves off the screen, while the middle image on V2 swings forward to fill the screen. As so often is the case with animation, we'll work backward.

6. In the Timeline, move the playhead to the one-second mark.

7. Apply the Basic 3D filter to each of the video clips in the sequence.

8. Open *Dance1* on V3 into the Viewer, and in the Filters tab set the following values:

Y axis rotation	−45
Center	x 160, y 0
Scale	60

9. Set keyframes for each of these values, which we'll animate.

10. Go back to the beginning of the sequence and set the values back to their default settings: zero Rotation, zero Center, and 100 Scale. Do not use the reset button to do this because it will remove the keyframes.

This is your animation for the beginning of the top layer. Next we'll animate the layer on V2.

11. Move back to the one-second point in the Timeline and open *Dance2* into the Viewer.

12. Set the following values with keyframes in the Filters tab:

Y axis rotation	45
Center	x −160, y 0
Scale	60

13. Go back to the beginning of the clip and set the Basic 3D values back to the default, which will swing open the clip on V1.

⯈ Tip

Constraining Dials: Holding down the Shift key will constrain the Basic 3D dials to 45-degree increments.

Let's now do the end part of the animation.

14. In the Timeline, move forward to the three-second mark.

15. Open each of the *Dance* video clips from the Timeline, and in the Filters tab, set keyframes for each of the six keyframed values, three in each clip.

These are holding keyframes. Between one second and three seconds, the values for these clips don't change. At that point they start to move and finish the animation at the four second mark.

16. At four seconds open *Dance1* from V3 in the Viewer and set its Filter values to:

Y axis rotation	−105
Center	x 370, y 0

You can leave the scale value at 60. This will swing the top layer open wide and move the edge off the screen. Now all we have to do is swing closed the clip on V2 so it fills the screen.

17. At four seconds set the *Dance2* Basic 3D filter values back to the default zero Rotation, zero Center, and 100 Scale.

That's it! You've created the basic animation that swings the images open to reveal both shots, holds them there for a while, and then brings one image back to fill the screen. You can use whatever timing and combination of animation you like, and this is only one of an unlimited number of motion animations you can create with this filter.

Flop

This filter can be a real lifesaver. If you have ever shot something in which someone is looking right to left and they really should be looking left to right, Flop is what fixes it. It reverses the direction of the image. Just be careful and watch out for words that might appear backwards, or hair parting that swings from side to side, and similar telltales that would give you away. The only control is a single pop-up menu, which lets you flop the default Horizontal and also allows you to reverse the image vertically or both horizontally and vertically at the same time.

QuickTime

Color Tint

Most of the QuickTime filters don't have much value or are redundant in FCE. One of the useful ones is **Color Tint**. This filter has one feature that is difficult to duplicate with any other tools. It allows you to create an X-ray negative effect (see Figure 15.12). It also has a subtle sepia tint, even less orange than FCE's Sepia.

15.12 Color Tint Controls with X-Ray Image

Color Tint also has Other, a wonderful tool. It allows you to set extremely different colors for light and dark. You can have a warm light color and a cold dark, a very nice duotone effect. The Brightness and Contrast controls really help with the duotone, letting you put in rich color while keeping the luminance from looking too washed out. Look at *Marker 7* in *Effects Builder*. It shows you the type of duotone effect that Color Tint can create.

Stylize

Find Edges

Find Edges is a neat filter that gives you a nice, stylized look (see Figure 15.13). Try it with the Invert checkbox on, which puts a hard, black outline on the edges. Both ways have their uses and can work well. Find Edges can be used to create interesting effects, especially when composited over other images or blended over itself.

Replicate

Replicate is a cool filter (see Figure 15.14). The default output produces only four images on the screen, but if you push the sliders, you can get 16 horizontal and 16 vertical. That's 256 very small images on the screen. It's a nice effect when it steps back 2, 4, 8, and 16.

15.13 Find Edges

In previous versions of the application you could create an animation by cutting up your clip and applying different replicate values to each clip to step up through the shot. Then cut to a second image that was also bladed into pieces to step back down through the values. Now that can easily be done simply by animating the filter values. Look at the two clips in *Effects Builder* at *Marker 8*. Being able to do this effect without cutting up the clip means that you can move the clip and edit the clip without difficulty.

15.14 Replicate Controls

▼ ☑ Replicate		⊗ ☑▾
Horizontal	◄ ⬜————————►	2	◄◈►
Vertical	◄ ⬜————————►	2	◄◈►

Video

De-interlace and Flicker

This has to be one of the most-used filters in FCE, if for no other reason than that it's used to remove video interlacing when making freeze frames. If you place a freeze frame of a clip with a lot of motion in it, the freeze will twitch horribly as the interlacing switches between the lines. The way around the problem is to apply the **De-interlace** filter to the freeze frame. The de-interlaced freeze frame will play back smoothly when edited into video.

The De-interlace filter has only a single control, a pop-up menu that lets you select a field. Choose whichever looks better. You can also use the Flicker filter to do this, which gives you three separate settings, letting you choose how much flicker removal to apply if there is only a minimal amount of jittering in the freeze frame. Flicker is also used to overcome that horrible shimmering effect you get when there are thin, horizontal lines across the screen, such as serifs in text, thin lines of newsprint on the screen, stripes in a shirt, Venetian blinds in the distance, and a host of other possible causes. These are all caused by interlace flicker, and Flicker, which probably should be called De-Flicker, helps remove it. It's particularly useful for minimizing flickering that can occur during scrolling titles as serifed fonts run up the screen.

De-interlace or Flicker should also be used before you export a still frame with motion. In that case, the frame will look like Figure 15.15. If you don't remove the interlacing on an image with movement, you get a still that looks like Figure 15.16.

The other use for the De-interlace filter is to help make video look more like film. The high temporal resolution of NTSC video, giving 60 discrete fields every second, is one of the reasons that video looks like video; but film, which has a lower frame rate and no interlacing, produces a more blurred motion, a softer look that we associate with film. Removing interlacing is the first step toward trying to recreate that ever-popular film look. The best way to create a film-look effect though is to use the G Film Effects filters from Graeme Nattress.

Summary

This is just the tip of the iceberg of some of the filters in FCE. I urge you to look through them and use the *Video Filters* sequence to explore its capabilities. By now you should have a fairly good idea of what you can do with this application and should be well on your way to creating exciting, interesting, and original video productions. We still have to look at an important group of filters for Color Correction, Keying, and Mattes, which we shall do next.

15.15 De-interlaced Still Frame

15.16 Interlaced Still Frame

Lesson 16

Color Correction, Keys, and Mattes

Setting Up the Project

One more time, begin by loading the material you need onto your media drive and reconnect the media if necessary. For this lesson we'll use the materials in the *Lesson 16* project.

Inside your project, you'll find in the Browser, the *Clips* bin, a master clip called *Dance*, and other sequences, *Keying* and *Color,* that we'll look at here.

Color Correction

Good exposure and color begins in the shooting. It's easier and always better to do it correctly to begin with rather than trying to fix it in post-production. That means lighting the scene well, exposing it correctly, setting your white balance correctly, and not leaving the camera's auto exposure and white balance to do the guessing. If you're producing work for output on a television set, it is essential that you view your color correction work on a properly set-up production monitor, not the computer monitor. The color and luminance values on television sets are very different from computer monitors. Do not trust the computer screen to display the colors and luminance values the way they will appear on TV. Watch your video monitor while you work, or at least a TV set. Don't try to rely on your computer monitor.

The color correction tools are professional-strength tools, so use them carefully. All of the color correction tools should be real-time capable, which can really speed up your workflow. Broadcast Safe is the perfect tool to use if you suspect your video is too bright for television. Just drop it on a clip, and you'll immediately see if it reduces the video level. It will have no effect if the image does not need correction.

Although **Broadcast Safe** can be used as a magic bullet, you do have quite a bit of control on the filter to set it to whatever parameters you want (see Figure 16.1). The default is **Conservative**. The values controlled by the sliders are based on luminance value standards from zero to 100. A value of 100 is considered peak white, and 0 is pure black. In practice, most cameras, especially consumer camcorders and prosumer equipment, shoot at levels much higher than 100, up to 109 and beyond, what's called superwhite. Televisions are designed to accept a video signal with peak white at 100, although they too have a good deal of tolerance, and most newer TV sets can readily accept values around 110 and 120.

16.1 Broadcast Safe Controls

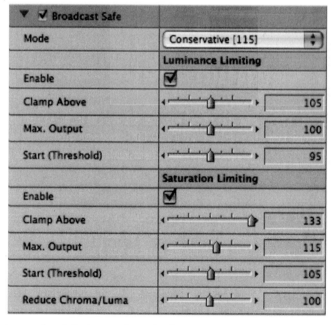

Notice that as the default, you limit both the luminance values and the chrominance values. If you want to keep the luminance in an acceptable range but do something outrageous with the color, you have to make sure

Custom—Use Controls Below is selected from the pop-up menu. Then uncheck the Saturation Limiting checkbox and go to town.

Color Corrector

Unlike most filters, Color Corrector, as well as the Chroma Keyer in the Key submenu, has two panels in the Viewer (see Figure 16.2). One marked Filter has sliders and numerical controls to adjust the values, and a useful button at the top lets you switch to the **Visual** display. The second panel with the name of the filter has the visual interface that you are most likely to use (see Figure 16.3).

Let's look at the visual controls for Color Corrector. At the top is a grouping of useful buttons. The Numeric button takes you to the Filter panel. There is also the little checkbox that allows you to toggle the filter on and off. The eye icon tells you that you're in the Visual panel, if you didn't realize that already. There is a small timeline that has the basic timeline controls and timecode reference.

16.2 Top of the Viewer Window with Color Corrector Tab

16.3 Color Corrector Visual Display

There is the grab handle, which lets you pull the effect onto a clip, similar to the grab handle in the Audio panel. On either side of the grab handle are some very useful buttons. The first to the right, with the number **1** on it, allows you to copy your Color Corrector settings to the next clip in the Timeline. The second button to the right, marked with the number **2**, can be even more useful. This copies the settings not to the next clip in the Timeline, but to the second clip down the Timeline. For instance, if

★ *Tip*

Before and After: With the visual display active in the Viewer, you can quickly toggle the filter on and off to switch between before and after views with the keyboard shortcut Control-1.

you have a two-camera setup for a wedding or a theatrical performance that basically switches back and forth between the two cameras and you want to color-balance one camera to the other, you need to color-correct every other shot in the Timeline. Clicking the **2** button will copy the settings to the next shot for that camera. You can quickly copy the settings to every other shot in the Timeline.

The two buttons marked with a **1** and **2** to the left of the grab handle act similarly. They let you copy the **Color Corrector** settings to the clip you're working on from either the shot before, the **1** button, or from the shot before last in the Timeline, the **2** button.

Let's look at the central control panel in **Color Corrector**, which has two color wheels, four sliders, and a few buttons. The left wheel controls the color balance of the image, and the right changes the hue, just like the hue control on a television set. Below are four self-explanatory sliders. The first controls the white levels; the second, the midtones; and the third, the black level. The fourth slider adjusts the Saturation or amount of color in the image. The three buttons stacked together on the right are auto setting buttons. These are the best place to start with any image. From the top, the buttons are Auto White, Auto Contrast, and Auto Black. To the right of that is an eyedropper, a color swatch, and a white **Reset** button, which doesn't work correctly in FCE.

☜Tip _____
Reset: To reset the filter in the Color Corrector visual display, hold down the Shift key and click on either of the white buttons to the lower right of the color hubs.

In the *Color* sequence, look at the pair of images at *Marker 2*. The first is probably a bit darker than it should be. The image right after it has the Color Corrector filter applied.

To use the filter, you should begin by clicking the **Auto Contrast** button, the middle of the three-button stack. Do not click on it repeatedly. You'll just keep shifting the contrast. Just click once. Next set the **Auto Black** and then the **Auto White**. Again, just one click for each button. Always adjust the luminance, whites, mids, and blacks before you start adjusting the colors. I usually start with the mids. A little adjustment there will spread the contrast levels nicely and brighten the image without increasing the overall level. Remember, as with almost all FCE sliders, if you hold down the **Command** key, you'll "gear down" the drag, giving you finer control.

The image at *Marker 3* in *Color* has been overexposed. With it is an attempt at fixing the problem. As you can see, you'll usually get a better result fixing an image that's been underexposed than one that's overexposed and washed out.

Color Corrector obviously is for color as well as luminance and contrast. At *Marker 4* in Color is another still image. Something's certainly gone wrong here. It looks like the white balance hasn't been set correctly. Color Corrector is the easiest tool to fix this. To correct it, start with the **Auto Contrast** button and set your luminance levels to what looks correct to you. It's not going to take much work. The exposure is correct; just the color is wrong.

What we're going to do is pick white in the picture and use that to set the correct color balance. There are a couple of tricks to this:

1. First, take the Saturation slider and crank it way to the right, terribly oversaturating the image.

This emphasizes any color cast in the image, making it easier to pick out what's wrong. The second trick is to find the right bit of white. The temptation is to use something that's very bright, but the problem is that what's very bright often is quite washed out and has almost no color information in it. Look for something that's white but not at full luminance or something that's neutral gray. Here's how you do it with Color Corrector:

2. Just to the bottom left of the **Balance** wheel is a tiny eyedropper. (Not the eyedropper next to the **Auto Contrast** button.) Use this to pick something in the scene that should be white or gray. In this image nothing is very oversaturated, so I'd pick something off the white roof of the van.

This will immediately pull the color back toward a truer representation of the image. You'll also notice that the button in the center of the Balance wheel has shifted toward the red direction. When I pulled the white, it gave the image a slightly more magenta tinge than I would have liked. Again, this was apparent because the Saturation was turned up. You'll want to fine-tune the color more toward the yellow-red direction of the Balance wheel.

3. Before you do that, slide the Saturation slider back down to normal, and you'll see that the image is close to looking correct.

4. Push the button in the center of the Balance wheel a little farther to yellow-red.

There's a little gotcha here. All of the color wheels are geared down by default. So you have to move the button a lot to get any effect. In the color wheels, as with Balance, you use the **Command** key to gear up. This is the only place in FCE that this occurs.

Limiting Color Effects

Some important functions are on the Filter panel only. These are the whole group of controls for Limit Effect Controls, Edge Control, and Mask Control. Without having the visual interface for the Limit Effect Controls and the other functions, they are quite tricky to use, although with some care you can effectively limit color control to only particular portions of the image. Look at the two stills at the beginning of the sequence called *Color*. The color effect is changing the color of the woman's jacket. I did this by turning on the Limit Effect Controls and isolating the color of the jacket. The settings I used are in Figure 16.4.

1. To begin to isolate the color of the jacket, turn down the color saturation to zero.

2. Turn the Chroma Center dial until you find the color that's being desaturated.

3. Then by increasing the chroma width, isolate just that area of color.

4. Once the jacket color is isolated, turn the saturation back on.

5. Then use Phase Shift in the upper portion of the controls to change the jacket color from its original lime green to a more conservative tan. You could also do this with the Hue hub in the visual panel.

Notice that two clips are stacked in the *Color* sequence. That's because I used another filter, the Four-Point Garbage Matte, to limit the area that I had to color select.

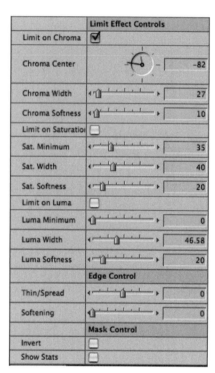

16.4 Limit Effects Control

Desaturate and Sepia

Desaturate

This is the quickest, easiest way to remove color. The default Amount of 100 is a fully desaturated image, pure black and white. I find it makes a somewhat flat-looking black and white. Desaturate does not only *de*saturate, it will also *over*saturate. Desaturate can go into negative values, which overchromas the image. It won't take much of a push into the negative numbers to get excessively colorful, especially if the scene already has a lot of color, particularly reds. To do anything other than desaturate quickly, you should use FCE's Color Correction filters.

Sepia

The default setting generates a rich brown color without being too orange (see Figure 16.5). Bringing down the Amount slider to around 60, blending in the underlying color, makes an interesting look.

16.5 Sepia Controls

Although the filter is called Sepia, the color picker allows you to tint the image any color you'd like. Sepia also has a Highlight slider, which increases the brightness in the highlight areas, punching them through the tint color. Pulling the Highlight slider into negative numbers will deepen the shadow areas.

Keying

Keying is used to selectively cut out areas of the image. The most efficient way to do this is chromakeying, the technique of removing one specific color from an image. It's how weather reporters stand in front of weather maps. The two commonly used colors are blue and green. Because of the way the DV format works, it's easier to chromakey green than blue. On the other hand, if your subject has to wear green for St. Patrick's Day, you'll have to use blue.

The key to keying is to shoot it well. Poorly shot material just will not key properly. For chromakeying, the background blue or green screen must be evenly lit and correctly exposed so that the color is as pure as possible. Video, and DV even more so, has many limitations of color depth and saturation that make good keying difficult.

FCE has tools to do keying, the best of which is the Chroma Keyer, in my opinion. In your Browser is a bin called Keying, which holds the elements we'll work with in this part of the lesson. Open the *Keying* sequence. This has a couple of still images to work with. On V1 in the sequence is a still of the Stanford University's Hoover Tower called *Background.pct*, and on V2 is the image to chromakey called *Blue.pct*. We're going to work with a quite difficult blue-screen image.

Color Smoothing –4:1:1

Color Smoothing –4:1:1 and Color Smoothing –4:2:2 are used to smooth color compression artifacts in heavily compressed material like DV and HDV. These filters are designed to reduce the effects of pixelization in digital video. When working in FCE with DV-resolution, you should use the 4:1:1 filter, which is the color space used by DV. You should apply the filter first to any clip that you want to key. The filter has no controls. You just drop it on the clip first and apply the Chroma Keyer filter to remove the green or blue that you want to key out of the image.

HDV material, however, uses a different color space, 4:2:0, for which there is no suitable color smoothing filter in FCE. If you need to key HDV material, I would suggest you look in Graeme Nattress' Film Effects filter, whose G Chroma Sharpen will do smoothing for 4:2:0 HDV material.

Chroma Keyer

If the material is properly shot and lit, there is no special trick to chromakeying in FCE, just a lot of shifting of sliders. I would ignore the Blue and Green Screen and Color Key filters and just work with the Chroma Keyer. Let's start by examining some of the controls in this perhaps daunting-looking filter.

1. Begin by applying Color Smoothing –4:2:2 to *Blue.pct* on V2. This may be the only instance in which you'll use this filter because FCE does not normally work with full-color space video.

2. Apply Chroma Keyer to the same clip.

3. Open the clip into the Viewer and go to the Chroma Keyer tab (see Figure 16.6).

16.6   Chroma Keyer Controls

The controls show a Color Range slider at the top, the rainbow-colored bar. Below that is the Sat (saturation) control and Luma (luminance) control. Each has a round radio button that allows you to reset the parameter and a square checkbox that lets you toggle the parameter on and off. Each of the controls has handles that can be adjusted. Pulling the buttons on the top of the sliders will increase or decrease the range of the effect, and pulling on the buttons at the bottom of the slider will control the tolerance, how widely the parameter will be applied to adjacent colors or saturation or luminance values.

16.7 Chroma Keyer
Buttons

On the right are three important buttons (see Figure 16.7). At the top is the critical eyedropper. Below that, in the middle, is a three-way toggle switch with a key icon. Its default position is colored gray, which shows the final output of the image. Click it and it will change to white, which will show you a black-and-white representation of what you're keying. Click it again and the button goes blue, which shows you the original source material. The bottom button with the keystone icon will invert the key, which can be useful in some instances.

4. Click on the eyedropper, click in the blue screen behind the flowers in the Canvas, and you're practically done. Almost instantly the bulk of the blue will disappear.

5. Check the matte by clicking on the **Matte/Key** button.

You'll see most of the background has been keyed out, as in Figure 16.8. This is a grayscale representation of transparency. What is white is opaque in the *Blue.pct* clip, and what is black is transparent. You'll see the black if you switch off the visibility for the background layer on V1.

6. Widen the Color Range slightly with the button pulls at the top and broaden the Luma controls a bit, and you'll have a pretty good key.

✏ Tip
Color Selection: If you hold down the Shift key, you can click on multiple points, and the Chroma Keyer controls will extend the range of values, color, saturation, or luminance as needed. Also, if you hold down the Shift key and drag a line through the area you want to sample, the tool will use the range of values along the line to set up the controls.

16.8 Matte Display

If you look closely at your key in FCE, you'll probably see a rather unnatural color fringe around the edges of the flower. This can be a little tricky to eliminate.

7. Push up the Edge Thin control a bit.

8. At the very end of the Softening control is a tiny little triangle. Give it a few clicks. This will move Softening incrementally.

9. Try adding a little Enhance, but not too much, or the edges will start to turn yellow.

Spill Suppressor–Blue and Spill Suppressor–Green

The Spill Suppressors are used if there is a blue or green cast on the edges of the image (see Figure 16.9). This often happens when you get reflected light from the blue screen wall falling on the edges of a curved object, like a person's shoulders. The Spill Suppressor replaces the blue in the image with black, like a shadow area. This is fine on the object you want to leave, but if the background color has not been keyed out sufficiently, it can leave a dark edging on the screen.

16.9 Spill Suppressor Control

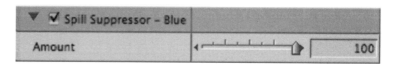

You might have to pull down the Amount slider substantially, although usually only a small amount will be sufficient to do the work.

Matte Choker

Adding another tool in the mix here may be helpful. The Matte Choker is useful, but it isn't in the Key package. It's in the Matte package, which we'll see in a moment. The Matte Choker is most commonly used as a keying tool, however, and adding it to the key will improve the image.

The controls (see Figure 16.10) are basically the same as the Edge Thin and Softening controls in the Chroma Keyer, but now you are adding a second line of choking to the key's edges after the Spill Suppressor has done its work. If you find that your keying is cutting too much into the image, you can also use the Matte Choker to bring back some of the cut-off image by pushing the slider down into negative numbers.

16.10 Matte Choker

Matte

Eight-Point Garbage Matte

A garbage matte allows you to roughly cut out a section of the image by selected points on the screen that define corners of the picture. In addition to the **Eight-Point Garbage Matte** there is a Four-Point Garbage Matte as well, the only difference being the numbers of points available (see Figure 16.11). Notice that in version 3.5 all of the points and most of the other controls are fully animateable, so you can change the shape of the garbage matte over time.

▼ ☑ Eight–Point Garbage Matte		⊗	
View Mode	Preview		
Corners			
Point 1	⊕	−360 , −240	◁◈▷
Point 2	⊕	0 , −240	◁◈▷
Point 3	⊕	360 , −240	◁◈▷
Point 4	⊕	360 , 0	◁◈▷
Point 5	⊕	360 , 240	◁◈▷
Point 6	⊕	0 , 240	◁◈▷
Point 7	⊕	−360 , 240	◁◈▷
Point 8	⊕	−360 , 0	◁◈▷
Edges			
Smooth	⇧⌐	0	◁◈▷
Choke	◁	0	◁◈▷
Feather	⇧⌐	0	◁◈▷
Options			
Invert	☐		
Hide Labels	☐		

16.11 Eight-Point Garbage Matte Controls

The controls allow you to set eight points on the image, beginning with Point 1 in the upper-left corner. The points go clockwise around the screen, starting with that corner (see Figure 16.12). It's best to try to keep the points in those relative positions. Because lines connect the points to each other, it's important to avoid having the lines cross each other. Bizarre shapes can be created with your image if the lines cross.

In the controls there are eight points that can be placed anywhere on the screen using the **Crosshairs** button. Click in the crosshairs for Point 1 and click in the Canvas. The point will be placed there. It's as simple and as difficult as that.

16.12 Garbage Matte Canvas Display

▷ *Tip*
Setting the Point: The easiest way to apply the garbage matte point is to click one of the point's crosshairs in the Filter panel and then mouse down in the Canvas, which will update as soon as it can. If you hold the mouse down and drag the point around the screen, the image will be pulled around on the screen as quickly as your computer can manage it. The faster your computer, the sooner this will happen.

Three **View Modes** can be selected from the pop-up menu at the top of the controller:

1. **Final** is the output as seen on the screen along with the underlying layers, but without any point markers.

2. Preview is the same as Final, only with the points indicated and with the point numbers. The number display can be toggled with the checkbox.

3. **Wireframe** shows you the matte outline, but only on the layer on which you're working, without cutting away the rest of the image to reveal any underlying layer.

Below the points are some important tools. The first is **Smooth**, which rounds out the corners in your matte. You can combine it with **Feather** to create soft-edged mattes with interesting organic shapes (see Figure 16.13).

Without Smooth applied, **Choke** is a subtle adjustment of the matte shape. Moving Choke into negative numbers will slightly reduce the matte, and pushing the value up will increase the size of the matte.

16.13 Matte without Smooth, and with Smooth and Feather at 20

Finally, an important but often overlooked checkbox is **Invert**. This feature allows you to create a matte around an object that you want to remove, and then rather than keeping the area you defined, by checking the **Invert** box, you'll cut it out.

Extract

Extract is a real beauty of a filter. It's a little unpredictable to work with, but with luck it will create interesting combinations of matte shapes, especially when used with a garbage matte to define a core area. **Extract** gives you deceptively simple controls together with a three-up display in the Canvas, if needed (see Figure 16.14).

▼ Video Filters	Source
▼ ☑ Extract	Matte
	Final
View	Source, Matte, Final
Threshold	38
Tolerance	50
Soft	50
Copy Result	to RGB
Invert	☐

16.14 Extract Controls

> ⭐ *Tip*
> **Do It First:** It's a good idea to apply your garbage matte before you reposition or scale your image. The points are based on the image frame. So if you move the image before you apply the garbage matte, it's hard to pin down where the points should be because they're not referring to the new shape and position and scale of the image, but to its original position in the frame. So apply your garbage matte, and make it the shape you want before you scale, center, or rotate the picture about the screen.

A pop-up menu lets you select if you want the extraction applied to RGB or to the alpha channel of the image. Applying it to RGB will make a high-contrast black-and-white image. By adjusting **Threshold, Tolerance**, and **Softness**, you can vary the image substantially. It gets really interesting when you apply it to the alpha channel instead of the RGB value. Then you cut through to an underlying layer with a great amount of control. It's useful for pulling an alpha channel from an image that doesn't have one.

Look at the file in the Browser called *TIFF.tif*. Apply the Extract filter to it with Copy Result to Alpha Channel, and you'll see that with hardly a

☆Tip

Matte Boundaries: Although you can extend the points out into the grayboard, the matte doesn't extend out there. If only it would. The matte is still bound by the edges of the frame. So if you hope that extending the points out from the screen so that Feather will not affect one edge of the image, give up. Feather will unfortunately occur around the frame edges.

tweak of the sliders, the white will disappear from around the word. It's set up at *Marker 1* in the *Effects Builder* sequence.

Mask Shape

Mask Shape is a useful filter that lets you easily control the shape of the image. The controls allow basic shapes (see Figure 16.15) and have Horizontal and Vertical sliders that let you adjust the default shapes. I'll show you a practical application.

An interesting use for Mask Shape is to create borders using color mattes. It's simple to do. Look at the clip stack at *Marker 2* in *Effects Builder*. On V1 is the *Dance2* clip with **Mask Shape>Round Rectangle** applied. On V2 is a color matte in pale yellow. The color also has Round Rectangle applied to it twice. The first time it's applied inverted. This leaves the matte with the picture showing through and fills the rest of the screen with the color. Applying the shape again, only slightly larger and not inverted, will cut the color outside in the Round Rectangle. I also used **Antialias** to soften the stair-stepping around the mask.

16.15 Mask Shape Controls

Mask Shape also allows you to create an animated highlight area. What in previous versions required multiple layers of video can now be done with only two. At *Marker 4* in *Effects Builder*, I have created an effect with a highlight area that follows an individual in a group as the camera pans over them.

1. To do this effect, first place two copies of the clip you want to do the effect on one on top of the other.

2. To the top layer, apply the Mask Shape filter. Nothing will appear to happen because the two images are identical.

3. To the bottom layer, apply the Color Corrector or **Brightness and Contrast** filter from the **Image Control** submenu.

Now you can see the area being masked off on the top layer.

4. Next, move to the middle of the clip, where it's easiest to see the layer you have to affect. In the Filters tab for the image on the top layer, use pop-up and the Horizontal Scale and Vertical Scale sliders to set the shape you want, as well as the Center point to position it roughly.

5. To animate the shape, start by setting the Canvas to **Fit All** in the Zoom pop-up, or by setting a value that lets you see the grayboard around the Canvas.

6. Go to the point on the screen just before the subject starts appearing as the camera pans, and using the **Crosshairs** button, set a Center value that's off the screen.

7. In this case we only need to animate the Center value, so set a keyframe there. If the image changed shape or size, you could animate the scale of the shape as well.

8. Because the pan is pretty constant, go to the point in the clip where the subject has exited the frame on the far side and set a new Center value off the left edge of the screen.

9. Next, step through the clip and see how the animation flows, adjusting the position of the shape to match the movement of the subject and the camera.

10. I also added a **Mask Feather** filter from the **Matte** submenu to soften the edges of the shape.

11. Finally, I animated the Brightness and Contrast filter to ramp down and back up the value of the Brightness to darken the image as the shape moves onto the screen, and bring it back to normal as the shape moves off.

Widescreen

This filter lets you take a standard 4:3 video and crop it to one of seven standard cinema shapes (see Figure 16.16) to create a letterbox effect.

This is a crop, not an overlay, so the area outside the image is empty. If you want to place a color there, you should put a color matte underneath it, as I did in *Final Letterbox*.

The **Offset** slider allows you to move the image up and down without altering the position. Negative numbers drag the image downward; positive numbers move the image upward, the opposite of the way the *y* axis functions in the Text tool.

> **☆ Tip**
>
> **NightScope:** If you apply Color Corrector to a clip, taking down the black level a bit, then use the Extract filter, followed by Color Corrector again with a green tint and the white level brought down considerably, as well as the mids choked down, you can create quite a credible Night-Scope look for your image. Look at the clip at *Marker 2* in Effects Builder. A touch of Gaussian Blur softens the hard-edged look of the Extraction. It needs a little fiddling, depending on the image, but it's fun, especially if you can add a little blurred glow to it with a composite mode, which we'll talk about in the next lesson.

16.16 Widescreen Controls

If you want to make a whole sequence widescreen—which is probably the point, rather than applying it to individual clips—nest the whole sequence, and apply the filter to the nest.

1. Make a new sequence, naming it something useful, such as *Final Letterbox* as I've done in the Browser for the *Lesson 16* project.

2. Drag your edited sequence into the new open Timeline window, in this case called *Edited Sequence* in your Browser. This is now a nested sequence, with the edited sequence nested inside the new sequence.

3. Select the nested sequence in the *Final Letterbox* Timeline, and apply the Widescreen filter to it.

4. To access the settings for the filter, simply select the nest in the Timeline and press the **Return** key or **Option**—double-click to open it into the Viewer. You can now go to the Filters tab to change the settings.

⋙ Tip _____

Recursive: Nested sequences are recursive. That is, any changes you make in the nested *Edited Sequence*, shortened or lengthened clips will also appear in the master sequence *Final Letterbox*.

If you need to use **Offset**, you may not want to do it here because it will offset all of the clips in the nest. It would be better to open the nest, use the Motion tab of any shots you want to offset, and move them up or down in the frame as necessary.

There are other ways to create the widescreen effect. You can use Four-Point Garbage Matte. Create the shape you want for the masked area, and use the **Invert** button. Or for a simple widescreen without the border, you could also use the Crop tool. Remember to drag with the **Command** key to get opposite sides to move equally. Or you could make a mask in Photoshop, a black area at top and bottom with transparency in the middle. I like this way best, particularly for projects such as commercials, because it lets me create interesting effects with the mask edges, such as graphic elements that overlap the widescreen line, different color masks, text, and logos.

Summary

With this lesson we've looked at some of the most important filters in FCE: color correction, keying, and creating mattes for our clips. We need to explore one more aspect of FCE before we're ready to put our creations out on tape, the web, or some other delivery format, and that is compositing, the topic of our next two lessons.

Lesson 17

Compositing

Compositing is the ability to combine multiple layers of video on a single screen and have them interact with each other. This capability adds great depth to FCE. Until now we have been looking primarily at horizontal editing. In compositing we're dealing more with vertical editing, building stacks of layers. Compositing allows you to create a montage of images and graphics that can explain some esoteric point or enhance a mundane portion of a production.

This kind of work has become the staple of wedding video production, for instance. Good compositing work can raise the perceived quality of a production. Compositing is used for a great deal of video production work on television— commercials, of course—but also on news programs and for interstitials, the short video that appears between sections of a program. Be warned, though, that compositing and graphics animation are not quick and easy to do. Most compositing is animated, and anima-tion requires patience, skill, and hard work.

Setting Up the Project

Begin by opening the *Lesson 17* project from your hard drive and going through the reconnect process. Inside your copy of the project *Lesson 17*, you'll find the *Clips* bin, two master clips (*Village and Ceremony)*, and some sequences.

As in the previous lesson, a couple of sequences contain examples of effects used in the lesson. They're called *Composite Stacks* and *Composite Modes*. Before we get into compositing, we should take a quick look at the Generators, because these provide us with some useful compositing tools.

Generators

We used the **Generator** pop-up menu to create text files as well as color mattes, but let's take a moment to look at what else is under that little A (see Figure 17.1). There's Bars and Tone or both HDV and DV NTSC and PAL, and submenus for Boris, Matte, Others (which are more video test signals), Render, Shapes, Slug, and Text. We're going to look at a few of the Generators.

17.1 Generators Pop-Up

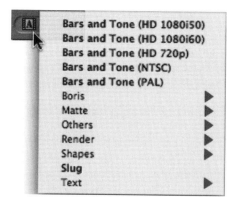

Render

The Render generators are a great tool and a hidden secret inside FCE's Generators. They allow you to create compositing tools that will alter the shapes and textures of video and graphics images. Be aware that the blackness you see in Render items and in the Shapes is not the emptiness you normally see in the Viewer or Canvas around text or animated images. What you see in the gradients and shapes is actual opaque black without any transparency, such as in the highlight in Figure 17.2.

Custom Gradient

Custom Gradient lets you create gradient ramps or radials, either from the default black and white or from two colors (see Figure 17.3). As with titles, you can create one in the Viewer and pull it into the Timeline, double-click on it, and use the controls in the Viewer while seeing your work updated in the Canvas. New in this version of FCE is the ability to animate the Custom Gradient's shape, color, and other controls.

17.2 Default Highlight

The default is a white-to-black gradient. The crosshairs let you pick where the white point or start color begins, and **Gradient Direction** controls the angle at which the gradient proceeds, the default being pure white on the left and going to pure black on the right. In a **Radial Gradient** only the crosshairs have effect; there is no direction. Generally you should leave **Dither** off. However, when a gradient shows *banding*—when what should have been a smooth transition from one color to another instead appears as sections of color with a clear edge where one color changes to another—then Dither should be turned on. Dither will add some noise to the image to break up the banding, which is usually caused by the way codecs compress the video. They often are not able to make the fine distinctions in color and tone needed to produce smooth gradients. **Gaussian** makes the gradient tighter looking and seems to have less of a ramp.

Creating gradients allows you to make wonderful, complex layered images using traveling mattes, as we shall see on page 303. By animating the motion of the gradients, you can make opacity vary and change over time, revealing and fading out layered images and graphics.

The Gradient generator doesn't provide anything that's not in the Custom Gradient, where you have more control than you do in the simple Gradient.

17.3 Custom Gradient Controls

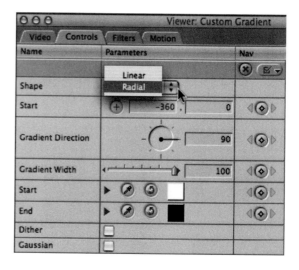

17.4 Highlight Controls

Highlight

The **Highlight** render is great for generating quick highlights that race across images or text (see Figure 17.4). The default sets the highlight to 90. I usually use it at 45 and with a much narrower highlight width than the default 10. When you combine it with a compositing mode, it produces effects that give a quick sparkle to your images. We'll work with it in the next lesson.

17.5 Noise Controls

Noise

Using composite modes, this Render generator can be used to create film grain–type noise that blends with your video (see Figure 17.5). It's perhaps a bit too "noisy" for most film grain, but it helps enhance the illusion. Small quantities of noise can also be used to break up banding, similar to the effect of Dither in the Custom Gradient.

Noise defaults to black and white, but the checkbox at the bottom of the controls can set color noise as well. You can also randomize it, which you probably want. Otherwise the noise looks stuck on top of the image.

Particle Noise

Particle Noise is a strange generator. It lets you create different shapes of particles:

- Circle,
- Square,
- Diamond, or
- Random

The shape, size, density, and color can be changed and animated. Particle Noise will generate shapes that play colored shapes over an image or can be used with composite modes to make a video clip out of randomized particle shapes as in Figure 17.6.

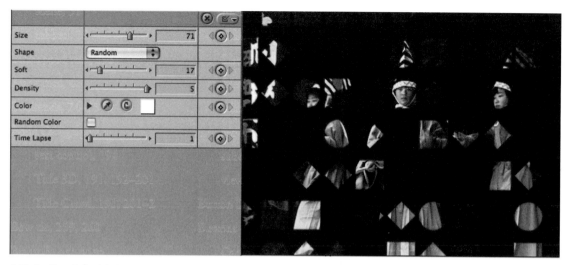

17.6 Particle Noise
Generator and
Controls

Compositing Modes

One of the best ways to combine render elements with images is to use compositing modes. If you're familiar with Photoshop, you probably already know that a compositing mode is a way that the values of one image can be combined with the values of another image. Final Cut has 13 compositing modes, including two traveling mattes, which we'll look at in the next lesson. For the moment, we'll deal only with the first 11. These can be accessed from the **Modify>Composite Mode** menu. The composite modes are:

- Normal, the way clips usually appear
- Add
- Subtract
- Difference
- Multiply
- Screen
- Overlay
- Hard Light
- Soft Light
- Darken
- Lighten
- Travel Matte—Alpha
- Travel Matte—Luma

Compositing Exercise

Let's begin by looking at the compositing modes available in FCE:

1.   Open up the sequence *Composite Modes*.

This sequence contains 11 iterations of two clips, one on top of the other. Each clip on V2 is composited onto the clip on V1 using a different compositing mode. There's an extended marker on each clip that identifies the compositing mode applied to the clip stack.

No two compositing modes are the same, although the differences are sometimes subtle. Some will make the output darker, some will make it lighter, but all in a slightly different manner. It's a wonderful tool for controlling and combining images.

The two last composite modes, Travel Matte—Alpha and Travel Matte—Luma, have special uses that we'll look at later.

2.   To change the compositing mode of a clip, select the clip on V2, and from the **Modify** menu choose **Composite Mode**, and choose a type.

You can also select the clip in the Timeline and right-click to bring up the shortcut menu and select **Composite Mode**.

Screen

One of the most useful composite modes is **Screen**, which will remove black from an image. It screens out portions of the image based on luminance values. Pure black will be transparent, pure white fully opaque. Any other shade will be partially transparent. This is great for creating semi-transparent shapes that move around the screen, very useful for making animated backgrounds. Many 3D and other animation elements are created against black backgrounds that can be screened out. Let's try the composite mode, and you'll see how it works, compositing the *Detonate* video on top of another scene. *Detonate* is one of the LiveType objects made into a movie.

1.   Open the empty *Sequence 1* if it isn't open already.

2.   Again, we won't be working on the sound, so let's switch off A1/A2 in the patch panel.

3.   Edit about six seconds of any of the *Village* shots into the Timeline. I used *Village1*.

4.   Take the *Detonate* clip from the Browser and put it on track V2.

5.   Select the *Detonate* clip on the upper track and use **Modify>Composite Mode>Screen**.

Instantly, the black background will disappear and an explosion will appear over the village scene as in Figure 17.7. You'll find the effect laid out at the beginning of the *Composite Stacks* sequence. I also scaled down *Detonate* a little so the explosion didn't obliterate the whole community.

17.7 Detonation over the Village

Animated Text Composite

One of the best uses of composite mode is to use it with text, especially animated text that's moving on the screen. The composite mode will allow the text to interact with the layer underneath.

1. To start, edit five seconds of another clip into the Timeline on V1. I used *Village3*.

2. Next, using the basic Text tool, create a title with the word *Village*. Use a large, chunky font and make it a bright color. I used Arial Black at 98 point in a fairly bright red.

3. Superimpose the text on top of the village shot.

4. Now we need to create the animation. Make sure you're at the beginning of the text block, and with the Canvas in Image+Wireframe mode, drag the text upward so that it's off the top of the screen.

5. Add a keyframe to the text block, either with the global motion keyframe button in the Canvas or with the Center keyframe button in the Viewer.

6. Move the playhead to the end of the village shot and drag the text block downward so that it's off the bottom of the screen.

So far you just have a simple text animation that scrolls across the screen from top to bottom, but adding the composite mode changes everything. The text will change and be textured by the underlying image.

7. Select the text block in the Timeline and use **Modify>Composite Mode** and pick one. I chose **Overlay**, but try some of the others and see what it does to the text as it moves across the screen.

The effect with the text animation is at *Marker 2* in the *Composite Stacks* sequence.

Instant Sex

Let's look at some more effects you can create with composite modes:

1. Let's open a clip from the *Clips* bin into the Viewer. We'll use *Ceremony2* because it has some nice highlight areas that will show off the effect.

2. Set the clip's duration down to five seconds and edit it into your sequence.

3. In the Timeline, move the playhead back over the top of the clip that was just edited into the sequence.

4. Drag the same clip from the Viewer to Superimpose, making identical copies on V1 and V2.

You could also use **Option-Shift**-drag to copy the clip from V1 to the space above on V2.

5. To the top layer, apply a generous amount of Gaussian Blur, something like 30. The image looks very out of focus now.

6. Turn down the Opacity of the clip on V2 to something like 40 percent.

7. Go to **Composite Mode** and change the clip on V2's setting to Add. I prefer **Add**, but try some of the others, such as Screen or Lighten.

8. Try adjusting the Blur amount and the Opacity levels to different settings.

This is a recipe for Instant Sex from the great After Effects artist Trish Meyer. Although it was created for After Effects, it adapts readily to Final Cut. The soft, blooming highlights make a wonderful, dreamy, romantic effect.

☞ *Tip*

NTSC Warning: If you are going to output to NTSC analog to be seen on a television set, be careful in using compositing modes, particularly Add. It will brighten the image, often beyond the luminance and chrominance values allowable for broadcast transmission. If the image is too bright or overchromaed, especially in red, it may bloom objectionably and smear easily when analog copies are made, particularly VHS copies.

Noise Exercise

Next let's bring up the noise. We can use Noise to add a film-grain effect.

1. Go to the Generators pop-up, and from **Render** select **Noise**.

2. Drag it onto V3, above the Instant Sex stack, or set V2 as the destination and use Superimpose to bring it into the Timeline.

3. Change the Noise layer's compositing mode to **Screen**.

4. Remember, the piece in the Timeline is a copy of the one you created in the Viewer, so double-click it to bring it back into the Viewer.

5. In the Controls tab, make sure the **Random** box is checked and the **Color** box unchecked.

In Color mode, Noise is too strong and generates too many sparkling bits to be useful for our purposes.

Toning It Down

At this stage the Canvas should look like a very snowy television picture (see Figure 17.8). Now we need to reduce the effect of the Noise.

17.8   Snowy Noise

1. In the Noise controls, set the **Alpha** level all the way to zero and pull down the **Alpha Tolerance** to something around 10 or 20, depending on how much graininess you want to introduce.

2. Also try using the Soft Light composite mode, but with Noise's Alpha turned up to around 120.

3. To see the effect the Noise layer is having, toggle the track visibility on and off with the green button at the head of the track.

Text

Let's not stop there. On top of your video, which should still have strong, glowing highlight areas, as well as a sprinkling of grain, let's add a text element.

1. For simplicity, use the standard Text tool to create the word *JAPAN* in any font you like, fairly large size and a nice, bright color.

I used Optima, bold and italicized, with a size of 168 in a fairly bright red, R 200, G 18, B 18. Create whatever text block you like, using any available font.

2. Place your text block on V4. I also used Image+Wireframe to move it lower in the frame.

3. **Option-Shift**-drag the *text* clip to the space above to create a copy on V5.

Your stack should look like Figure 17.9.

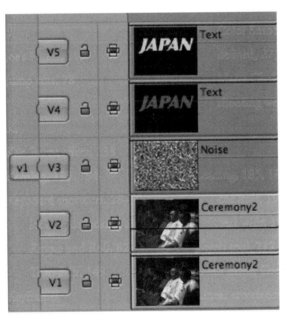

17.9 Two Video Layers, Noise Layer, and Two Text Layers

4. Go to the controls for the text file on V5 and change the color to bright yellow, something like R 223, G 223, B 18.

5. Next, apply a Gaussian Blur filter to the top text layer, maybe something in the 30 range. This will make it quite wispy-looking.

6. Change the composite mode for the text on V5 to **Add** so that it combines with the layers beneath.

Making the layer blurred and then compositing will make it look like a glow over the image (see Figure 17.10), but you may not want that top glow layer on the image all the time.

7. Ramp up the Opacity on the glow layer quickly over a few frames.

8. Hold the Opacity at full level for four or five frames.

9. Quickly ramp it down again. When you play it back you should just get a quick flash of yellow glow.

17.10 Composited Layers and Effects

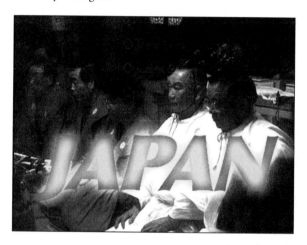

Look at the sequence *Composite Stacks*. I've built the five-layer stack with the quick opacity animation at *Marker 3*.

Drop Shadow Exercise

Another variation is to use a composite mode to create a different kind of drop shadow, using this type of glow layer technique, only behind the text rather than on top of it (see Figure 17.11). Rather than using yellow in the glow layer, we'll simply keep the same color as the text layer.

1. You should still have in your *Sequence 1* the five-layer stack we created. Let's start by deleting the top text layer that became our glow.

2. Once again, **Option-Shift**-drag the text on V4 onto the empty V5 to make two copies of the text stacked on top of each other.

This time, rather than working with the upper text layer, let's work on the lower text layer.

3. Double-click the lower of the two text layers on V4 to open it into the Viewer. In the Motion tab, change the value Scale up to about 110 percent.

17.11 Drop Shadow Glow Layer Behind

4. With the Viewer still in the active window, go to **Effects>Video Filters>Gaussian Blur**.

5. Set the blur value to something around 20.

6. At this point the color will be too rich, so change the composite mode to **Overlay** or **Darken**. Try a few different ones to see what they look like.

The drop shadow glow layer stack is built in the *Composite Stacks* sequence at *Marker 4*. This is a different-looking shadow than you usually see. Instead of being directed to one side, it flares out from the text as though the light is coming from the front, projecting the text onto the background.

These glow effects can also be created and animated using Title 3D's edges and drop shadow effects.

Bug

A bug is an insect, a mistake in software coding, and it's also that little icon usually in the lower-right corner of your television telling you what station you're watching. There are lots of different ways to make bugs, but I'll show you one using Photoshop and compositing modes. In your Browser in the *Graphics* bin is a Photoshop file called *Logo.psd*. Double-click it, and it will open as a sequence with two layers. The bottom layer has the bug already made up with the Photoshop effect. The top layer that is visible in the Canvas doesn't have the effect applied, and that's the one we're going to work on. If you want to just work with the bottom layer that's made up for you already, you can skip the first section of this tutorial.

Photoshop Effect

1. Make sure in your User Preferences that your External Editor for still images is set to Photoshop (or Photoshop Elements).

2. Right-click on the visible layer in the *Logo.psd* sequence, and from the shortcut menu choose **Open in Editor**.

3. Once Photoshop has launched, select *Layer 2*, and from the little F in the bottom left of the Layers palette, add a Layer Style, choosing **Drop Shadow** (see Figure 17.12).

17.12 Add Layer
Style>Drop
Shadow

4. Change the Drop Shadow Angle to 145 and the Distance to 15. Leave the other controls the same.

5. Check the Inner Shadow checkbox to add the shadow. Set the Distance to 5, and the Choke and Size to 10.

6. Also add a Stroke. Set the Size to 6. I made the color blue (see Figure 17.13).

7. Click OK, and you've built the effect.

There is one more step to take before going back to FCE. The effects have to be applied to the layer. The easiest way to do this is to add a layer underneath the effects layer.

8. Add a new layer to your Photoshop composition, and in the Layers palette, drag it below *Layer 2*, which holds the effects.

9. Make sure *Layer 2* is selected. From the Wing menu, choose **Merge Down**, or use the keyboard shortcut **Command-E** (see Figure 17.14).

10. Save your file and go back to Final Cut Express.

17.13 Drop Shadow Panel with Inner Shadow and Stroke

17.14 Merge Down

✷ *Tip*

Distinctive Logo: There are any number of different ways to give your logo a distinctive edge by using the power of layer styles. Rather than use the Inner Shadow and Stroke method, you could also use Bevel and Emboss. Change the Technique pop-up to Chisel Hard, and push the Size slider until the two sides of the bevel meet. This will give you maximum effect. Remember that the logo is going to be very reduced in size. Also, in the bottom part of the Bevel and Emboss panel, try different types of Glass Contour from the little arrow pop-up menu.

Compositing the Photoshop File

Back in FCE *Layer 2* in the Photoshop sequence, *Logo.psd* will have been updated and will include your new effects.

1. Open a new duplicate *Sequence 1* and drag some video into it. I used *Village2*.

Now normally you're going to want your bug to run the duration of your sequence, which might be an hour or more. Because you can't drag out still image layers to an unlimited duration once they're in a sequence, you need to set the duration of the bug while it's still in the Browser.

2. The simplest way to work with this is to first open the sequence *Logo.psd*. Now drag your newly minted effects *Layer 2* out into the Browser (or the original *Layer 1* if you prefer).

This will be a copy of the *Layer 2* in *Logo.psd*. With *Layer 2* as a single-layer image, before you place the bug into the final sequence, you can change its duration in the Browser. Here you can make the duration of the still image anything you want—anything up to 12 hours anyway, which is the duration limit of any FCE sequence.

3. Set the Duration for the bug logo to the duration of the sequence you want to cover. Now you can drag the layer into your final sequence.

The first step is to change the logo's composite type. Several compositing modes will work for this, but I like to use **Composite Mode>Multiply** (see Figure 17.15). This will make the white of the logo almost transparent. For a slightly brighter look, try **Soft Light**, and for an even more transparent look, use Overlay.

At the current size, the logo is probably a bit intrusive. You might want to scale it down a bit and reposition it in the corner of your choice, bottom right being the traditional location on American television. It will now be your unobtrusive watermark on the screen. Some people also like to use effects such as displacements or bump maps, but for something this small, I don't really think it's necessary. The simple transparency effect of a composite mode is enough. The one I created is at *Marker 5* in *Composite Stacks*.

Summary

This short lesson should give you a taste of and a little practice in using composite modes in Final Cut Express. They are a great way to blend images, text, and generators together into a single composition. But

17.15 Logo with
Composite
Mode>Multiply

there's more: We still have to look at the two most important composite modes, the travel mattes, to which we'll devote the next lesson.

Lesson 18

Travel Mattes

Travel mattes, or traveling mattes, are a unique type of composite mode that uses the underlying layer in a composite stack to define an image's transparency. It allows the application to create a great many wonderful motion graphics animations. We'll look at a few, which I hope will spur your imagination and get you started on creating interesting and exciting projects.

Setting Up the Project

For this lesson you'll need to launch the *Lesson 18* project and go through the reconnect process if necessary. Inside your copy of the project *Lesson 18*, you'll find the *Clips* bin, three master clips (*Village*, *Dance*, and *Ceremony*), and a number of sequences. As in the previous lesson, there is a *Composite Stacks* sequence.

Travel Mattes

Technically these are compositing modes as well, although they function in a special way. The two travel mattes are **Luminance** and **Alpha**. In a travel matte the layer to which it's applied will take its shape and transparency from either the Luminance value or the Alpha (the transparency) value of the layer directly beneath it. Because it tracks the layer, any animation or change in the layer below will be reflected in the tracking layer. This makes Travel Matte an extraordinarily powerful tool.

303

Soft-Edged Split Screen

Let's use a travel matte composite mode with a gradient to create a soft-edged split screen. Sometimes when doing a split-screen effect, you like to have a soft, blurred edge, instead of the hard edge the Crop tool gives you, which we saw in Lesson 14. The Crop function does have an Edge Feather function; unfortunately, this feathers all of the edges, not just the edge that splits the two images. That's where gradients with composite modes come in. At *Marker 1* in *Composite Stacks* I've created a soft-edged split screen. One clip is on V1, another on V3, and sandwiched in between is a custom gradient.

★ *Tip*
Clip Visibility: Rather than switching off the visibility for an entire track, which will lose your render files if you have any, simply switch off the visibility for a single clip. You can do this by using the Clip Enable function. Right-click on the clip you want to hide and choose Clip Enable to deselect it in the shortcut menu. You can also use the keyboard shortcut Control-B. Another option is to Solo just the clip you want to see, and switch off the visibility for other clips. You can do that from the Sequence menu or with the keyboard shortcut Control-S.

1. To build this effect, start out by laying the clips into the *Sequence 1* Timeline on V1 and V2. I used the still images *Rich.pct* and *Anita.pct* from the *Graphics* bin.

2. Offset each to left and right so the heads are separated enough to leave room for the soft-edged split. You'll have to toggle the Visibility of the top layer on and off as you make this adjustment.

3. From the Generators, select **Render>Custom Gradient**.

4. Make sure the playhead is over the two clips and V1 is set as the destination track. Use the Superimpose function to sandwich the custom gradient onto V2 between the still images.

5. To the clip on top, apply **Composite Mode>Travel Matte—Luma**. You will immediately start to see that much of the image has become transparent.

What immediately happens is that half of the top layer seems to disappear. The top layer's transparency is created by the composite mode that is looking at the layer directly beneath it to determine what should be transparent. Whatever is white in the layer below will be opaque in the top layer. Whatever is black will be transparent in the top layer. Different values of gray will create different levels of transparency.

In our exercise, what we need to control is the shape of the gradient, how quickly it falls off from white to black, and where that fall-off happens.

6. Double-click the Custom Gradient in the Timeline to open it into the Viewer and go to the Controls tab.

7. To make things easier, grab the Video tab and pull it out of the Viewer, positioning it to the left. Now you can see the gradient on the left, its controls in the center, and the output of the effect on the Canvas to the right (see Figure 18.1).

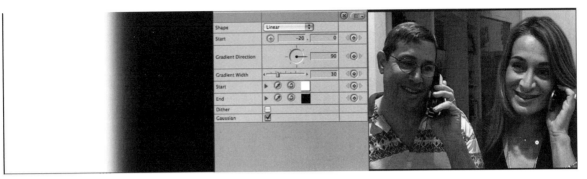

18.1 Viewer, Controls, and Canvas

8. Begin by setting the Start *x* value to 0, 0, and pull down the Gradient Width to about 40.

That's about it; you just need to adjust the *x* value at it so the gradient doesn't bleed too much into the right image. Perhaps even tighten the gradient some more. Turning on the Gaussian checkbox will make it easier to get a tighter gradient fall-off from white on the left to black and transparency on the right.

Highlight Matte

Next we're going to create a **Highlight Matte**. This allows us to create a highlight area, like a shimmer that moves across an image or as here across a layer of text. Let's set up a simple animation:

1. Edit only the video of five seconds of one of the clips into the Timeline to use as a background layer. I used a section of *Ceremony1*.

2. Next we'll add text on top of it. As in the previous lesson, for simplicity use the standard Text tool to create the word *JAPAN* in any font you like, fairly large size, and a nice, bright color. I again used Optima, bold and italicized, with a size of 168 in a fairly bright red, R 200, G 18, B 18. Create whatever text block you like, using any available font.

3. Superimpose your text block on top of the video and use Image+Wireframe to move it higher in the frame.

4. Next, duplicate the text block and make a copy on the layer above, V3, by **Option-Shift** dragging it upward.

5. Open the top text layer and make it a very pale version of the text color on V2. I made it a pale pink.

6. Set V2 as the destination track so you can superimpose between the two text layers.

7. Select **Highlight** from the **Render Generator** pop-up menu, and superimpose it onto V3 between the text layers.

Let's work on the highlight:

8. Double-click the Highlight to bring it into the Viewer. Go to its Controls tab and move the **Highlight Angle** around to 35 degrees.

9. Set the **Width** and **Softness** to about 5 and 10, respectively, leaving off **Dither** and **Gaussian**; the latter only tightens the sharpness of the fall-off.

Your Canvas should look something like Figure 18.2.

18.2 Highlight under Text

Animating the Highlight

The next step will be to animate the Highlight. In previous versions you had to animate in the Motion tab, which limited your animation possibilities, but in this version you can do your animation in the generator's Controls tab.

1. Put the playhead at the start of the clip.

2. In the Controls tab of the Highlight, set the Center x axis to –600, which should take it off-screen left, at least away from the text file on V4.

3. Add a Center value keyframe in the Highlight's Controls tab.

4. Move to the end of the clip (**Shift-O**). Now set the Center x point to 500.

Over the five seconds of the clip, the Highlight bar will sweep slowly across the screen. Of course, we still don't see the background layer.

5. Next set the Composite Mode of the text file on V4 to Travel Matte—Luma.

If you're at the start or end of the clip, you'll see the red text layer on V2 as well as the background. As you scrub through the sequence, you'll see that the text highlight area will softly wipe onto the screen and then wipe off again as the Highlight layer slides underneath it. The pale text file's transparency is being directly controlled by the luminance value of the layer beneath it. The matte layer, the Highlight in this case, is invisible. The four layers are at *Marker 2* in *Composite Stacks*.

Glints

We've seen how we can put a highlight across an image. Next we're going to do something a little more complex, creating a traveling highlight, but one that goes only along the edges of a piece of text—a highlight that glints the edges.

1. We'll begin again with a base layer from one of the clips available in the Browser. I used the first five seconds of *Ceremony2* for this, editing onto V1.

2. Next we add the text to V2. Again make it big, a fat font, such as Optima in bold, with a font size of about 180, right to the edges of the Safe Title Area and beyond. Set it a little below center in the frame. For my font I used a *y* value of 70.

Next we'll create a moving highlight area:

3. Use FCE's Custom Gradient from the **Generators** pop-up menu, **Render>Custom Gradient**.

4. Superimpose the Custom Gradient on top of the text and background clip so that it has the same five-second duration.

5. Open the Custom Gradient from the **Timeline**, and using the Control tab of the **Viewer**, change the Shape pop-up menu to Radial.

The Radial center is very large and on the left edge of the screen. We want the radial highlight to be much smaller and higher in the frame.

6. Set the Gradient Width to 35 and make sure both Dithering and Gaussian are not checked.

7. Change the gradient's Start coordinates to *x,y* of 0,–100, centering the radial in the screen as in Figure 18.3.

Animating the Radial

To animate the gradient, we want it to move from left to right across the screen and then back again, staying at its current height. At the start you want the gradient off one side of the screen.

18.3 Radial
Gradient in
the Viewer

1. In the Custom Gradient's Controls tab, set the Start *x* point to –600, leaving *y* at –100.

2. Make sure you're at the beginning of the Timeline and keyframe the Start value.

3. While in the Controls tab, type **215** to go forward to 2:15 (two and one-half seconds), about halfway through the clip.

4. Set the Start *x* value way over on the opposite side of the screen, about 600.

5. Go to the end of the five-second clip, and set the Start *x* value back to its start position of –600.

Over the five seconds of the clip, the radial gradient will sweep across the text and then back again. So far, so good. If you scrub the timeline, or play through with **Option-P**, you should see the gradient swing from left to right and back again.

18.4 Five-Layer
Video Layers
in Sequence

6. To make the glow appear only on the text, start by copying the text layer on V2 and placing the copy on V4, on top of the gradient. Do this with **Option-Shift**-drag. Your stack should look like Figure 18.4.

7. Open the top text layer into the **Viewer** and use the controls to change its **Color** to white, pale yellow, or whatever glow color you want to use.

This layer will be the glow on top of the text; the radial gradient will be the matte it follows.

8. To the top text layer, apply **Composite Mode>Travel Matte—Luma**.

Immediately the gradient will disappear and the glow will be composited on top of the bottom text layer. Figure 18.5 shows the text with the glow but with the underlying video switched off.

18.5 Text with Glow Composite

Polishing the Glow

That's a nice effect. You could be happy with it and stop there, with the glowing layer animated across the screen with the Custom Gradient layer.

What we really want, though, is for the glow not to race across the whole text, but to run just along the top edge of the text. It's not hard to do. We just need to add a few more layers.

1. **Option-Shift**-drag two more copies of the text layer on V2 up to the top of the stack onto V5 and V6.

These will completely hide the glow, so we want to create a mask that will hide most of the text except for the very edges.

2. Open up the Controls for the topmost layer and set its Origin point slightly to one side, away from the side where the glow starts.

3. Also set it slightly lower on the screen if the glow is traveling above the text or slightly higher if the glow is traveling below the text.

I increased the values of both *x* and *y* by 6. This will make the text look slightly fatter than it is, so we want to make a matte that cuts off the bits of text that protrude beyond the correct shape of the text. That's what the layer beneath is for.

18.6 Glint on Text

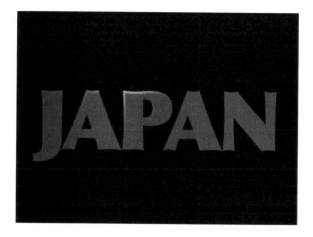

4. To the top layer, apply **Composite Mode>Travel Matte—Alpha**.

The Travel Matte layer disappears, and you're left with just a glint that travels along the edges of the text (see Figure 18.6).

Alpha Mattes and Luma Mattes. An alpha matte uses the transparency of the layer below, like text layers, to create transparency in the layer to which the composite mode is applied. A luma matte uses the luminance values of the layer below for the composite mode. Generators, like render shapes, have no transparency, but they have luminance values. Whatever is white in the matte layer will be opaque in the layer above, and whatever is black will be transparent in the layer above. Shades of gray give different amounts of transparency.

One More Touch

At the moment, the glint brushes across the upper-left edge of the letters as it moves back and forth across the screen. If you want to be really crafty and add a little something special, you can shift the glint side as it swings back and forth.

1. For the first pass of the Radial Gradient, leave the settings as they are.

2. When the glint reaches the far right side of the screen at 2:15, in the Controls tab of the text layer on V6, set a keyframe for the Origin point.

3. For the next frame, while the Radial Gradient is still off to the right, change that offset text layer's Center *x* value to –6, leaving the *y* value as it is.

Now when the glint passes back from right to left, it will be on the upper-right edge of the letters.

The glint stack is at *Marker 3* in *Composite Stacks*.

Video in Text

I hope you're getting the hang of this by now and are beginning to understand the huge range of capabilities that these tools make possible. Next let's try an even more complex animation with traveling mattes, the ever-popular video-inside-text effect, the kind of technique that might look familiar from the opening of another old television program, *Dallas*.

To look at what we're going to do, open the *Composite Stacks* sequence and go to *Marker 4*. If you click on the clip on V2 called *HDV Sequence* and press **Command-R**, you will render out the section of sequence defined by the length of the clip. That's what we're going to build.

If you want to make really enormous letters that fill right to the top and bottom edge of the screen and that are wider than the screen, you would, in an early version of FCE, have to create this in Photoshop or Photoshop Elements. We can use Photoshop to create multilayer, oversized sequences that we can work in FCE. If you're working in DV, you can also use FCE's HDV capabilities to generate an oversize sequence.

Making Text

We need to start with really big blocks of text.

1. Start by creating a new sequence and opening it.

I called the prebuilt one in your Browser *HDV Sequence*, so you should give yours a different name. It's probably in DV format, so we need to change it to HDV.

2. With the sequence open, go to **Sequence>Settings** or use **Cmd-zero**.

3. In the lower-left corner of the settings window, click on the **Load Sequence Preset** button, and from the pop-up choose **Apple Intermediate Codec 720p**. You could use 1080i as well, but 720 is a little closer to DV size.

4. From the **Generators** go to **Boris>Title 3D**.

5. Go to the Controls tab and click on the **Title 3D click for options button.**

> **Tip**
> **HDV Multilayer Sequence:** If you're working in HDV format, I've created an oversized Photoshop file with the text built into it that you can use in HDV. It's in the *Graphics* bin called *Stage.psd*. It's based on a 1080i format, but if you need it for 720p, simply scale it down to fit.

✏ Tip

RAM: You will have difficulty doing this portion of the lesson if your system resources do not meet the minimum requirements to support HDV content. In which case, rather than creating an HDV sequence, use the *Stage2.psd* that's on your DVD inside the *Graphics* folder which is in the *Media* folder.

6. In the text window, click on the **Reset Style** button to go back to the default white text, and then make your text.

I created the text using the word *JAPAN*. Pick a chunky, broad font. Don't use a thin, wimpy, serif font. I used Arial Black, but you can use whatever you have at hand. Make the type size large, something like 96 point to start, but we'll make it even bigger. You will also need to open the tracking up a little, or kern the letter pairs so the letters don't overlap vertically, particularly the P and the second A.

7. Click the **Apply** button in the text window, switch back to the video tab, and edit the text into the HDV sequence. It should be fairly large, but still not fill the screen.

Nesting

We now have a large HDV-format sequence as well as a standard-definition DV sequence called *Sequence 1*. We need to nest the large-format sequence inside the smaller-format sequence.

1. Begin by opening up *Sequence 1* from the Browser.

2. From the **Generators** button, select **Render>Custom Gradient**.

3. Make the Custom Gradient five seconds long, and edit it into the sequence. This will be our animated background layer.

4. Make sure the playhead is over the Custom Gradient in the Timeline, drag your HDV sequence from the Browser to the Canvas in the Edit Overlay, and drop it on Superimpose. That will make the nested sequence five seconds long as well.

5. Double-click on the nested sequence inside *Sequence 1* so that it opens into its own tab in the Timeline window.

6. Double-click on the text layer in the sequence to open it into the Viewer, and switch to the Controls tab.

7. Uncheck **Lock to Scale X**, which gives you separate vertical and horizontal scaling.

8. Push up the **Scale X** value as far as it will go, still keeping the letters in the screen. Don't touch the *y* value for the moment.

9. Switch back to *Sequence 1* in the Timeline window.

The text should extend beyond the edges of the screen, which is fine. The Controls tab for the text should still be in the Viewer, and we'll use this to adjust the size of the text while watching the text in the Canvas for *Sequence 1*.

10. Now increase the **Scale Y** value until the text stretches up to the Safe Title Area guides in the Canvas.

We've now made the text for the sequence.

Separating Letters

We're going to not only move images in the text, but we're also going to move a different image in each letter of the text. We're going to do that inside of the HDV sequence, adding images above each letter, which will all appear inside the nested sequence in *Sequence 1*. The text file will be the matte for the video that's on top of it. Because we want different video in each letter, we need to separate the word into its individual letters.

1. Inside your HDV sequence, **Option-Shift**-drag the text layer from V1 onto the layers above again and again, until you have a stack five text layers tall, or one for each letter.

After you've created the layer stack, then you need to crop each letter so that only it is visible.

2. If the Canvas is not already in Image+Wireframe mode, switch to it now.

3. Select the text on V1 and use **Sequence>Solo Selected Item(s)** or **Control-S** to solo it, so that none of the other layers is visible.

4. Use the Crop tool to pull in the right side of the text layer that's in your sequence. Crop it between the J and the A until only the J is visible (see Figure 18.7).

18.7 Cropped Text Layer

5. Select the text layer on V2 and solo it with **Control-S** to make only that layer visible.

The number in the center of the Canvas will tell you which layer is selected.

6. With the Crop tool, move the right crop line from the right until you are between the A and the P, and then move the left crop line so that it's between the J and the A, isolating the second letter.

7. Select the text on V3 and repeat, moving the right crop line to the right until all of the *P* is visible, and move its left crop line so that it's between the second and third letters, A and P.

8. Repeat for the other two layers until each layer has one letter visible on it.

9. When you're done, be sure to switch off Soloing on the last layer with **Control-S** so that all of the letters are visible again.

Adding Video

We're now ready to put in some video. We'll work only with video here, no audio.

1. Decouple the audio patches and set V1 as the destination track, and make sure the playhead is over the stack in your HDV sequence.

2. Find a clip in the Browser that you want to place above the text on V1. I used *Ceremony1*.

3. Drag the clip to the Canvas to Superimpose, slotting the clip into a new V2 between the J on V1 and the A now on V3.

4. Roughly position the clip in the Canvas so that it's sitting on the left side of the frame over the letter J.

The next step will be to apply a **Composite Mode**.

5. With the clip on V2 selected, right-click on it in the Timeline to call up the shortcut menu, and choose **Composite Mode>Travel Matte—Alpha**.

The image doesn't have to be the whole size of the frame or positioned in the center of the frame. It can be placed anywhere at any size, so long as it covers the letter.

6. Grab a corner of the image and resize it. Hold the **Shift** key and distort the image shape if you want (see Figure 18.8).

Next we need to add some more video to the other layers:

7. Set V3 as the destination track and find a clip in the **Browser** to superimpose over it. I used *Village3* for this one.

8. Superimpose it onto V4 and change its **Composite Mode** to **Travel Matte—Alpha**.

9. Scale and distort the image in the Canvas and position it so that it covers the letter A.

The next clip will take its matte from the text now on V5 and fill the letter *P.* I used *Dance2* beginning about three seconds into the shot.

10. Find the clip to use and Superimpose it above V5.

11. Set the composite mode to **Travel Matte—Alpha**.

12. Scale and position in the Canvas.

I used the beginning of *Ceremony2* to super above V7.

13. Repeat the process, which will create a new V8, above the second letter *A.*

18.8 Distorted Image Composited over Text

I used *Dance1* for the next track.

14. Repeat the process to create a new V10 to be matted by the letter *N* on V9.

Your 10 layers in the sequence should now be made up of five layers of text interspersed with five layers of video scaled and positioned to fit the text layer below it (see Figure 18.9).

Edging

One last thing we want to do in this sequence is to add an edging that borders the letters and helps separate the text and the video from what will be the background layer.

1. Let's start by **Option-Shift**-dragging a copy of the text layer on V9 right up to the top of the stack to create a new text layer on V11.

2. Double-click the text layer on V11 and go to the Motion tab to reset the Crop values. Use the little red **X** button next to crop. This will cover all of the video with the letters.

3. Switch to the Controls tab in the Viewer and click the **Title 3D click for options** button to bring up the Title 3D text window.

4. Stroke through the text to select, and then switch to the fourth tab in the text window, the Edges tab.

5. Activate one of the edges and set an edge to taste. I used a plain edge, but set the **Position** pop-up to **Outside** so it didn't cut into the video, and selected a rich blue for it.

18.9 Ten-Layer Stack

6. Switch to the third tab on the left, the Color tab, and in the top left corner deactivate, uncheck, **Fill On**. This will leave the text fill open with only the edging around the letters.

Animating the Nest

Let's switch over to *Sequence 1*, which is 720×480, smaller than the nest inside it. We want to animate two elements: the nested sequence so it moves across the screen and the custom generator so the background has motion as well.

1. In the Canvas, make sure the View pop-up has Image+Wireframe turned on, and set the Zoom pop-up on the left to Fit All. Your Canvas should look like Figure 18.10.

2. Select your nested HDV sequence and press the **Return** key, which will open it into the Viewer. Double-clicking won't do it, because that will just open the nested sequence in the Timeline window.

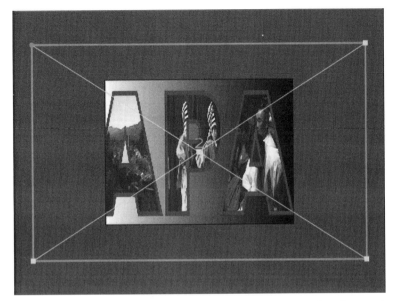

18.10 HDV Sequence
Composited on
Custom Generator

3. Go to the **Motion** tab, and with the playhead on the first frame of the sequence, set a Center point keyframe.

4. In the Canvas, holding down the **Shift** key to constrain the movement, drag the nested layer off the screen to the right. A Center value of 1,000 did this for me.

5. Use **Shift-O** to go to the last frame of the sequence, and holding the **Shift** key again, move the image over to the left side of the screen. I used a Center value of –1,000.

Over the course of the five seconds, the text will travel from right to left on top of your Custom Gradient. Next we want to animate the colored background. This is a new feature in FCE 3.5, which was not possible in earlier versions of the application.

6. Double-click the Custom Gradient and go to the Controls.

7. You still should be on the last frame of the video, so set keyframes for all of the parameters. If you're not sure what you'll need to animate, keyframe everything.

8. Set whatever values you want for the gradient. I used these settings:

Start	x –109, y –95
Gradient Direction	135
Gradient Width	80
Start Color	White
End Color	Red

9. Use the **Home** key to go to the beginning of the video and change the Custom gradient values. Although you could have animated any parameters you wanted, including the color start and end values, I only changed Start and Gradient Direction to make the gradient swing around.

Start	x 127, y 80
Gradient Direction	320

I have built the animation at *Marker 4* in *Composite Stacks*.

Grunge Edges

Next we'll do something different. We're going to grunge up the edges of a clip.

1. Start out in Photoshop, making a new image that FCE will resize for digital video. Start by using the Photoshop NTSC DV preset at 720×480. If you don't have Photoshop or Elements, the file I made up is in your Browser. It's called *Grunge.psd*.

2. Make the new image completely black.

3. Take the **Rectangular Marquee** tool and draw a rectangle that's about 50 pixels in from the edges of your image.

4. Fill the selection with white.

5. Now have some fun. Drop the selection (**Cmd-D**) and grunge up the edges of the white box. Start with Photoshop's **Smudge** tool (**R**), which you can use to pull the white into the black and black into white. Or you can use one of the PS filters from the **Distort** group, maybe **Ripple** or **Ocean Ripple** set to a small size but a high magnitude—or combinations of various tools.

I like to smudge up the edges a bit first and then apply the filter so it doesn't come out too repetitive. Do it by mostly pulling the black into the white, because the filter will expand the schmutzing effect. Avoid doing an effect that goes beyond the edges of the frame. It will look cut off when you composite it with the video. You should end up with something that looks like the *Grunge.psd* image in your Browser (see Figure 18.11).

6. Import your Photoshop file into Final Cut Express.

7. In a new DV sequence, place your Photoshop file on V1 and place a video clip on top of it on V2.

8. Apply **Composite Mode>Travel Matte—Luma** to the clip on V2.

18.11 Grunge.psd

In the Browser is a sequence called *Grunge Sequence* that contains *Ceremony2* on V2 and the Photoshop file *Grunge.psd* on V1. To the video clip I applied Composite Mode>Travel Matte— Luma.

Look at *Marker 5* in *Composite Stacks*. Here I've laid a gray color matte on V1, and on V2 I placed the nested sequence *Grunge Sequence*. With the Canvas in Image+Wireframe mode, I scaled and rotated the nested sequence in the Canvas (see Figure 18.12). As you can imagine, you can work up millions of variations on the basic idea.

18.12 Scaled and Rotated Grunge-Edged Clip

Day for Night

Color mattes don't have to be used only for backgrounds or graphical elements as we looked at in earlier lessons. They can also be used as a color filter. Day for Night is the now seldom-used technique of trying to shoot in daylight and make it look like a moonlit night. Old Westerns almost always used this technique. Basically, you stop down the camera and shoot through a blue or a graduated blue filter. Let's do something similar:

1. Start off by laying the clip you want to affect on V1 in a new sequence. I used *Village3* because it presents a typical daylight problem, the bright sky.

2. Darken the image, using a filter such as with Color Corrector.

I pulled down all of the levels—**Whites**, **Mids**, **Blacks**, and even **Saturation**. Even with the levels pulled quite far down, the sky remains bright and pale (see Figure 18.13). Next we'll use the **Color Matte** to add the blue night filter.

18.13 Darkened Image with a Bright Sky

3. Create a deep, dark blue color matte and Superimpose it onto V2.

4. Create a **Custom Gradient**, and with V1 set as the destination track, Superimpose it so it sandwiches itself onto V2 between the video and the color matte.

5. Set the **Composite Mode** on the color matte to **Travel Matte—Luma**.

All that's left to do is to set up the gradient.

6. Open the controls, leave the default at **Linear** gradient, and change the **Direction** to 180.

Next you need to use the crosshairs to place the start of the gradient. There is a start point but no end point for the gradient. If you start at the top of the Canvas, the blue will carry too far down into the image.

18.14 Day for Night Gradient Filter

7. Zoom down the size of the Canvas to something like 25 percent.

8. Place the start point for the crosshairs out in the grayboard above the image.

9. Tighten the **Gradient Width** so that it falls off more sharply.

10. Make the end color of the gradient somewhat less than pure black to give the lower part of the image a cold, blue cast.

The sky should be dark blue, but the center of the image should still show some light and color (see Figure 18.14). The stack is at *Marker 6* in *Composite Stack*s.

Summary

That brings us to the end of this packed lesson on compositing. We're almost ready to export our material from Final Cut Express out into the world, which is the subject of our final lesson.

Lesson 19

Outputting from Final Cut Express HD

Remember that I said earlier that the hard, technical part of nonlinear editing was at the start, setting up and setting preferences, logging, and capturing; the fun part was the editing in the middle; and the easy part was the outputting at the end? We're up to the easy part, the output. Because it's so simple, this will be a short lesson.

The two basic ways of outputting are:

- Exporting, if you're going to another computer application or CD or DVD or web delivery
- Going back to tape, if you're going to traditional tape delivery

Because it's probably the most common requirement for Final Cut Express users, let's look at outputting to tape first. We'll see exporting later on page 326.

There are basically two ways to get material from your computer to tape:

- Record to tape
- Print to video

Record to Tape

You can get your edited material back out to tape in several different ways. The simplest one, and perhaps the most commonly used way, is to record to tape. Before you do that, you should always:

- Make sure everything that needs to be rendered in the sequence is rendered.

- Make sure you are set to **FireWire** in the **View>Video Out** menu.

- Make sure you mix down your audio. Go to **Sequence>Render Only>Mixdown (Command-Option-R)**.

Mix down the audio even if you have only a single stereo pair of audio. It's much easier for your computer and your drives to play back a mixdown file than it is to mix your audio on-the-fly. Also, the default audio quality playback is set to Low. If you just record to tape without mixing down, you will get low-quality playback. However, whenever you mix down your audio, it's always done to high quality, and that's what you want when you record to tape.

Put the playhead at the beginning of the timeline, put your camcorder into VCR mode, switch on record with the VCR controls, and press the spacebar. This is a fast, effective, and simple method. It's probably a good idea to have some black at the beginning of your sequence and have the playhead sitting on it, so that when you begin recording, you're not recording a still image for a while. You should record at least 10 seconds of black before pressing the spacebar to begin playing back your sequence.

There is one other trap in recording to tape, either manually or with Print to Video. If you have set your Render Controls in Sequence Settings down to low values to speed up rendering, that's the playback quality you'll get. You cannot now switch to high quality and automatically force a re-render. You have to switch to high quality and then reset each effect that was rendered at low resolution to force it to re-render at high quality. There is no force re-render function, unfortunately. This is also true of exporting to tape and can be an issue in Final Cut.

Using playback from the Timeline has some disadvantages. You don't get to put in bars and tone and neat countdowns and slates and black leaders and trailers, unless you physically add them to your sequence. If you want these features, you can use Print to Video.

Print to Video

Print to Video is under the **File** menu. If you have a sequence selected in the Browser or an active Timeline, you can call up Print to Video from the **File** menu or use **Control-M**. This brings up the dialog box in Figure 19.1.

In this dialog you can set any number of options for program starts and ends. You can add bars and tone and set the tone level, depending on the system you're using. Several different digital audio standards are used, if you can call anything that has variables a standard. Different systems use –12, –14, –16, or –20dB as digital audio standards. Analog uses a variety of other standards around 0dB. If you are going to send your video to a duplication house, check with them before selecting a tone level.

19.1 Print to Video Dialog Box

The Slate pop-up lets you use the:

- Clip Name
- Text, which you can add in the text window
- File, which is any still image, video, or audio file

So if you want to record an audio slate, selecting the file and navigating to it with the little Load button will play the sound during recording.

You can use FCE's built-in countdown, using a form of Academy leader. Or you can use a countdown of your own by selecting File in the Countdown pop-up menu.

Notice the checkbox in the bottom left that provides the ability to automatically begin recording. When you start Print to Video, FCE will write a video, and if necessary, it will write an audio file of any material that needs to be rendered. Every time you use Print to Video, it will have to do this, even if you've just used Print to Video. After it's finished writing the video and audio files, FCE will prompt you before it begins recording. Accept by clicking OK, and the computer will take control of the deck and send it into record at whatever point it's parked on the tape.

You can use either Record to Tape or Print to Video to make a VHS recording. Connect your DV camcorder or deck to your computer, and connect its analog output to your VHS deck. It's probably a good idea to have the VHS deck in turn connected to a video monitor or TV set so that you can see what you're recording. Then set the VHS deck to Record, and use the DV device as a digital-to-analog converter to get your movie onto VHS.

Export

You can access the different formats and ways of exporting from FCE from the File menu. From here you can export to **QuickTime Movie** or **Using QuickTime Conversion**.

QuickTime Movie

Let's start with QuickTime Movie, the first of the two Export options. When you export a QuickTime movie, Final Cut is listed as its creator type, so that if you launch the resulting movie, it will launch FCE. Because Final Cut is a QuickTime-based application, the exported movie will also play using the QuickTime Player and will work in any other QuickTime-based application on the Mac, such as iMovie or iDVD.

You can export a sequence as a digital file in several ways:

- From the active Timeline window directly from the sequence you're working in
- From an active Viewer
- From the Browser by exporting a sequence or clip

Click on the item and go to **Export>QuickTime Movie**. This brings up the dialog box in Figure 19.2. Here you can rename your sequence, and you can select whether you want to export **Audio and Video** or **Audio Only** or **Video Only** from the Include pop-up menu. Here you also have the option to export **Markers** through a pop-up menu (see Figure 19.3). To export chapter markers to iDVD, select **Chapter Markers** from the pop-up menu.

The checkbox at the bottom of the dialog box, **Make Movie Self-Contained**, is an important one. This checkbox defaults to being on, but if

> ★ **Tip** _____
> **In to Out:** If you want to record only a portion of your sequence, select the portion you want to record by marking it with In and Out points in the Timeline. Then in the Print to Video settings window, select In to Out from the Print pop-up menu in the Media portion of window. When you press OK, playback will begin at the marked In point and run until it reaches the Out point.

19.2 QuickTime Movie Export Dialog Box

you uncheck it, FCE will generate a reference movie. This is a relatively small file that points back to the original media source files. It will play the contents of the sequence as you laid them out.

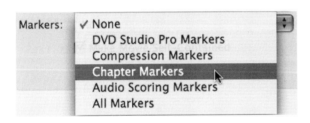

19.3 Exporting Markers Pop-Up Menu

The reference movie will play back from the QT player, and it can also be imported into other applications such as iDVD or compression programs such as Sorenson Squeeze. The reference movie is treated just like any other QT clip inside these other applications. FCE and the importing application do not need to be open at the same time for this to work.

The advantages of making reference movies are the speed in generating the file and the comparatively small file size. If anything in the FCE sequence needs to be rendered, it will still have to be rendered for the reference movie, and the audio files will also be duplicated as a mixdown of your tracks. You do need to have access to all of the source media included in the sequence, because a reference movie only points to existing media source files on your hard drives. It's not a complete video clip in itself. Be warned: if you delete any of the media needed for the reference movie, it will not play. It will be a broken QuickTime file. If you send it to somebody on a CD, they won't be able to play it. It will play only on a machine that has access to the media.

Export to QuickTime Movie is an important tool because it is the only way to export a sequence from FCE without recompressing the video. All other exports, including Export Using QuickTime Conversion, will

> ✎ *Tip*
> **Anamorphic Material:** iDVD still does not support the use of anamorphic material from DV, only native widescreen HDV. To get around this problem, you need to use software like Anamorphicizer or the excellent myDVDedit.

recompress the frames, producing some degradation of the video image, albeit very slight.

❧*Tip*
Export for Soundtrack and for

LiveType: These export functions
are the same as exporting to Quick-
Time Movie. The only difference is
that exporting to Soundtrack,
Apple's music-creation application,
is preset to export audio scoring
markers. Export using either of these
defaults to make a reference movie.
A little thing to watch out for: if you
do an export to Soundtrack with
scoring markers and then do an
export to QuickTime Movie, the preset will still be set to export audio
scoring markers.

QuickTime Conversion

Export>Using QuickTime Conversion is the catch-all for every form of
file conversion from FCE. I would have liked for Still Image export to be
separated, but it's hidden in here as well (see Figure 19.4).

19.4   QuickTime Conversion Export

How to Make Chapter Markers. The last thing you should do to a project before exporting is to set up chapter markers to use in iDVD. It could not be simpler to create them.

First, you need to ensure that the marker is in the correct location. It has to be placed on the Timeline Ruler, not on a clip. To put a marker in the Timeline, make sure nothing is selected in the sequence. Use Command-Shift-A to De-select All.

Add the marker by pressing the M key. Press it again to call up the Edit Marker dialog box (see Figure 19.5). To create the chapter marker, click the Add Chapter Marker button. <CHAPTER> will appear in the Comment field. Do not alter this.

If you want to give the chapter a name that will carry over to iDVD, enter it in the Name field. That's it. Close the dialog box, and you're done.

Notice that you can also enter scoring markers here in the same way to use with Soundtrack.
You should bear in mind a few rules about chapter markers:

- DVDs will accept no more than 99 chapter markers.
- Chapter markers cannot be closer than one second from each other.
- You can't have a chapter marker within one second of the start or end of the sequence.
- A chapter marker is automatically created for the beginning of the exported material.

It's probably a good idea not to put in chapter markers until after you have completely, positively, and finally finished editing your show. Otherwise, you may have to redo or at least reposition all of your chapter markers to get them into the right place.

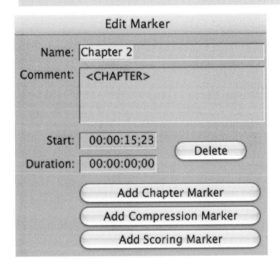

19.5   Edit Marker Dialog Box

Video Export

Final Cut Express has several video export choices for QuickTime Conversion. The **Format** pop-up allows you to choose from a variety of formats including:

- 3G, a format used by handheld devices such as cell phones
- FLC, an 8-bit format used for computer animations
- iPod, for podcasting size and format for display on an iPod or on the web
- QuickTime Movie
- AVI, a PC video format
- DV Stream, DV audio and video encoded into a single track for use with iMovie
- MPEG-4, a format designed primarily for cross-platform web compression

These are the video formats. Some, such as AVI and QuickTime, allow you to use several different codecs. DV Stream is used by iMovie, not by FCE. Do not export to DV Stream if you're going to a video-editing application other than iMovie.

In QuickTime Conversion, the **User** pop-up is contextual; that is, what is offered here is determined by what's selected in the **Format** pop-up. If you select QuickTime in the Format pop-up menu, the **User** pop-up menu offers common Internet settings (see Figure 19.6) based on QuickTime using H.264 as the codec. This is a good place to start if you want to create a video to show on the Internet or put on your .mac homepage.

19.6 QuickTime Conversion User Pop-Up Menu

✓ **Default Settings**
LAN/Intranet
Broadband – High
Broadband – Medium
Broadband – Low
Dial-up
Dial-up – Audio Only
Streaming – Medium
Streaming – Low

Codec and H.264. Codec is a shorthand way of saying compression/decompression, defining the mathematical algorithm that's used to compress and play back your media. H.264 is a specific codec that became available in QuickTime 7. This is now the default compressor, and an outstanding codec, used by iPod video and one that will be used for HD DVD creation. It's highly scalable, while preserving image quality, and excellent for web use in particular. It's not a production format and cannot be used in video editing applications, but it's great for content delivery. The only problem with it is that it requires the user to have QuickTime 7 or later installed, which may limit its availability, particularly for PC users, who often don't have the latest versions of QuickTime.

If you want more control, click on the **Options** button to bring up the Settings window (see Figure 19.7). The Video and Audio tabs give you full control over your media. It takes a great deal of practice and testing to become proficient at compression for the web. Try various data rates, frame sizes, and frame rates and compare them to the default web settings that come with selecting QuickTime in the **Format** pop-up menu.

Exporting with QuickTime Conversion allows you to use a variety of different codecs for compression in addition to H.264, such as, among others:

- Animation
- Cinepak
- DV-NTSC

19.7 QuickTime Settings Window

- MPEG-4 Settings window
- Motion-JPEG A
- Photo-JPEG
- Sorenson Video 3

To export to other QuickTime codecs, such as the excellent Sorenson Video 3 codec, use the **Options** button and then click on **Settings** to select the correct video and audio settings (see Figure 19.8). For Quick-Time video on the Internet, if you don't want to use H.264, you might set the Compressor to Sorenson Video 3. Try various data rate settings: 1,000kbps will give good results. Set the frame rate to 15fps. Size should be set to 320×240. Sorenson Video 3 is older technology and will produce comparable results to H.264, which will be larger and have a better frame rate for the same size file.

You should also compress the audio. IMA 4:1 at 22,050 works well for most material. For music you might use a music compressor such as QDesign Music 2 and a sample rate of 44.1K, the audio CD standard. These settings will produce a fairly large file, suitable for use on high-speed connections.

Photo-JPEG is an excellent codec used for file-size reduction. An important codec is Animation, which has a high data rate. Animation is a loss-less compression codec often used to transfer material between various

Standard Video Compression Settings

Compression Type: Sorenson Video 3

Motion

Frame Rate: 15 fps

Key Frames: ○ Automatic
● Every 24 frames
○ All

Data Rate

Data Rate: ○ Automatic
● Restrict to 1000 kbits/sec

Optimized for: Download

19.8 Sorenson Video 3 Settings

applications. One advantage of the Animation codec is that it can carry alpha-channel information with the video. This allows you to create a sequence in one application and bring it into FCE without loss and with its transparency information. Or you could export an FCE sequence that has transparency and bring it into another application such as After Effects, keeping the transparency you created in FCE. When you export with the Animation codec with an alpha channel, make sure that for **Colors** you select **Millions+**. The plus is the alpha channel. The Sound dialog box allows you to set an audio compression scheme as well as setting the sampling rate you want to use.

To create video CDs, you'll need an application such as Roxio's Toast that allows compression to the MPEG-1 codec. This is a heavily compressed codec, but a remarkable one in that it can play back off the very low output of a CD and still produce a full-screen, full-motion image. To create a DVD, you need another application such as iDVD. When exporting to iDVD, you should use either a self-contained or a reference QuickTime Movie, and iDVD will do the compression to MPEG-2 for you.

To export to Flash, which is the most widely available video format on the web, you'll either need to use a separate application like Sorenson Squeeze or get the On2 Technologies export module.

Exporting to QuickTime Conversion allows you to add filters to your clips or sequences. Most of the QuickTime filters are available directly within FCE, with one notable exception, **Film Noise**, which is under the **Special Effects** submenu (see Figure 19.9).

This filter adds an old-time film look to your video, as if it were scratched and dirty. A small QT movie runs in the bottom-left corner showing you how much schmutz you've added to the picture. Here you can set amounts of Hair that appear on your video, from very low to quite furry. Notice the buttons that allow you to Save and Load, letting you create favorite preferences for the filter that you can access again and again. In addition to Hair, the pop-up at the top will take you to another panel to

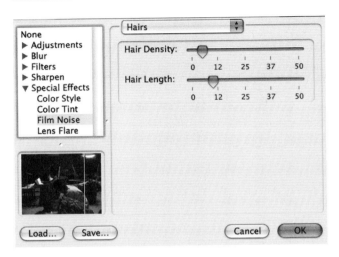

19.9 Film Noise Hairs Panel

set Scratches, where you can set the amount of damage on your video, and another to set Dust and Film Fading, which allows you to tint the film. The sepia is quite subtle, and the 1930s color film is suitably garish.

Still Image Export

Two other types of QuickTime Conversion export are often used: **Image Sequence** and **Still Image**. Image sequences are useful for rotoscoping, frame-by-frame painting on the video image, and other animation work, and provide high-quality output without loss. You can set any frame rate, and exporting will create one picture for every frame you specify. Make sure you first create a folder in which to put your image sequence, because this can easily generate a huge number of files.

Finally, QuickTime Conversion allows you to export still images. This is how you get frames of video out to your computer for web or print use. Your stills will only be 72dpi—probably not good enough for fine printing. Software such as PhotoMagic or Photoshop plug-ins such as Lizard Tech's Genuine Fractals can help improve the image's appearance.

The **Options** button for Still Image export, which uses the same dialog box as Image Sequence, includes a Frame Rate box. Don't be confused; leave the Frame Rate blank if you want only one frame.

The still you're exporting may very well be in rectangular pixel aspect ratio. This is not a problem if you're going back to a video application, but in print or on a computer display, the stills will look squashed. Photoshop will fix this problem for you. If the still image comes from DV, in Photoshop go to **Image Size**. Switch off the **Constrain Portions** checkbox and change the size to 640×480. You'll end up with a 4:3 image in the correct pixel aspect ratio. Check **Resampling** and select **Bicubic** whenever you resize in Photoshop.

If you're going to export stills for web or print work that come from video, especially video with a lot of motion in it, you'll probably want to de-interlace it. You can do this either in FCE or before you export the frame. As we saw in "De-interlace and Flicker" on page 264 in Lesson 15, you select **Video Filters>Video>De-interlace** from the **Effects** menu. Or you can de-interlace in Photoshop as well. It's in the **Filters** menu under **Video>De-interlace**. I normally do it in Photoshop because I think its De-interlace feature works better than FCE's built-in one, which simply drops one of the fields. In the Photoshop De-interlace filter, you have an interpolation option, which works very well.

Audio Export

FCE can export to several different audio formats, including:

- AIFF
- AU
- Wave

It cannot export to MP3.

If you select AIFF in the Use pop-up you'll get common audio file settings (see Figure 19.10).

✓ Default Settings
  11.025 kHz 16 bit Mono
  11.025 kHz 16 bit Stereo
  11.025 kHz 8 bit Mono
  11.025 kHz 8 bit Stereo
  22.050 kHz 16 bit Mono
  22.050 kHz 16 bit Stereo
  22.050 kHz 8 bit Mono
  22.050 kHz 8 bit Stereo
  44.1 kHz 16 bit Mono
  44.1 kHz 16 bit Stereo
  44.1 kHz 8 bit Mono
  44.1 kHz 8 bit Stereo

19.10 AIFF Export Use Pop-Up Menu

Notice that the selection does not include any of the DV sampling rates, although AIFF is the most commonly used format for audio files with Final Cut. Instead of the **Use** pop-up, use the **Options** button, which is also context-sensitive and offers a wider range of options, including 32,000 and 48,000, the DV sampling rates. AIFF export options also offer a large number of compressors to reduce the file size of the audio (see Figure 19.11). Generally, audio for video is not compressed, except for web use or in DVD creation.

Archiving

Now that you've finished your project, you should think about archiving your material. The original videotapes on which you shot the project should be your primary archive. Using the **Project** feature that we saw in the Capture window in Lesson 7 on page 103, you can recapture all of the video for your project.

You need to store the project file. This is most important because it allows you to recapture your material and rebuild your project. The best way to

19.11 AIFF Export Options

do this would be to burn it onto a CD. You should also put on the CD whatever graphics files you created for the project. Not the FCE titles, which are retained in the project file, but any Photoshop or other images you may have used. You should also save any music or separate sound you used in the project. And don't forget to save any Voice Over tracks you created. Everything other than the video clips that made up your movie should be burned onto your archive CD.

To restore the project, copy all of the material back from the CD onto your computer. Open the project file and reconnect the existing files. Next run the capture process, clicking on Project in the Capture window to bring your video material onto the computer. The Capture window will prompt you for each tape it needs in turn. When all of the material is back on your computer, your project will be restored and ready to be re-edited.

Summary

We've now gone through the whole cycle of work in Final Cut Express HD version 3.5, including setting up your computer, working with the interface, capturing your tape raw material, either analog or digital, editing, transitions, titling, special effects, and compositing. Now finally we have returned our finished project to tape or outputted it for everyone to see and enjoy. It's been a long road, but I hope one that was exciting, interesting, and rewarding for you. Good luck with all of your future video projects and with your work in FCE.

Index

What's on the DVD?

The companion DVD for *Final Cut Express HD 3.5 Editing Workshop* is a hybrid DVD. The DVD portion of the disc is a 12-minute video introduction to FCE aimed primarily at iMovie users making the transition between the two applications. In the video I go through some of the principal differences between the two as well as a few issues to watch out for to make the transition easier. Watch the video to see an extra tip on creating a special video transition in FCE.

The DVD-ROM portion of the disc includes unedited, raw footage for the tutorial projects, which contain sequences that guide you through the material. The disc contains:

- Over 11 minutes of DV and audio files
- 27 graphics files
- 15 FCE3.5 tutorial project files
- QuickTime preview movies of all FCE transitions
- Extras folder with:
  - Demo filters for:
    - CGM
    - CHV Plugins
    - G-Filters
    - Lyric Drawing Plugins
    - V-Key Chroma Keyer
  - Timecode Calculator
  - Custom Editing Workshop button bars
  - Lens flare effect in DV, and HDV 1080i and 720p